BIG-GAME
FISHING
The Great Adventure

 The Oxford Illustrated Press

© Graeme Pullen, 1987

Printed in England by J.H. Haynes and Co. Limited,
Sparkford, Yeovil, Somerset.

ISBN 0 946609 44 6

The Oxford Illustrated Press, Sparkford, Near Yeovil,
Somerset.

Published by:
The Oxford Illustrated Press, Sparkford, Near Yeovil,
Somerset.
Haynes Publications Inc, 861 Lawrence Drive, Newbury
Park, California 91320 USA.

British Library Cataloguing in Publication Data
    Pullen, Graeme
    Big game fishing : the great adventure.
    —(The Great adventure series)
    1. Big game fishing
    I. Title. II. Series
    799.1'6 SH457.5
ISBN 0-946609-44-6

Library of Congress Catalog Card Number 86-82903

CONTENTS

To anglers everywhere.
If you dream long and hard enough that dream may become
a reality.

ACKNOWLEDGEMENTS

For me, writing the acknowledgements was the most difficult part of the whole 85,000 words of my first book. Not that the people were difficult to recall, but who was I to acknowledge? I've always been a loner, no brothers or sisters ensured I had no confidante — nobody with whom I could express any inner feelings. Now, at the tender age of 34 I find I have crammed into twenty years' intensive fishing what most fishermen would be happy to see in a lifetime. I've paid the price of being an individual, but in all honesty would not have it any other way. I've had experiences that many will never see. Have travelled to 34 different countries and been privileged to view changing cultures in other worlds. I'm not a politician, nor do politics have any interest for me, but I feel the world is changing just a little too rapidly for the likes of myself who like to sit and enjoy, for a while, what I see in front of me.

Everything I have done within this book I have done myself, alone, even down to typing this manuscript one-fingered, over the period of a year. So, rather than acknowledging assistance with this book, I would rather acknowledge those who have helped me generally with advice and tips. These are as follows: Chris Dawn, previous features editor of *Angling Times,* now editor of *Trout Fisherman* magazine, who urged me to start putting pen to paper. On the photographic side I have to thank Terry at Longworth Photographic for his patience with someone who still doesn't know his ASA from his DIN! I might not understand the technicalities of the camera, but I seem to have the knack for being in the right place at the right time. Then there is Pete Perinchief, previous Director of Fisheries for Bermuda Tourism. It was he who really showed me the pressure that can be applied to a fishing rod, and since then, I have, as they say, never looked back. I am sorry to say I have little respect for most of my fellow men, but Pete is one of the few men I do respect. Another is my father. John Pullen. Taken from me too young, he gave so much pleasure and happiness to others with his antics and laughter. I couldn't have asked for a better old man; he has to be at the top of the tree for my respect. The old bugger.

Next there is Bernard Hunkin, a Mevagissey shark and wreck skipper who took me under his wing and so generously gave me his tips on pollack fishing. A small man, but with a mountain of a heart, and an elfin grin crinkling his craggy face, he just gave help. Then there's Alan Dingle, the man on whose boat was landed the biggest mako in British angling history: 500lb. I took my first ever boat trip with Alan and even though I spent most of the day heaving my kidneys over the side, he goaded me into winding up three dogfish and a 20-lb conger. That conger did the trick, and I was into the sport in a big way. Unfortunately I still suffer from sea-sickness.

Henry Spearman. My old sports teacher at Courtmoor Secondary School. A hard man, he gave no quarter, and if he thought you could take another two seconds off the hundred he'd make sure you would do it. A superb sportsman and marvellous cricketer, he is a Hampshire man and proud of it. I have a great deal of respect for this man, who taught me through my sports career that if I was going to do anything with his name attached, I'd better do it properly. Strange as it may seem I've tried to apply this philosophy to other areas in my life. It's not easy. Self discipline has a price on its head. Henry also taught me English, though God knows he couldn't have envisaged me as a writer! My grandfather on my mother's side, drove me through my business life harder than Henry Spearman did on the track.

Henry John Pettifor. Or was it John Henry Pettifor? He was just the 'Old man' to me. A self-made man who built a business empire from nothing but sheer hard graft. A Londoner who moved his family down to Hartley Wintney to avoid the bombs of the Second World War. Seems a sensible precaution. All these people have taught me something in life that has helped me dedicate myself to the sportfishing world.

Lastly, it wouldn't be fair to acknowledge the men without making mention of the ladies too. Mum. Well, what can you say? She's stuck by me through thick and thin, moaned when I've been fishing all night, but has still done my flask and sandwiches. All mums are the same, but Joyce is exceptional — a toughie who deserved a little less worry through life, but who's made it nevertheless. A survivor. Then there's my first wife Valerie. Valerie carried hot meals 300 yards down a freezing Norfolk beach for me, only to be asked to carry the cod back to the car; she also typed my first articles. Shame it didn't work out, but I guess everyone is entitled to make a mistake every 34 years. Lastly Hilary. Present lady in my life. Doesn't fully understand what makes me tick, but helps in every way she can anyway. Probably thinks I'm crazy . . . no! she *knows* I'm crazy. She gave me the confidence to eat publisher's rejection slips for breakfast. What do they know?

Finally an acknowledgement to the good Lord above. I've been at sea in places where he could have quietly snatched me with ease, but instead he's let me view some of his wondrous creations without asking for the admission fee. One day he will though, but I cannot complain. I have memories to last for years.

I close with the fisherman's prayer . . . 'Lord grant to me to catch a fish, so large, that even I, when telling of it afterwards may have no need to lie' . . . There are no lies in this book.

FOREWORD

Putting pen to paper started when I was sweet sixteen. Seeing my name at the bottom of an *Angling Times'* letters page gave my ego an amazing boost. Was I really in print? Wow! I was suddenly famous for a day though I seem to remember my school friends were less than impressed. Writing can be a chore or a pleasure. If it's new innovative work then it's interesting, even exciting reliving experiences again. If it's repetitive 'work' it can be absolute hell trying to get it down on paper. I don't find writing comes easily, I have to work at it. Photography comes more easily, and I find it enjoyable when it all goes right. Deflation comes when your editor tells you he had to replace your beautiful colour shot with somebody else's advert!

Writers who have influenced me are: Brian Harris of the old *Angling* magazine, which was years ahead of its time — it was his first account of a trip abroad in the late sixties that gave me this unquenchable thirst for foreign fishing; Ian Gillespie, now alas no longer with us, who wrote amusing yet factual stories; the late Dick Walker who gave so much in his writing, for so many anglers; Bernard Venables who wrote as descriptively as an artist uses a brush; and Zane Grey, probably the greatest pioneer writer of big game stories ever — I still read his books when I need some reminder of this fantastic sport and he's never been equalled in my own eyes.

This book is just a tiny portion of my fishing career. I have spent just as much time fishing England's beautiful stillwaters and majestic rivers, and I hope I will find the time to write accounts of all these freshwater experiences. Life for me is governed by the seasons. In winter there is the pike, the cold weather cod and trips to the southern hemisphere. In spring come the daffodils, primroses, and of course the trout, taken on fly tackle in pleasant surroundings. In summer the sharks move inshore, the tench bubble in the lakes, carp cloop on the top and barbel glint on the river bed. When the leaves float earthwards in September, despair not, for the perch, pike and bass come into the calender, which of course takes me into winter again.

Itchy feet I most certainly do have, and I hope I never stop in one country for the rest of my life. Though travelling for me is exhilarating, it really is nice to come back to my own little house, dump the suitcase, post off the films and have a nice cup of tea, even though the only place in the world I have had a decent cup of tea is Mauritius, where they make it with vanilla flavouring and hot milk! It's like pies, mash and licquor in the East End of London. Once you've had a taste there really is nothing quite like it. That's how the world of sportfishing can, and should be.

I say to you this. If you have the chance to travel then take it. There are a few places left where the air still has that magical quality, where man, the sea and the wind are all that matters. Go now, before it's too late. I have been fortunate in so far as I have made my own dreams a reality. Dreams are the food of adventure, and I shall endeavour, within the confines of this book, to give you a taste of my own.

G.J. PULLEN
Fleet, Hampshire.
27 June 1986.

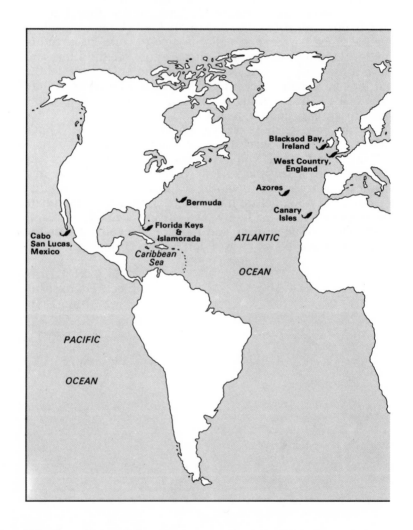

The locations of the adventures described in chapters 1 to 13.

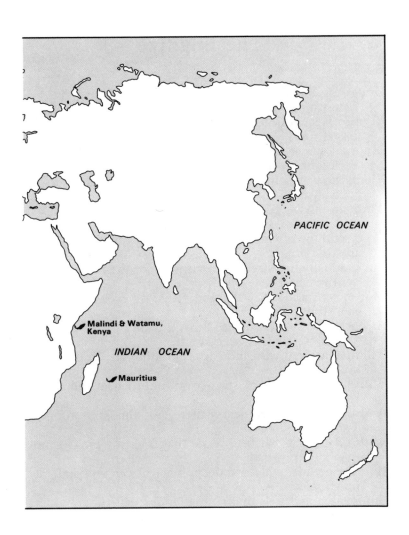

PACIFIC OCEAN

Malindi & Watamu,
Kenya

INDIAN OCEAN

Mauritius

The Fugitive

Under the earth's deep crust I rise, to bubble eagerly
    beneath the hill,
My bed is smooth to my surprise, this pleasant land I
    travel finds,
My thoughts at rest as down I rush, to gather speed with
    each long thrust,
Along the way some friends join me, companions
    journeying to the sea.
Through village quaint and time well worn, down hill
    and valley and cornfields shorn.
To meet a town whose pipes leak fluids, that all combine
    to stifle lungs,
But gradually my strength returns as for the fresh sea my
    soul yearns,
More towns and cities clog my veins, till even breathing
    is a strain,
As chemicals from factories flow, a scum of soap and oil
    shows, where fish once swam,
Till man arrived with industry, polluting air, land soil
    and me.
With faltering strides I stagger on, until I hear the
    seagulls' song,
And then I know I'm nearly there, but almost dead until
    I share,
With reverie the salt fresh taste that frees my lungs from
    man's foul wastes.
Into the oceans, wide and deep, where I can rest and
    maybe sleep.
But wait . . . what is that strange foul smell? . . .
It's man's pollutants and my death knell.

ANNA WENTWORTH.
10th November, 1976.

The First Big Sharks

FLORIDA KEYS

I jostled my way down the elevator at Miami International Airport, competing with fellow humans for a few inches of metal on the slow descent to the baggage claim. This was my second trip to Florida for a vacation, the previous year I had travelled over with the features editor of *Angling Times,* Chris Dawn. We'd both done some research into what to fish for and where, yet had come away slightly disappointed. The largest fish was a 40-lb amberjack boated by Chris, while the largest fish I tied into was a specimen blackfin tuna of $17^1/4$lb. I remember it won me a citation, probably for being the dumbest angler on that particular trip.

I collected my bags from the baggage claim and as always on my foreign trips waited anxiously for my rod tube to come through the side door. Would it be intact? Would it be in ten vastly differing lengths? Would it come at all, or had it been ripped off? A hand on my shoulder made me spin round. I was confronted by a massive, coloured, Security Officer, beaming at me from behind the customary reflective sunglasses.

'Hey man, I figure this toob o' fishin' poles gotta be yorne. I seen your leapin' sailfish on your blazer badge.'

I offered my thanks and quickly inspected the tube. Everything taped up. Padlock in one piece.

'Yes, thanks a lot. I was beginning to think I wouldn't see it again. Me and my old tube have been quite a few thousand miles.'

He picked up my suitcase and we walked down the corridor.

'That's OK. I can manage,' I said, trying to avoid being charged several dollars for a porter's fee.

'No problem man, I go fishin' myself, so I don't mind carryin' your gear. Where d'you go to from here?'

'I've got to pick up a rental car from Alamo, then it's

pedal to the metal on 895 East until I hit the turnpike. If I don't get picked up for speeding by then I'll bomb it down the 'Pike to Islamorada.'

A huge grin spread across the coloured man's face, displaying a set of gleaming teeth that would look great on Liberace's keyboard.

'Hey, that's a good spot man. I had a 52-lb tarpon from there once. Where you going out from — Bud 'n' Mary's?'

'No, I'll probably try there late on. I want to try a guy called Jim Taylor. He works out from Whale Harbour with a 40-foot gameboat. Specialises in shark and big amberjacks.'

He stopped, mouth open like the Blackwall Tunnel, the whites of his eyes reflecting in the glow of a street lamp.

'Jesus man, what you wanna mess with them fish for? They can be M-E-A-N. I figure you ain't so dumb that you don't know they EAT people over here?'

I smiled, a little taken aback at his obvious distaste for one of my favourite species. I sensed we might be parting ways, and the free suitcase carrying would cease forthwith.

'Well, I've never pulled on a real big one before, and this year I said to myself "Graeme — you're going to pull against a really big fish this year." See what it's really all about.'

He put my suitcase down and adjusted the tie on his uniform.

'I'd just like to know one thing' he said, eyes narrowing as he delivered the question. 'Did you have the reading light on in the plane?'

I thought carefully for a second, sensing some sarcastic reply.

'Well yes, I did actually.' He straightened up, a relieved look spreading over his face.

'Thought so.' He turned and started to walk away. 'I figure you got sunburned already man — nobody with any brains in his ass goes fishin' for shark over here. Let alone big mothers!'

A feeling of nausea swept over me as I drove through Key Biscayne. It was dark and I was pushing to get to the hotel before they sold my room. I always made a point of phoning in and letting them know when I expected to get in, because sometimes they were double booked. I slowed a little as I realised that eating three McDonald's cheeseburgers chased by a pint of milk, was the cause of my sickness. There was no moon as I specifically timed the trip to coincide with the new moon period, a phase that had been proven beyond doubt to be *par excellence* for billfish in Mexico. A canopy of stars spread themselves overhead, the pure silence broken by the garbage eminating from the radio station.

'This is your local WXYZ Radio Station (or whatever) playin' music through the night to keep you bright! Tomorrow's weather looks real good, as though we're in for one of those settled spells. Highs in the 90s, lows in the 70s tonight. Winds light to moderate, 10 to 15, south-west, seas 2 to 4 feet.'

I punched to another channel, and finished the rest of the journey having my ears beaten with country and western music.

I checked in at the hotel, knowing full well from previous trips that I was likely to have the usual over-booking problems. I walked up to reception, trying to look as happy and radiant as possible. We got off to a civil start.

'Good evening sir, may I help you?'

'Yes. I have a reservation. I'm afraid I'm a bit late but I did phone through to let you know I was coming.' She let the smile drain from her face.

'What name sir?'

'Pullen. Initial G.'

'Poollaan?'

'No. Pullen. Initial G.'

'Oh, Pullemm.'

I fixed her with one of my 'KILL' stares.

'No. Pullen. P-U-L-L-E-N! From Fleet, Hampshire, England. U.K. Britain.'

'What initial sir?'

'G.'

'C?' I dropped my head and stared at the floor in disbelief. Was this really happening to me? Or was I still asleep in the plane and would wake up on the set of some Benny Hill Show.

'It's G. GEEE. For Graeme.'

'Sorry sir, we have nothing under that name.'

'What about the vouchers?' I fumbled amongst my passport bag and proudly thrust a sheaf of vouchers at her, smiling benignly. 'See. It's on the vouchers. Pullen. Initial G.'

3

She took the vouchers, spread them out across the desk and put on her glasses, observing them closely. 'Sorry sir, our company doesn't accept these vouchers. Also you owe ten nights at $3 a night for State Tax. These vouchers aren't stamped "Tax Paid"!'

'Wha—Wha—Wha—.' I struggled to subdue an apoplectic fit. 'Listen Miss. I've got jet lag. I'm here on a fishing trip. My vouchers are stamped "Inclusive", that means tax as well. I want to go to bed, that's all. Just sleep. Now why don't you take the vouchers, take my passport and sort it out on your computer in the morning. Please. PLEASE. Just give me a room for the night. I'm booked anyway.'

She looked at me, at the vouchers, at my passport. She thumbed through the passport and found an excellent resemblance to Omar Sharif and Burt Reynolds. She punched out a cipher on the computer keyboard, then took a key from the wall behind her.

'I'll just keep these till the morning, and we'll sort it out when the manager comes in. Here's your key. Room 505. Thank you sir. Have a nice day!' She wheeled and was gone, leaving me, mouth agape staring at the computer keyboard. It glared back at me. Giving it a two-fingered salute, I picked up my cases and left for the elevator.

The tube wouldn't go through the elevator doors. To prove the point, the doors closed with my cases and half the tube inside, and me and half the tube outside. When it closed on the tube it slid back and forth as though trying to eat its way down to me. Thankfully somebody came, pressed the 'Hold' button, and I was in. On the fifth floor I jammed a suitcase across the door, threw everything out of the man-eating elevator and whipped my suitcase away. The doors slid together with a satisfying thud, and descended with a sneer.

I stumbled to the door of 505, piled my baggage in a heap and put the key in. I twisted it, turned it, and did everything that was humanly possible, short of snapping it off in a rage, but the door wouldn't open. I extracted the key slowly. Maybe one of the teeth was blocked. Then what I saw printed on the smooth surface of the key, made my blood boil high enough to make a cup of tea. Room *405!*

After breakfast the next day, I drove 3 miles along Upper Matecumbe to Whale Harbour, to find Jim Taylor. A pelican glowered at me from one of the mooring posts, its

4

drooping ungainly pouch large enough to take a skipjack tuna. The *Ace*, Jim's boat, was moored up in the corner berth; someone was hosing down the stern.

'Hi. Are you Jim Taylor?'

'Naw. I'm Ritchie. The crewmate. Jim's just gone to get some ice. You gotta be Graeme.' The voice came from a 6-foot 2-inch ex-marine with a beard. You know the size. You knock his beer over, look at him, then offer to buy him three crates of Budweiser.

'Yea. What's the fishing been like. Any sharks?' He played the hose within inches of my feet, then turned it off.

'Sure. Fishin's been real good lately. Dolphin in the weedlines, some 20-lb wahoo, plenty of big 'jacks, and the sharks are always there. You caught big sharks before Graeme?'

'Not very big. I've taken blues, porbeagle and thresher to a hundred and a half, and a few marlin. Other than that, nothing really big.'

'Well climb aboard matie, we'll be off in a few minutes.'

I loaded my gear and cameras aboard, viewing the boat to see what my three hundred and fifty bucks was buying. It was a beamy boat, large cabin, toilet, bunks, cooker, freezers for bait. I looked inside and saw several blackfins, obviously for bait. The boat had a sort of patio, with plastic tubing settee and armchairs, side plastic spray canopies, outriggers and tuna tower. Yes, it looked alright. I walked to the stern and looked in the fish boxes. Some ballyhoo were lying, ready rigged on single strand wire leaders. Obviously an efficient set up. A bronzed blonde-haired figure rolled down the quay.

'Hey there Gray-ham. A'm Jim Taylor. You ready to pull on some fish?'

I tried to look taller and more macho. 'Sure, ready to go.'

He climbed up to the tuna tower, and the big twin diesels burbled into life. Ritchie slipped the ropes and the *Ace* manoeuvred her way out of the marina. I sat in the fishing chair like a modern-day Hemingway, marvelling at the fact that I was finally here. The fish didn't matter; it was the actual fishing that counted. We motored out to the channel between the flats, and Jim opened the big engines up. The bow lifted and foam spumed from the stern. Ritchie brought out a couple of 30s and stood them in the holders. Then he put a pair of 50s in each outrigger holder. I watched intrigued as he ran each bait back to the required position, set the reel drags and clipped the two outriggers up. I was fishing. I soon got fed up watching the ballyhoo baits skip and splash in the wake behind us, and started to doze off in the warm morning sunshine.

'Get some oil on Graeme, you're gonna burn up else. We got the blue-water coming up in a few minutes, so start looking for some weedlines.' The voice came from Jim, some fifteen to twenty feet up in the tuna tower. Obviously he would see any weedline from his vantage point long before me, but he wanted to keep me awake. Another half hour of weed-searching and I started to doze again. A can of Budweiser hung from my fingers as I balanced on the arm of the chair, propping my head up. The sun burned my shoulders, frying me. The constant throbbing of the big diesels lulled me, the wash of the blue-water past the hull, whispering a lullaby.

'RIGHT RIGGER! FISH BEHIND THE RIGHT RIGGER!

I jerked awake, looking around to see what the hell was going on. Ritchie ran to the right side of the boat, shading his eyes against the surface flat. 'He's still there,' shouted Jim, 'Watch that flat line.' Suddenly the flat line in front of me twanged, and the rod folded over, reel screaming.

'GRAB IT, STICK THE SONOFABITCH!'

I grabbed the rod and struck three, four times. The line zeeee'd off the reel, and I held the rod at 45 degrees. Ritchie cranked in the other rods like a demented mechanic trying to start the President's car with a starting handle. He shouted up to Jim.

'OK Jim ease her off, we got a hook-up!'

The engines slowed, and I tried to gain line. The fish had slowed but the momentum of the big boat meant I couldn't gain line.

'Wahoo Jim' shouted Ritchie. 'Bout 20-lb or so. Ease him in Graeme, don't jerk on him.'

Slowly I pumped the fish in, until I saw the long barred, tiger stripes on the flanks of a torpedo shaped fish. As Ritchie leaned out to grab the leader it gave a series of violent head-shaking movements, jarring the rod top down to the butt. His fingers closed on the wire, and the gaff went home. With the fish safely aboard, I felt the sense of ease which all fishermen know, of having secured my first prize.

I'd taken plenty of big wahoo before in Bermuda, but they're a species I never tire of. That first searing run, makes them seem about three times as big as they really are. We resumed trolling and after some two miles Jim spotted a weedline. We dragged the baits past it three times before a yellow shape flashed out from underneath the weed on an intercept course with the baits. One of the 30s folded over, then as I leapt up to grab it the two 50s on both outriggers buckled over. I stood in the middle of the boat looking from one rod to the other, wondering which had the biggest fish on. Being a sportsman I settled for the 30, which yielded a 12-lb female dolphin. Ritchie wound in an eight pounder on one 50, and I took the other. It was a small fish of some 5lb. Jim climbed down the ladder from the flying bridge.

'How d'you fancy some amberjack Gray-ham? We can motor out to the "Hump" and try dropping for some if you want.'

'Sure, whatever you say Jim.'

The rest of the journey to the Hump proved uneventful, with the exception of something that chopped the bait off on the starboard flatline, probably a barracuda. Jim located the Hump, an undersea mountain some 12 miles offshore, by looking for birds working on the surface, and the white water of a rip caused by the gulfstream boiling over it, and disturbing the surface. Ritchie put away the four rods, and brought out fresh ones, a pair of 20s and a 130. 'We're gonna get some fresh blackfins for bait first Graeme. We troll through the rip using these small plastic artificial squid.'

The rods were set and in no time both were bent double with 5-lb blackfins pumping away at the other end. If God made blackfins that grew to 200-lb they would never be landed! They have got to be the hardest fighting of the small tuna family, the most difficult time being when they are under the boat, head pointing down, tail throbbing like a motor as they try to pull away. Having secured six blackfins for bait, one was rigged on a double hook wire leader, and the *Ace* manoeuvered over the Hump. I sat in the fishing chair, slotting the rod butt in the gimble. Jim shouted from up in the tower, 'OK Ritchie, tell him to drop.'

Two big egg sinkers towed a 4-lb blackfin down into the depths of the azure water, spiralling away until it was out of sight. I lightly thumbed the spool to prevent an overrun, and watched as it dwindled down, showing rust marks on the side plates of the spool. Ritchie slapped me on the shoulder. 'OK Graeme. Lock her up and jig it.'

I put the lever over, waited for the line to tighten and tried to jig. Now jigging with a set of 130-lb class gear is not too much fun. I must have raised the rod top all of two feet when it suddenly slammed back down, hitting the gunnel. Ritchie roared and hit me on the shoulder hard enough to hurt.

'Wheeeooo! We got one Jimbo, stick him Graeme, set the steel on that sonofabitch!'

I heaved back five or six times on the heavy rod. All that happened was the line left the spool in fits and jerks.

'Let him run Gray-ham' shouted Jim, 'then when he stops, work him hard!'

Eventually the runs slowed and I was able to get some line back on the big 12/0. The heavy rod was cumbersome and I called for the shoulder harness. I've never been one to make life harder than it need be, and the shoulder harness took the full weight of the rod and reel, allowing me to fight the fish better. Several more short runs and I had everything under control. The higher I got the fish in the water, the more it would be affected by the pressure. All small points in my favour. After ten minutes the sweat was pouring off me, but the spool was a lot fuller than when I had first hooked up. The leader came to the surface, Ritchie leaned out and grabbed it, Jim cut the engines and the gaff flashed down. Ritchie stood up and heaved on the gaff.

'Gimme a hand Jim, it's a big one.' Together they heaved the fish aboard, and it fell with a crash on the deck. I looked open-mouthed at the sheer size of it, its cavernous mouth and huge eyes. They both pumped my hand. 'He'll top 70lb Gray-ham, maybe even go to 80. That's a good 'jack for a first fish. You wanna catch another one?'

I nodded, and the fish was dragged to the side, despatched with a wooden club, and the rod made ready.

'That's too big a rod for me' I told Ritchie, 'give me an 80 to try. I think I could work it better.'

Fifteen minutes later and I was back into another big amberjack. Only slightly smaller, it was a thinner fish and seemed to put up a better fight on the set of 80. A third fish followed this and probably fought even harder. It was in the 60-lb range. 'I've got my own 30-lb outfit with me Ritchie. Can I try that?'

8

The message was relayed to Jim, who shook his head in disbelief.

'You use what you like Gray-ham. But if you tie into a 90-lb 'jack you're gonna spend an awful long time whipping it on that light tackle!'

An hour later and I was sweating on a big 'jack. My 30-lb Conoflex rod was hopelessly bent double, and the sheer depth of water meant I had to gain line in inches. The rod was fine for small conger and ling of 20lb in home waters, but 200 feet down with an unknown weight on the end, it wasn't man enough for the job. Eventually I landed the fish, thankfully only about 40lb. Suddenly I had tired of catching amberjacks.

It was late afternoon, and I climbed up to see Jim on the flying bridge. It was so quiet and peaceful, the throb of the engines was indistinct, and the fantastic azure blue of the Gulfstream seemed like a dream come true. The sea breeze was fresher up here, and I could see other gameboats trolling on the horizon.

'What do you think the chances are of getting a shark.' I asked Jim.

'Well it's pretty late in the day now to start sharking, but if you like we can go inshore to about 150 feet, anchor and drop a couple of shark lines down.'

'What are the chances?'

'Fair. No more. Simply because we don't have much time. But if you're finished on the 'jacks we could give it a shot for an hour.'

'Let's do it then. I'm pretty shot from that last 'jack, the rest will do me good.'

An hour later and the *Ace* was rolling at anchor on the edge of the green reef water and blue of the Gulfstream. Two big 130s were resting in the rod holders, lumps of iron and concrete tied to the bends of the hooks to hold them down in the 5-knot current.

'No rubby dubby or chum Jim?'

'Nope. Don't need it. These mothers can smell blood from those fresh blackfins a mile away. If there's anything down there, it'll smell those babies out.'

Sharking is a slow business: hours of inactivity broken by spells of screaming panic. After half an hour Jim was dozing up in the tower, and Ritchie was lying reading a book, can of Budweiser in his massive hand. I sat back in the fishing chair, feet up on the gunnel, my fingers resting on the dacron of the big reel. I sat twanging it, humming a tuneless song. The sun beat down mercilessly, as only it can at sea when the wind drops away. Twang-twang-twang 'Home, home on the range, where the fish and the fishermen play — twang-twang-twang.' TWANG! That's funny. One twang too many! I half opened my eyes and watched the rod top. It was stationary, moving only with the rock of the boat. TWANG! This time the tip dipped and kicked straight. Down there in the depths somewhere — something was chewing on a whole blackfin tuna. TWANG!

'Hey Jim, something's chewin' on the blackfin!'

Ritchie dropped his book and jumped to the rod, feeling the taught dacron from the reel spool. The rod top jumped again and line was dragged from the spool of the 12/0. Jim shinned down the ladder and helped Ritchie crank the other set of gear up out of the way. 'Stick him Gray-ham. You gotta nail him now!' I struck three times, barely raising the rod against the incredible power below.

'No, No! Jesus you gotta get the steel in these mothers Gray-ham, otherwise he'll jes' swim aroun' holding that bait in his jaws. When he gets fed up of playin' tag with you he just opens his mouth and spits it out — NOW STICK HIM!'

Gritting my teeth I heaved back seven, eight, nine, times thumping the rod until it jarred the whole of my body. The shark's response was to rip off even more line. I hung on grimly, the power of the run lifting me bodily out of the chair. My feet skidded on the wet deck and I fell back. 'Steady Graeme, that sonofabitch can drag you over. Just lean back and let him run. That's a real big fish!'

My knuckles turned white with the strain of holding the big rod, my tee-shirt soaked with sweat.

'Can I have the harness please?' I croaked. 'No you're gonna have to wait until we get this other set of gear up.'

Finally Ritchie grabbed the trace on the other gear, cut off the lump of concrete weight, and swung the blackfin inboard. Jim fired up the big twin diesels, and slipped the anchor rope.

'Get him the shoulder harness Ritchie,' said Jim. 'We're gonna lose this guy over the side if the drag on that Penn locks up.'

All the while I hadn't moved my hands from the rod butt

where they clung like a man on the window sill of life. It was pointless trying to touch the reel handle, the pressure was so great from the running fish, I wouldn't have gained an inch. Ritchie helped me put first one arm, then the other through the shoulder harness, and snapped the holding clips onto the reel lugs. The straps dug into my back as they twanged taught and I leaned against the running fish. Painfully I opened my fingers and flexed them, taking the entire strain with my back. I put on my fishing gloves, and gripped the reel handle. The spool was about three-quarters empty, and Jim started the boat in reverse, trying to get me some line back on the reel. For fifteen minutes I cranked feverishly, gaining and losing line. Then the line ran straight up and down, going tighter all the time.

'DAMN!' Jim put the boat in neutral. 'Ah tell you that's a real big shark Gray-ham, he's acting like he might be a tiger. Don't seem like a big bull or hammerhead. You got yourself 400-lb of unhappy fish, Mister!' I tried to smile at this, but as my back was beginning to cramp up, it more than likely came over as a grimace. Ten minutes later and I was *really* tired. My back hurt and my fingers were cramped. At 3.45 pm, after about half an hour the hook tore out.

The trip back in was very quiet. Jim was straight faced, and Ritchie hardly spoke. Back at dock Jim apologised for our poor luck.

'Sorry you didn't get your shark Gray-ham. But at least you got some good 'jacks, let's go weigh 'em.'

The biggest dolphin weighed 12lb, and the amberjacks tipped the scales at 38lb, 65lb, 78lb and a massive 82lb! Hardly a day of failure.

'You booked up tomorrow Jim?'

'Why. You wanna try again?'

'Sure. I told you I want to catch a big shark. They're obviously out there, so let's go get' em!' A smile spread across Jim's face, and Ritchie beamed at the thought of another day's pay.

As we walked to the bar Jim shouted. 'Whoooeee! Man — we are going to kick-ass on some sharks tomorrow!' It was a phrase that was to remain with me all my fishing life.

The following morning found me walking under the palm trees at Bud 'n' Mary's marina. It was 6 am. The sub tropical heat hadn't yet been fired up by the sunrise, and it was still dark. A gentle breeze soothed the whispering palm leaves, and fry dimpled the surface between the boats; surely a most hazardous life, being a bite-sized fish with so many predators prowling the warm waters. Very often, for reasons known only to those who write, paint or dream, the serenity and isolation of remote islands seem to capture the imagination.

For me, travelling has always been something of an adventure. Something perhaps only men can understand, a primeval yearning that precludes the emotional female of the species being involved. At some time or other, wherever I may travel, there comes a period in the trip when I need to spend an hour just walking, dreaming what might have been, what might be, or what should be. Sometimes so high is the feeling of elation and well-being that I want to shout to the world. At other times I have sat watching roseate clouds on a winter sunset, feeling so emotionally down, you could carry me away, sobbing like a baby. I have no idea where the feelings come from, or why. Maybe it's something to do with the isolation of being an angler of solitude. Too many years spent at the waterside, alone. Too much time for thinking. Yet it seems as though I have a purpose in life other than catching fish. They say a man can go mad at sea, from being alone too long, without hearing another human voice. God knows I've spent hours, days, weeks, months alone, happy with things until I've begun thinking too much.

The thing I miss most is a relationship with a woman who understands these feelings, and can share them with me. But women are such different creatures: basic animals who require, in the main, only loving, warmth, companionship and of course children. From there they cannot seem to extend feelings. They can't hate like a man, or see the need for a man to be among the company of men. They cannot accept that physical violence is a necessary outlet for men, nor understand the reason behind a man's desire to kill a living animal or fish. Their instincts are maternal and protective. A man's are physical, violent and often destructive. Of all the women friends I've known, and these have been limited, only one ever had the feeling to appreciate all this. We spent half a night sitting around a campfire up at Lake Powell in Arizona, discussing the problems of actually putting an emotion down on paper. She was also a journalist

12

which helped somewhat in the understanding of all this. I mention it all because I know there are other loners, other individuals who feel the same things, yet believe they are alone in the world. There are many who feel the same, but the very existence of being an individual precludes the sharing of such emotions.

I wandered over to Indian Key bridge and heard the tarpon rolling downtide of the buttresses. Light worms glowed as they drifted out of the Gulf and into the Atlantic on their spawning ritual. Silhouetted against the black sky was the island of Lignumvitae, an island that began life thousands of years ago, a living coral reef jutting up from the sea floor. As great quantities of water began to freeze into glaciers at the earth's poles, the sea level dropped, exposing the top of the reef and forming an island composed of fossilised coral rock. As time passed, storm tides and waves left seaweed, driftwood and other organic debris stranded on the bare rock. This material began decaying and forming small pockets of soil in depressions in the coral rock. Then came a few seeds from nearby tropical islands, floating on the sea or carried by the winds, while others came in the digestive tracts of migrating birds. With the passing of each generation, a complex and diverse tropical hummock colonised the remains of this coral reef. As I leaned on the bridge it seemed a fragile balance that nature maintained between construction and destruction!

I walked back, climbed into the car and drove down to Whale Harbour. By the time I had my sandwiches made at the corner shop, Jim and Ritchie were on the boat, and the sun was over the horizon. I knew as I climbed on board the boat that I was going to catch. Jim knew it. Ritchie knew it. All fishermen know it. And if, when you return to dock the fish boxes are still empty you simply blame the weather, the wind, the clouds or the moon. If everything was right, you say to yourself, we would have caught!

The trolling out to the 200-foot mark gave us about fifteen 'chicken' dolphin, fish in the 3–5-lb pound range. Then Jim anchored us and the *Ace* swung round on the Gulfstream and the obligatory blackfin tunas were consigned to the depths with lumps of concrete or iron. I settled down in the chair to wait. After two hours the big Penn Senator started up like a diesel engine, gradually gaining momentum until it was shrieking. In two minutes I had the harness on, another two and the other rods were in; five, and the anchor was slipped and we backed towards the departing fish. After twenty minutes of following the fish, I had regained only some fifty yards. Jim cut the engines and walked back down to me.

'Can't figger this one Gray-ham. He's still got too much line out. What sort of drag are you getting?' I took a couple of pulls of line off the reel. The drag was smooth, but still with many pounds of pressure on it.

'We'll try to get ahead of him, and work his head up. You're gonna get wet, when the water comes over the stern, so be prepared for it — and don't give him no slack, y'hear!' As the *Ace* crashed back through the waves I wound like a demon to keep the line tight. SUPERB! I gained a hundred feet. We repeated the process and suddenly I could feel him moving. I leaned back hard on the harness and pumped hard. In fifteen minutes Ritchie claimed to see it through the depths.

'He's coming in sideways Graeme, no wonder you had trouble moving him. He's either wrapped up in the leader, or foul-hooked.' The leader showed, Ritchie hauled on it, and suddenly Jim leapt up on the gunnels, feeding two shells into the chamber of his twelve-bore shotgun.

'You hold him up when he breaks surface Ritchie!' shouted Jim. 'I can't get a spinal shot unless you keep him on top for a couple of seconds.' He swung the twelve-bore to his shoulder and waited for Ritchie to ease the big fish up to the surface. Just as he was within range it swung under the stern and wrapped the steel trace round the tip of the rudder. I felt the back of the boat tremor, as the huge form thrashed and writhed only six feet back from the boat. Ritchie dropped the wire leader, wringing his gloved hand. 'Damn! Damn! Damn! He's foul-hooked in the guts Jim, I couldn't hold him, now he's wrapped on the rudder. The hook'll probably pull!' Jim ran to the stern and followed the thrashing form with the gunsight. 'It's no good, he's too deep, I can't get to him.' In another minute the hook pulled and I jumped to the stern to see a massive white-bellied shape spiralling back down the depths. 'What was it?'

'A damn great hammerhead. He was big too — maybe three, three fifty. Jesus, what a blow! Man, you are real unlucky Graeme. What you want to do, stay here or try out at the Hump?'

14

I was tired from hauling up the hammerhead for an hour, and decided a couple of amberjack would be easier. We up-anchored and trolled out to the Hump. As we circled amongst the birds Jim yelled from aloft.

'Over on the starboard, a good sized hammerhead. He's chasing blackfins. Run a bait out when I tell you!'

It was a full two minutes before I could make out the single tail fin cutting through the waves. He was swimming fast, the dorsal half in and half out of the water. As we quartered his route, Ritchie looked up at Jim for the signal. Jim's gaze was intense as he tried to time the drop so that it crossed the hammerhead's path. Then he cut the boat's engines.

'OK — NOW!' Ritchie dropped half a tuna over and I thumbed the reel as Jim put the motors on to drag the bait past its nose. With eighty yards of line out, he again cut the engines. I had a rough idea where the bait was from the angle of line in the water. The shark's fins suddenly disappeared. 'Watch out — he's going for it!' I had trouble keeping my hands still, they wanted to reel like crazy to take the bait away from this eating machine, which I now decided maybe I didn't want to catch.

'Spool it back again Graeme, he's gotta be right on top of it by now — and I know he can smell it — he had that "I wanna kill something today" look about him.'

Suddenly the arc in the dacron line jerked, then tightened.

'He's got it Jimbo — OK G.J. spool it back to him till I tell you'.

The line ran from the spool across the tips of my fingers. I thought of that creature below the surface crunching up the tuna bait. It could be me, or Ritchie, or Jim. Boy, I sure didn't have any craving for any swimming lessons!

'OK Stick him — reel man reel — let him know you're there!' I wound and struck several times, pausing only to let several yards of line be ripped off the reel. The first run was probably eighty yards. The second shorter, and the third non-existent. I locked down the drag and heaved the rod back, then cranked furiously on the forward motion. Wind-drop-pump-drop-wind-drop-wind. I began to breathe fast, and I felt my heart pounding. Pump-drop-wind, line came in easily, maybe he was only small, and Jim had over-estimated its size.

15

'Only feels small Jim. I can move him real easy.'

'He's big, don't worry Gray-ham.'

'No, he's only about 80 or 90, I'm gaining all the time.'

'You'll find out how big he is when he sees the boat. He's up round the 200 mark. How tight is the drag?' I pulled on it and it barely moved.

'Pretty loose Jim, I haven't touched it.' I liked the tight drag which allowed me to gain line quickly, and as I wasn't convinced this shark would go over 100lb, I horsed it some more.

'I see him' said Ritchie. 'Nice fish, he's hooked in the corner too.'

Suddenly the fish stopped, saw the boat and decided it liked the darkness of the depths better. The rod bowed over, the harness creaked, and I started to LIFT OUT OF THE CHAIR! I scrabbled with my feet trying to get a grip on the deck, and felt the veins of my neck start to bulge.

A voice from above boomed down. 'What's he doin' Ritchie, what the hell is the man doin'? Grab him before that sonofabitch drags him overboard!' The pressure was so great I didn't have the strength to take a hand off the foregrip and loosen the star drag. By the time Ritchie got to me I was extended over the stern, rod pointing straight at the fish. He fumbled with the drag, and it purred off line, zzzzzz, zzzzzz, zzzzzz. I dragged myself back into the fishing chair, and resumed the fight.

'Take it easy Graeme' said Ritchie. 'We got all the time in the world. That ol' hammer ain't goin' nowhere!'

I composed myself, adjusted the drag and resumed the fight with the fish. Another fifteen minutes and Jim and Ritchie had it balanced on the gunnel, tail flailing the air. CRASHHHH! It hit the deckboards and went berserk, rods, tackle boxes, fishing chairs, cushions — everything got thrashed around.

'Man he's a mean bastard beating up on my boat' laughed Jim. 'I've a good mind to throw him back!' The expression on my face at such a statement made an even bigger laugh, and we decided on an early start back. A small crowd had gathered to watch the weighing, and I watched myself, with a deep satisfaction as I saw the scale go past the 200 mark — 204, 209, 210lb. A roar went up, and I was the subject of much back slapping. Needless to say I slept well that night!

I had decided on one more try with Jim. I'd lost two good

fish through bad luck, and now my luck had changed I wanted to ride it as far as I could. All fishermen are superstitious to some extent, and I'm proud to say I'm no different. The next morning was perfect, a light north-westerly breeze held the *Ace* against the flow of the Gulfstream as we drifted in about 250 feet of water. Gulls wheeled overhead, a few cotton wool clouds drifted by on the horizon, and as far as I was concerned, all was well with the world — I wanted for nothing — EXCEPT — yes, a shark! Aren't we fishermen selfish? Mind you I could have asked for a night out with a lady of the night in New York, but then again that probably works out as expensive as big-game fishing.

The first take came on the 80. It purred out line, and I knew it wasn't going to be a big fish. After several minutes I had a 102-lb bull shark in the boat. Another half hour later and one of the 130s took off, reel singing. This one produced a 50-lb bull shark that had swallowed the whole blackfin tuna like it was its last meal in the sea. Then there was a period of inactivity. We all started to doze. Then the 12/0 sang its song. This fish was more powerful, and fought a ranging battle, far better than the previous two. It took me half an hour to get it in, as it had swum round two of the other lines. Jim and Ritchie had nearly as much fun untangling the mess, as I did fighting the shark! It proved to be a hammerhead, a beautifully shaped killing machine of 204lb.

We now had three sharks aboard and I was feeling a bit tired. The sun beat down, and while Ritchie re-baited I took the opportunity to make a ham and mayonnaise sandwich, grabbing a can of beer from the cooler. What a life! I lay back on the settee, feet off the end, eating food and letting the rocking of the boat relax me. People who haven't been out on a good day have no idea how peaceful and beautiful the sea can be. Mind you I've thrown up with the best of them, on days that couldn't even be classed as rough, yet somehow the lovely warm days with fish in the boat make you forget.

I was woken from this pleasant euphoria by a yell from Ritchie.

'FISH ON! get your ass in the chair Graeme, and I'll get you the harness!' The rod was bent double in the holder, line coming from the reel in short grunts. The drag was terrible on this gear, and I had secretly hoped I would never have the opportunity of catching a fish with it. Too late, this sucker was well and truly on, and I had to make do. I screwed the drag right up when Jim and Ritchie weren't looking and worked that fish so hard I thought my eyes would pop! The other two were so intent on cranking the other rods in they didn't see what a bad time I was giving this poor fish. 'Leader up!' I shouted.

Ritchie looked up. 'What? Already? Holy Christ, watch that swivel in the tip ring!'

I stopped winding with about three inches between the swivel and tip ring, and backed the drag off in case the shark made any sudden lunges. Ritchie grabbed the wire, and Jim put two shells into the spinal column at the neck of the shark. It turned out to be a big hammerhead that later turned the scales at 140lb again. I stripped down to shorts and lay on the bunk in the cabin, hoping to regain strength in case we had another take. Four sharks a day in ninety-degree heat was more than enough for one fish-crazed Englishman!

The baits were changed and dropped back down, two hours of the trip remaining. I decided to freeline a small bonito, streaming it away in the flow to fish about twenty feet deep. I fished it on an 80-lb outfit, and lay back down in the settee. I'd just started to doze off when zzzzzzzzzz! Line poured off at an astonishing rate. I grabbed the rod, and standing up, tried to set the hook. Now an 80-lb class of big game gear is very heavy, and one simply doesn't stand up to strike if one wants to retain one's sexual attributes. After the third strike, pain compounded itself in my groin and I let out a high pitched squeal. Cross legged I stumbled my way to the fishing chair clutching a partly bent rod! I jammed the butt in the gimble and managed about three pumps before my hook flew from amidst a welter of spray.

'Mako' shouted Jim.

'Throw the goddam hook' said Ritchie.

'Oh, damn!' I said, massaging vital organs.

Half an hour later there was another tremendous run before the bait was dropped. 'That was a sailfish Gray-ham, tried to take a whole bonito!'

As I wound in to inspect the bait, the big set of 130 took off, streaming line against a heavily set drag. I gave Ritchie the 80, and climbed in the chair. I managed to put the harness and gloves on before I picked the rod up. It was a good job I did. This fish was so powerful it was all I could do to keep the rod off the gunnel. A quarter of a spool disappeared in the time it took Ritchie and Jim to clear the other rods away. The anchor rope was put away, and the engines fired up. Half a spool had gone, in a constant speed that was frightening. This thing had picked up the whole tuna and was simply swimming along unconcerned!

'You got the one you wanted Gray-ham' shouted Jim. 'That mother is the biggest we've hooked in three days. Don't mess around with the drag on this one boy, he'll drag you in so fast we won't be able to catch you! Hey Ritchie, put some new shells in the chamber of the shotgun, and put a knife over on the stern by Gray-ham, we may have to cut this monkey off, if the Englishman can't handle him!'

He turned with a grin from ear to ear. 'Only joshin' G.J. — honest!' Three-quarters of a spool of dacron had disappeared and the sideplates on the big 12/0 reel were getting too hot to touch! 'Throw some water on the reel Ritchie, we don't want it seizing.'

After fifteen minutes I still hadn't got one turn on the reel handle. We were pacing the shark with the boat and all I had done was keep pace with it. The rod was bent so hard the straps bit into my shoulders. The sun blazed down and I felt the fatigue from the previous four fights. Half an hour passed and I had gained a few yards of line. Still no appreciable improvement on the reel capacity though. My back ached and I tried several different positions trying to ease the discomfort. How I longed for a proper fighting chair with footplate and bucket harness. No such luxuries on the *Ace*. If you wanted to land a shark you did it the hard way — sheer graft! Forty-five minutes and I felt physically sick. I wanted to give the rod to Ritchie, but pride prevented me from asking. I hadn't come all this way to hook up a huge shark, then have to go home saying my 5-foot 8-inch torso cracked up under the strain! Jim turned the stern of *Ace* to a different angle and I gained some line. Frantically I thumbed the sideplates and pinched the dacron against the butt in a fruitless effort to stop the big fish regaining it. No point — it all slid back beneath the surface. I felt like crying! Ritchie appeared at my side, kneeling down beside me.

'You look like you could use a drink G.J. If I pour it in your mouth can you swallow OK?'

19

I nodded and swallowed some Millers. It was cold from the ice, and hurt the back of my throat. 'How big is he Ritchie? How big?'

'I figure he's over 300, maybe up to 400.' He looked at Jim who was standing with his back to the morse controls continually jockeying the boat's position to keep the stern to the fish. 'How big you reckon Jimbo?'

Jim shook his head, face expressionless. 'I dunno Ritchie, I'd like to see a bit more line on the reel; we could lose him if he decides to take the reef.'

Ritchie pulled some line to check the drag, then put it up a quarter of a turn. 'Try to work him some more Gray-ham — he's still a long way down.'

'I—can't—Ritchie . . . I—feel—exhausted!'

He knelt beside me again, like a mother urging her son to do his homework. 'Try to move him in one turn pumps Graeme. Heave up, make a sharp drop, then spin the handle real quick. Don't jerk. Make a smooth motion out of it. He'll come, believe me — I seen a lot of these — but you GOT to move him. He'll lay there all today and tonight, and remember — he's gaining strength a whole lot quicker than you!' With such sound advice I worked the fish as suggested. To my surprise I began to move him, slowly at first, then gaining quickly.

'He's comin' Jim. Hey, look Ritchie the spool's half full!' Both men cheered. 'Well ALRIGHT Gray-ham — let's go get him!'

I worked the fish with renewed vigour until the reel showed three-quarters full. To my amazement the leader suddenly appeared. The line had been wound on under such pressure that it was like a stone to the touch, compacted onto the spool.

'Leader up!' shouted Ritchie, grabbing it. 'Get the twelve gauge Jim!'

That was as near as I got to that damn shark for another twenty minutes. An hour and a quarter had passed and Ritchie had hold of the leader no less than seven times. Each time he could only get the shark near the boat and it would sound, a power I was unable to resist. Jim paced up and down impatiently, he wanted that shark as badly as I did. We planed it up again, and the leader showed above the surface. A massive form was some twenty feet beneath it, twisting and turning in the current.

'How long he's been on that fish Ritchie?' asked Jim. He looked at his watch. 'An hour and a half Jim.' Neither man smiled, my personal battle with this fish had become theirs, they wanted, no, needed that fish for the sake of man's pride of conquest over beast. This fish had beaten us as far as we were likely to be beaten. I couldn't hold on much longer. I'd already spent a total of nearly two and a half hours on the previous four sharks. I was nearing total collapse. Jim knew it. Ritchie knew it. I certainly knew it, and I had a feeling the shark knew it. Jim strode across the cabin, snapped shut the twelve gauge and stalked back, his face impassive. 'Ritchie when I plane it up with the boat next time, you grab the leader and you damn well better hold him this time. I'm going in fast and there's gonna be spray comin' over the back. Gray-ham I know you're shot, but you gotta do it one more time. You're gonna get wet, and I don't care if you hurt so bad you wanna scream. You DON'T take your eyes off Ritchie. Keep the rod over his left shoulder when he goes for the wire, and keep the goddam swivel away from the tip ring. Has everybody got it?'

'Sure Jim.'

'I'll do my best Jim.'

'OK Let's get him, he's done messed around with us long enough. If we don't get him this time I'm cuttin' the line!'

Cut the line? Oh no! Not that!

'Everybody ready?' He revved the boat's engines, then yelled 'Here we go!'

I felt the *Ace* surge backwards as the twin props bit water, the chop cascading over me, blinding me temporarily with the stinging salt. I winced as the salt ran into the strap cuts on my back made by the harness, but wound line on that reel as though my life depended on it. The double line showed. Then the leader. The shark started to pull away but Ritchie took a turn of steel cable round his hand and held on doggedly. I virtually stood up in the chair as I leaned back, the last of my strength going into helping Ritchie hold that leader. 'Keep him, KEEP HIM' screamed Jim, jockeying the morse controls. Suddenly I felt the give, that subtle thing that tells you it's over, finished. The shark started to come again. Ritchie pulled the wire slowly, hand over hand and I watched for the swivel. It neared the tip ring and I screamed out 'Swivel up, he's all yours Ritchie!'

21

Jim stood by Ritchie's side, the twelve gauge only inches from Ritchie's face. 'Yahoo! Here he comes Jim!' A massive ten-foot length of killing machine appeared at the back of the boat, rolling in the swell, jaws agape like the doors of hell. I saw Jim actually squeeze the trigger, no jerk-off, just a smooth action. . . BOOOOMMM! The water kicked as the shot ripped into the neck of the huge fish. 'Hold him still' shouted Jim. 'NO WAY' screamed Ritchie — 'You do it!' BOOOMMM! The second barrel blew a hole in the shark's head and Jim leapt to the stern and drove the head of a flying gaff into the lower jaw. A rope secured to the gaff head was connected to the stern cleat. I suddenly realised it was all over. The shark was ours.

After an hour and a half the shark was ours. I looked at Jim who was already laughing. Ritchie lay gasping on the deck, still clutching the leader wire. . . all he said was 'Jesus — the things we do for Englishmen!' The fish was too big to bring aboard by hand alone, so we rigged up the gimble and winched it in. I couldn't believe the size of it. My big shark — and though I was to take several more over the years, that first truly big one will remain etched in my memory forever. So too will the comradeship, and teamwork that was involved in its capture. It was a three-man shark. One of the hardest fighters I have ever taken. It proved to be a bull shark, and was the biggest taken by Jim that year. Back at dock it weighed 455lb.

I can remember those immortal words — 'So you wanna catch a big one — Huh?' I did. And I had.

2

Hammerheads and Marlin

MAURITIUS

Winter in England can be a dismal affair at the best of times. Usually I spend my weekends hunched over a pair of pike rods at a local lake, waiting for those bobbins to slither and slide towards the butt ring. As you get older, the desire to catch every fish in the lake, river or ocean subsides. It doesn't matter that you can't catch what you want today. Tomorrow is only a few hours away! So it was that I found myself on a jet bound for the warmer climes of the Indian Ocean.

Travelling expectantly to a new venue has always been half the fun for me. Strange countries, with even stranger customs hold that certain mystique that keeps the adrenalin flowing. Mauritius is a relatively small island situated some 1,200 miles off the east coast of Africa, with Australia and India on the east and north-east respectively. This tropical paradise remains, as Mark Twain discovered it: 'of brilliant sunshine, blonde virgin beaches, sea lagoons as clear as crystal, balmy sea breezes and lush vegetation'. Once home of the extinct dodo, I was hoping for some piscine activity that would prove to be far from extinct. Doubtless there are dozens of, as yet, undiscovered angler's paradise islands, but Mauritius itself held the reputation for being a potential big-fish venue.

My flight was from London to Cairo, Khartoum, Nairobi and finally Mauritius. On landing at the airport, officials thought we were carrying a few more passengers from the Nairobi section than immigration allowed, and so we had to spend an hour sitting in the aircraft, while a fumigation spray was administered. Not the most auspicious of welcomes. I was met by Mimma Hulkhory from the Tourism Office and escorted to the La Pirogue hotel in the west of the island. There were two places renowned for producing the goods. The most successful big billfish area was out on a bearing south west from the Le Morne mountain, which continued under the sea for some distance. This in turn attracted the baitfish on which the big billfish fed. The Black River empties into the sea at the side of the Le Morne mountain, creating a break in the natural surround of the barrier reef. Tucked into the bay here are two fishing organisations: the Centre-de-Peche Club, which offered boats for charter and accommodation, and the Bonanza Big Game organisation, run by the I.G.F.A. rep, Maurice-de-Speville. I decided on a session from both, so, after checking into the hotel, telephoned the Centre-de-Peche Club to arrange some boat bookings.

It was the end of February, so there were still plenty of billfish about, a point which did nothing to make my first night's sleep enjoyable! Mauritius boasts five 1000-lb fish having been caught there, and indeed there are monsters swimming that drop-off that would spool many a 12/0 reel! One year there filtered a message on the angler's grapevine of a massive specimen in a market in the north of the island. It had no head. It had been gutted. Yet the remains of that commercially caught fish tipped the scales at 900 kilos! That's 1,900-lb and more than most men would want to bang a hook into. I would be happy just to catch the odd fish or two.

The 7 am taxi journey from the hotel to Centre-De-Peche proved to be a somewhat traumatic experience in itself. For the first mile or so I thought the effects of the previous nights' imbibing was still having some adverse effects. Then I realised that the body of the taxi was indeed moving at a different rate to the chassis, and appeared to be unattached. The sugar cane workers calmly stood aside as we careered along, bouncing and rattling, the driver's hand held permanently on the horn. (The following day I was late getting up so naturally asked the driver to put the pedal to the metal. That in itself was a mistake, as the odd nut and bolt started to come loose with the increase in speed). Somehow however, I arrived safely, if somewhat jaded. I would hate to think what would happen if the driver lost his temper, or wanted to have a carve up with a fellow taxi driver.

Eventually I found myself sharing a boat with a Frenchman and his wife, both of whom had failed to connect the previous day. Apparently the skipjack tuna, on

24

which the big marlin feed, were too large to use as livebait. I naturally assumed a big skipjack to weigh around 8–10lb, and began rigging up my 12-lb graphite spinning rod. The mate fingered this tackle, laughed and tossed it aside. He was obviously unimpressed with the diameter of the line, and presumably labelled me an 'amateur'.

An hour later and the diving birds were sighted; the big konahead lures were brought in and replaced with small plastic squid. As I looked round I saw the mate running back my 12-lb outfit in open bale position. I watched in that sort of slow motion, watching the bale snap shut just as we ran through the school of fish. The two 50s we were trolling as flat lines took off with fish attached, and the line on my 12 exploded in his hands as a big tuna hit! This made him jump and he tossed the outfit down on a seat, confirming his opinion of light tackle fishing. What I hadn't reckoned on was the size of the skipjacks which were *averaging* 20lb apiece. Now that's a helluva skipjack on a fixed spool reel. However, I was now in the position of not being able to back down, so I set about re-tying a Bimini twist and running back a new Hexhead lure. When we ran through the next school I had a hook-up, and watched in amazement as line poured from the spool. I increased the drag slightly, bounced the rod a few times to set the hook, then backed off the drag and waited for the tuna to wind itself up. By the time the boat had slowed I was looking at a half empty spool, with around 250 yards of line out in the wake. By altering the drag and watching the line stretch I killed that tuna in twenty minutes without waiting for the boat to be backed down. He proved to be a new Centre-De-Peche record, on 12-lb class, at 19lb, and was only some 61lb below the world record.

The rest of the day was spent in search of smaller skipjack for bait but none were found. I had prudently brought over my 50-lb class Fenwick outfit on the plane, hoping to do battle with one of the smaller marlin. When I learned that a 500-pounder, together with two 700s had been landed, I thought discretion the better part of valour and left it in the hotel room.

Next day I was out on Maurice-de-Speville's private launch from the Bonanza organisation's jetty just down the beach. This time I was on my own in the boat, Maurice being unable to make it. I've always been lucky when on my own, but had that fisherman's sixth sense that today would be different. For starters, we were a little late getting away from the quay and by the time we reached the diving birds, we heard on the radio that another crew already had a hookup. Two miles out and we saw the dots on the horizon of the other gameboats churning through the birds and fish in an effort to secure livebait. By the time we arrived on the scene the activity had died down a little, but every tuna we hooked bled a little, and so were unusable as livebait. To make matters worse, just thirty yards away an angler hooked up on a billfish and disappeared into the horizon for an hour or so.

Suddenly we had a triple header on the squids and one of the tuna proved to be scissor hooked. It was bridle rigged on a set of 130 immediately, and the skipper started to feed line down from the rod top. At the same instant the line was ripped from his grasp and I shouted as a marlin gouted water not fifteen yards off the stern. I leapt in the chair, and after the line came tight, drove the hook in. It was great to feel that satisfying weight as I came up against a three-figure fish. Line purred from the International Reel and I started to ease the drag on as he slowed. The harness was clipped around my shoulders and then snapped onto the reel lugs. Bracing my feet against the footplate of the fighting chair I began to work him. After only two minutes I could move him — a sure sign that he wasn't the big fish I'd been looking for. After about fifteen minutes he was billed aboard, a gleaming fish in the 100-lb range. The other two tuna we had kept in a bucket had unfortunately expired, so we re-rigged the small squids and pushed the engines on to catch up with the tuna school. We soon saw another two, one of which would make a good livebait, and it was consigned to the depths on the bridle rig.

The rest of the day was spent slow-trolling at around 1 to 1¹/₂ knots, just enough movement to tow the tuna out behind us. I lay in the sun, still trying to appreciate that the temperatures back home in England would be hovering around freezing, with a biting wind! Late in the afternoon the skipper spotted a flock of diving birds. We tracked them with the boat but the school of fish were obviously moving too fast for us. I walked forward to see what the skipper thought about winding the skipjack in, putting it in a bucket to keep it alive and running up on the tuna school. He assured me that very often the marlin would stay like we were, just tracking the baitfish, and only moving in to feed when the tuna went into a frenzy. Half an hour later and the flock of birds were several hundred yards away. Suddenly I saw the outrigger pole bend slightly and the line snap down. I was already sitting in the chair, so easily threw on the drag when sufficient line had run off. As I drove the steel in, water erupted off the stern, and a billfish wagged its head in defiance.

The first run fooled me into thinking it may be a big fish, but again, once I got to leaning back on the harness I could gauge the size of the fish, and I guessed it to be no more than 100lb. Sure enough, twenty minutes later it lay alongside, another hundred pounder, almost identical to the first! Catching two fish this small in Mauritian waters was almost unheard of, the average weight being up around 300lb. However I was more than pleased to catch two Pacific blue marlin in one day, and returned to the Bonanza headquarters a happy angler. Back on dock a 370-lb blue was being weighed, and next in line was a 300-lb-plus black marlin. They were out there somewhere!

After sampling the delights of the watersports over the next few days, I moved to the north west of the island to try my luck from the other big game centre there. Roland-de-Speville runs the Du Peche Nord organisation, and accommodation can be found just three hundred yards along the beach at the Trou-Aux-Biches hotel complex.

After a couple of days settling in here, I had the opportunity of watching the ancient ritual of the cavadee festival. This ceremony is celebrated in honour of the Lord Muruga, and includes an awesome ritual where the Tamil people pierce their cheeks and tongues with long needles. Although an extremely colourful festival I found myself having a severe case of camera shake as I photographed them performing this. The air was thick and heavy with the scent of flowers, perfumes, bodies and smouldering hot coals. During the procession from the river bank to the temple, the Tamils who have been pierced, carry a huge wooden arch called a cavadee. This is smothered with beautiful yellow alamanda flowers and young leaves of the coconut tree. A devotee usually undertakes to carry the cavadee in fulfilment of a vow, or as thanks for recovery from a serious disease.

The ceremony left behind, I went to the north-western resort hotel of Trou-Aux-Biches. Bungalows situated right on the beach made this a haven for the watersports enthusiast and sun worshipper; it suited me fine. That evening I spoke with the owner, Roland-de-Speville, who told me that although the marlin fishing wasn't as good as that found down at Le Morne mountain area a 300-lb billfish had just been caught and so I should set a day aside to try for one. First though, I wanted to spend some time reef fishing, which I elected to do the next day.

The morning was a classic as far as January weather in Mauritius was concerned. It was hot and humid and my clothes were saturated by the time I reached the restaurant just 200 yards away. The humidity takes a while to get used to but as the sun climbs in the sky the day does become drier.

I met the three crew who were to join me, exchanged greetings and boarded the gameboat. They were all engineers and crew in Roland's employ, and were more than pleased to have a few hours off work to go fishing. Their tackle was produced, and left a lot to be desired. A gallon petrol can, fortunately empty, clattered around the deck as they dropped their weight over the side. Weights were pieces of iron and rock. A simpler handline would be harder to find, and doubtless worked well until someone tangled their feet up in the huge mess of 40-lb monofilament crumpled over the deck like some man-eating clock spring. On the journey out we ran about a hundred yards off from the barrier reef, so I ran a couple of magnum rapalas, superb inshore trolling lures, from my rods in quest of predators. We reached the intended rock mark without having to tend the rods, and thus began the serious business of fishing. A chunk of tuna fillet was impaled on a rusty hook and dropped to the bottom, which was a considerable distance once outside the reef. Furious jerks by the arms and back muscles indicated a bite, and every so often a fish flopped over the side. Deciding the depth was more than I could tackle, I ran out a tuna head on a shark rod, and dropped my 12-lb class outfit over the side to drift at mid depth. Gradually the heat of the sun, the gentle rocking of the road and the companionship of other anglers came to the fore and anaesthetised us against the problems of the world. It was fishing as it should be. There were no glass rods. No lever drag reels with which to attract the unseen adversary. No fancy lures or rigs designed to do a specific task. A simple handline, a length of line and a hook baited with hope was all we had.

After three hours the sun became too hot even for the Mauritians and we lounged in the canopy shade drinking beer before departing to the dockside. I looked at the array of colours in the fish box. Well-known wildlife and fish artists recreate the majesty of the leaping blue marlin; the cobalt blue colours of the sail from a sailfish; the garish flashing yellow of a dolphin. Yet I defy any man, photographer or artist, to recreate the beauty that lies in a box of freshly caught reef fish. Clumsy fighters they may be, with an appetite of a starving wolf, but they made up for their lack of sporting vigour by portraying all the natural colours that God created.

That evening while sitting on the beach I thought about our so called 'sporting' ethics. I have caught trout, billfish and tuna and have returned them gently to fight another day. Yet surely the reef fish, although a poor proposition when it comes to bending the rod, should have the same chance? And why should some species be allowed a second lease of life, while their fellow fish suffer expiration in some fish hold?

Next day I was up early, and had forgotten the philosophical problems of the previous day. Today I wanted to pull on something. Little was I to know what would follow. The day began routinely enough with us steaming out with a couple of konaheads on flat lines, and two bonito lures running from the outriggers. As soon as we saw some birds out came the konaheads and on went a couple more squid for the bonito. At nine o'clock the obligatory flock of terns was sighted, and we motored over. In no time at all two of the 30s were bent over, ratchets chattering to the tune of hooked fish. These first two fish were bleeding and thus were retained as future deadbaits; what we wanted was livebait. We relocated the terns and ran through again. Small gouts of water sputtered up behind the lures as the skipjacks tried to grab the skipping squids. Two hung themselves on and we brought them aboard. One was bleeding from the gill, the other very slightly from the eye. We decided to rig the latter on a bridle mount and see if it would last as our marlin livebait but before long a trickle of blood came from the corner of its eye and the skipper pulled it in.

I was leaning over the stern watching this, with my face only three feet from the surface, when suddenly a massive shape came into my field of vision. A grey-brown shape, snake-like in movement flashed right up and crashed into the stern, jaws crunching on the prop. I saw its head twist convulsively, then let go and swam under the boat. This happened in no more time than it takes to read this, probably faster. I staggered back, mouth open, frozen with the primeval fear of having countered death at its closest. I backed into the skipper who amazingly enough was still discussing our poor luck in catching four tuna, all of which had bled, as though nothing had happened. He looked up at my pale face and wide eyes.

'A shark's just bitten the boat! He's underneath now!'

They both looked at me with blank expressions. I tried again. 'LOOK, THERE'S A HUGE HAMMERHEAD UNDER THE BOAT. WE MUST DO SOMETHING!'

They leaned over the stern with me. Nothing. Only the exhaust bubbles spiralling into the wake, the waves softly lapping at the stern. They must think I'm crazy I thought to myself, yet I know I saw it. I've caught hundreds of sharks. This hammerhead was like nothing I'd ever seen before, it was huge.

Just as they were about to turn away it came out. Eight or ten feet of solid muscle, swimming fast, that hammer-like head methodically cutting through the water, scanning for the source of the tuna blood. They saw it at the same instant, pointing, screaming excitedly, yet I heard nothing. Things started to go into slow motion as the shark sliced through the water away down the wake. If he'd failed to locate the source of food he'd disappear and my chance would be gone. The skipper was screaming as he shook the trace in his hand. It was about five feet of wire coupled to heavy duty mono. No good for shark. Its rough hide would chafe through that in ten minutes. I dunked the remains of a tuna in the stern, shaking it to get the guts and blood in the water, banging the back of the boat with my free hand. Anything, anything to make that shark turn round. In fifteen seconds he had gone, the proverbial needle in the haystack. The mate and skipper were uncoiling a steel shark trace, rigging up the 130 and baiting a whole tuna, all at once. He was gone. The skipper looked up and swore. I didn't need to speak Mauritian to know what he said. The mate tossed the tuna into the bucket, turning as he too cursed under his breath.

Suddenly, from the corner of my eye I saw the line from the outrigger hanging limply in the water. I'd still left a big konahead out there at the back of the wake. That sixth sense told me that the shark was so hungry he might, just might, be attracted to a fast cranked lure. I started winding feverishly, frantically, until the line came tight, sprang from the rigger clip and came taut to the rod top, I felt the weight of the lure, maybe sixty yards back, and wound like fury to get it up on the surface where it would kick and splash. The mate shouted that it was a waste of time, yet still I cranked that International handle. We could see the lure spluttering along the top; 'Yes! he's right behind the lure — LOOK AT HIM GO!'

The hammerhead was scything, slashing after the lure, jaws snapping at the plastic skirt. Suddenly the skipper and mate were in action as they realised we had a chance, and dropped a whole tuna over the side. The lure came in, I clunked it over the stern and the big shark shot under the boat. In three seconds he reappeared so close I could have reached out and tapped his huge dorsal with the gaff handle. God, he looked big! The tuna winked and flashed in the blue of the water and then the shark homed in. We watched the cold, calculating way the shark approached, killed, then rolled upside down jaws ripping into the tuna's flesh. A cloud of blood coloured the water and the shark twisted and thrashed under water as it gorged on the meat. I leapt in the fighting chair, then away went the line, the spool picking up speed until it was a blur. The mate counted in seconds, then with over one hundred yards of line out, slapped me hard on the shoulder and I jabbed up the lever drag with my thumb. I felt that line draw slowly tight, felt the clutch start to creak as the plates groaned, then bent my back and heaved the rod back, six, seven, eight times. The fish shook his head, obviously worried by the tugging of steel in its jaw, and decided to move to pastures new. The reel drag whined, groaned then screamed as the line roared away, the shark's incredible strength lifting me bodily from the seat, my arms outstretched in front, forearms bulging, eyes popping. Where the hell was the harness?

31

The mate snapped the clips onto the reel lugs and I felt that wonderfully satisfying pull as the straps bit into my shoulders. It was a macho thing, that awesome power of being physically dragged from the fighting chair. Men only. Death a few seconds away, all that stuff that men and boys love. Better than making love to a woman. Like a twenty-minute orgasm. I loved it. It was what I had travelled 7,000 miles for, and all the old battles with other big fish came flooding back. I wanted this fish. I wanted to whip him into submission. But always that inherent fear: maybe this was the one that would kill me, the reel would seize and I would get dragged over the side; my heart give out under the strain; I would die from exposure in the sun; physical damage would be done to my back.

These weren't entirely fanciful fears — they had all happened to other people. I wanted to make damn sure I was on top. I wanted to WIN! That first run must have taken some 120 yards from the reel, and by the time both fish and boat had slowed I was looking at a dwindling supply of line. The secret of whipping big fish is to start working on them as soon as that first run stops, so I stretched my legs out stiff against the footplate, stood up, and leaned hard back, making the leather harness creak. That provoked a response alright, and I had to back down as another thirty or so yards disappeared! The skipper looked at the mate. The mate looked at the skipper. I looked at both; we were in agreement this was no 100 pounder. Originally I had thought he looked about 200lb but things always look smaller in the water due to the light refraction and I revised this to over 300lb; the skipper thought maybe over 400lb.

The hammerhead is a hard fighter, and this one was no exception. We had hooked him up at 9.30 and it was now 10.05. I should have made some headway on him, but everything I had gained had been dragged back out by the shark. The sun was beginning to push the temperature up, and I downed a cold beer, pouring some over my wrists. Slow down, I thought. Take it easy. He's going to come. You know he's going to come. Just wait for the chance. At 10.15 I sensed that certain something that tells you the fish is getting tired, he's puffing a bit. The continual strain has taken its toll. I thumbed up the lever drag a little and bent the 130 blank as much as my five-foot-eight frame could stand. The line sang in the freshening breeze, the leather shoulder harness creaked like an old sloop's mast in a storm.

Then he started to give, slowly at first, and I had him coming smoothly, getting three turns of the International's handle to one pump. The double showed, then the steel trace. The swivel came to within three inches of the rod tip and I backed down the drag. I could do no more. My part was completed now, it was up to the skipper and mate. As their gloved hands closed around the wire I felt the fish move off. No less than three times was that wire in the mate's hands. And three times he had to let go otherwise he would have joined the hammerhead in its own environment. The fourth time a rope was looped around its curious shaped hammer head and tied off on two cleats. He was mine! With the fight over I flopped back in the chair without realising the chair was backless. I crashed out backwards avoiding a crack on the head as the rod jammed against an arm. Not exactly a macho image after landing a big shark but who cared? I was knackered and both skipper, mate and myself had a good laugh.

Getting the shark aboard was the next problem. It had taken me 56 minutes to whip the fish, a huge male hammerhead that later tipped the scales at 378lb, undoubtedly a 400 pounder if it hadn't dried out in the sun all day. It took a further half an hour to get it into the boat, and only then could we see the tremendous length of the fish. He must have measured well over eleven feet, and was my biggest hammer to date.

The rest of the day was spent trolling a livebait for billfish, but despite a long journey down the coast to the lighthouse we saw no action. On the journey home we dispensed with baits and I ran three lures. My own big Jet lure, and two bonito lines. Just before we ran through the gap in the reef I picked up two big skipjacks and a 15-lb wahoo.

So finished my first encounter with the fabulous, and as yet quite untouched, potential of the Indian Ocean island of Mauritius. That it has big fish swimming its coastal waters is not in dispute. It's how best to put them in the boat that's important. The following few days were spent touring this fabulous island, and I covered a story on the island's horse racing. With a father and grandfather in the racing game as trainers I was amazed to learn that the Mauritius Turf Club is the second oldest in the world! The horses were kept up in the mountains during the months of highest humidity and only raced during the cooler weather. With all the backache from capturing the big hammerhead I felt as though I'd taken a fall at Beechers in the Grand National! Next year I would return for that 1,000 pounder. In fishing there's no greater incentive than the thought of what tomorrow might bring.

3

Tope and Monkfish

THE WEST COAST OF IRELAND

Think of our own home waters and the species of gamefish seems fairly limited. Yet it includes a fish that in my own opinion is a fighter of the highest calibre: the tope. I have already caught its bigger cousins around British waters — blues, porbeagle and thresher — but because of its size the tope is considered a poor relation. A smaller, primarily bottom-feeding shark, it rips line from the reel at an alarming rate.

Although I had caught the odd tope among the mixed ground fishing of the English Channel, it was Ireland that initiated me into 'skinny water' fishing at its best. After that first trip I have returned each year, sometimes twice a year, to fish in its truly magnificent waters. The west coast of Ireland remains a paradise on earth for English anglers, who still have that yearning to fish in pure waters, untouched by over exploitation of trawlers or industrial pollution. Many remote areas of the west coast are almost fifty years behind modern times and enjoy a peace, serenity and pace of life that is all too rare today.

If you arrive in Dublin on the ferry, a four-hour drive across bumpy roads and open pasture is necessary to get to the gradual rise of land mass that marks the west coast: a ridge of purple-mauve mountains that skirts the deep clear Atlantic Ocean. My initiation into the world of tope came in Co. Mayo's Blacksod Bay, a huge expanse of water surrounded by the Belmullet peninsula, where the opening to the ocean is guarded by Achill Head, one of the highest and most impressive mountain cliffs in Europe. My skipper was Vincent Sweeney, his craft the *Girl Emer*, a cabin cruiser that often had to ply the route from Blacksod lighthouse out to the treacherous waters of the Blackrock. The tope run the main feeder channel of the bay, hunting right up to the sleepy town of Belmullet itself. The depths are not more than twenty feet thus making this true 'skinny water' fishing.

I was guiding a group of anglers on their first trip to the area and the lads sharing *Girl Emer* with me were Jerry Airey from Hornchurch in Essex, and Paul Neal from my home town of Fleet in Hampshire. After a long drive down the Belmullet peninsula we arrived at the base of Blacksod pier, the sentinel lighthouse towering above us. It was here that Vincent and his family live, braving the wild weather that often races in across the Atlantic Ocean from its birth place near the eastern seaboard of the United States. Weather conditions along this peninsula can change from day to day, even hour to hour. Mountains that stand clear against the deep blue sky in the morning can quickly become clouded with hazy cumulous; puffing, blooming structures that soon drop down over the moorland to develop into that light misting drizzle known locally as 'soft' weather. It can stay like this for a night and a day, invariably developing into a blustery gale and heavy rain. Many is the time I have sat quietly beside Vincent's smouldering peat fire, watching the glimmering coals as the wind has whipped down the chimney and blown the odd puff of smoke out into the room. It rattles windows, bangs barn doors and funnels through the tiniest crack, seeking you out, making you shiver and poke the embers in the fire for that extra bit of warmth. At sea are only the brave or the stupid — either saving lives, or hopefully being saved. Outside, the reefs of rocks known to the local fishermen rise from their placid slumbers and strive to grow from the sea, fighting each wave, throwing it high in the air to be whipped away on the howling wind. During such time, any sensible person stays indoors, for there is only one winner in such conditions.

When the wind has eased it is time the fisherman must ready his tackle, for invariably the sun will break through, settling the scudding clouds and smoothing the surface of the bay waters, for then, as warmth and calm descends from Achill and the western approaches, the tope move in, harassing mackerel shoals and scouring the seabed for the rippling flight of a startled dab or flounder. It was on such a day that Vincent guided the *Girl Emer* up into the bay waters, following the feeder channel from the sea entrance towards the town of Belmullet, the echo sounder flickering monotonously as it told us of the seabed's contours. Close to the town the channel splits filling two huge bays, and it was here that the anchor chain clattered over the deck, dragging with it the rope, until the steel blades bit into the sand, and *Girl Emer* settled in the tide, held by the taut rope.

We used a mixture of dubious origin to attract the tope that is concocted of old mackerel minced with bran and pure pilchard oil. Dispersed via a meshed onion sack it is sunk near the seabed on another rope with the help of a 2-lb lead, where its noxious vapours can finger their way down through the currents that use the filling channel as a highway. Any tope crossing that path will change course and home in to the source of the smell. As it nears the boat, three or four separate smells will be located by the hunter thus reducing its area of search. Our hookbaits ooze pilchard oil and hopefully will be found by the tope.

Aboard *Girl Emer* Vincent places a mug of hot tea on the gunnel near my rod. As I close my fingers round its hot plastic outer casing the reel fires out a banshee wail as a tope hits the mackerel bait and runs for the channel, crunching the flesh in its razor-sharp jaws. I knock the mug over, curse as its hot liquid splashes my arm, but manage to grab the rod and release the check. Smoothly the line races from the reel spool and slants down towards the stern. After fifteen seconds it stops, then I hear my own heart hammering in the silence that envelops me, the line across the index finger of my left hand stationary, my only connection to the bait thirty yards away. Ten seconds drag interminably then with a jolt the line is torn from my finger, the inertia of the revolving spool making loops of line fluff up. Thumbing it carefully the snaking coils smooth out and I lock the reel into gear, let the line come tight then hammer the rod up . . . once . . . twice . . . a third time, hard on the running fish. The tope kicks into third gear and melts line from the reel, a protesting star-drag 'zeeeeing' a spray into my face. Thirty seconds into the fight and another reel shrieks as another tope races away from the boat, this time with Jerry's bait held across its jaws. Too early he strikes and the still Irish air is broken by a series of Essex expletives. As my own fish planes to turn into the tide a third rod bends. This time Paul lets it run without any resistance and we are shortly connected to two of these greyhounds of the sea. With lines threatening to cross I pressure my own tope, horsing it towards the side where a waiting Vincent stands patiently with gloved hand. Suddenly its form is showing under the surface, a sleek grey missile, pectoral fins flared wide, that scimitar head shaking savagely as it tries to dislodge the steel in its jaw. On the surface it thrashes the water to a foam. A 'green' fish held hard on the 140-lb mono leader by Vincent, is grabbed by the dorsal and pectoral, then scruffed noisily into the boat. Once on the deckboards its main aim seems to be to cause as much discomfort to those in its proximity as possible. We have no need to kill this superb fighting fish (being poor eating quality) so it is carefully weighed, tagged with a Central Fisheries Board plastic tag and slipped back to give another angler sport. These tope are nomadic, travelling from the west coast of Ireland down to the warmer climes of Morocco in the Mediterranean, and the Canary Islands in the Atlantic. Nobody knows why they travel so far on this migration, but the ocean currents are like a serengeti of the seas, giving birth to a multitude of food chains that are interlinked throughout the world.

This particular fish weighed 31lb which is quite large for a male; the females are usually the real heavyweights. Paul's fish topped out at 27lb and we took a further seven from the channel before the current eased, and the fish left to chase the mackerel and brit out into the open sea. On that, our first day, we set a record for the number of tope taken in one day from the bay.

Exactly one year later I was in the same place, in the same boat with the same bait. The long smell trail exuding downtide from the rubby-dubby bag was beckoning strongly, but during that entire week we took just three tope. Jerry took one, and I landed one. We did of course have superb fishing with other species: thornback skate that flopped lazily onto the bait causing the rod top to dip twice indicating their presence; golden-flanked pollock that rose from the depths of the Ushbourne shoal reef to engulf rubber sandeels; hard fighting fish that kiss double figures; speckled, rust-coloured rock cod, their cavernous mouths scooping up the plastic muppet lures we used as attractors; needle-toothed ling that darted out to snap up any mackerel fillet that fluttered enticingly near their rock hideouts, some 200 feet beneath *Girl Emer's* hull. But the tope, as the saying goes, were notable by their absence.

It was the memory of that first tope run that drew me into

38

organising a fourth expedition to the west coast. This time I was accompanied by Jerry Airey and my local tackle dealer Nigel Newport. This time we returned in June, to see if it was true that the larger tope packs hit the bay at this time of year. The rocks looked the same, the rain still felt warm, and the gales were still chilly. But the faces of friends looked older. When I look in the mirror I see the same face, the same lines, the same marks — but to others no doubt I must be changing as well, getting older. They say for every day a man fishes the good lord tacks a day onto his life. I smile every time I hear that.

Aboard the anchored *Girl Emer* again, Vincent made us hot mugs of tea, and we put four rods over the side. I promise you that inside a minute we had four tope all screaming line from respective reels. With a fish apiece headed in different directions it remained for Vincent to play the fish on the fourth rod. The teas again got knocked over, lines crossed and re-crossed in a cat's cradle of monofilament yet somehow we boated all four tope! Three were over 30lb, one a shade under, and all this before we even had time to put the rubby-dubby bag over! It had remained up on the bow, its noxious mixture trickling down towards the stern. When the fish were all returned the first job was to put the bag in the water where the tope could enjoy the smell and not ourselves. The tea was re-brewed and before it could be poured into the mugs two fish slammed into the mackerel baits. We landed and released them, shading 30lb. From that moment we had no chance to even replenish the rubby-dubby, instead dispensing it straight out of the fish box with a scoop, to leave an oily trail across the surface.

By 2pm the tide slackened and so the tope pack left us. With the *Girl Emer* looking like the scene from Custer's last stand we stood and laughed. Rubby-dubby was everywhere, plastered over jeans, fishing smocks and the *Girl Emer*. Tackle boxes lay across the deck, their contents spilled in all directions. Fingers were investigated, skin scuffs and line cuts treated with ointment and plasters. Rods lay strewn all over the place in tangled heaps. We had been hit by the biggest pack of tope ever known to local anglers in living memory on this west coast. In $3^{1}/_2$ hours, we'd been subjected to 45 runs resulting in 24 tope landed, the smallest being $25^{1}/_2$lb, the largest 38lb; the average weight being

31lb. With the bull huss and dogfish landed during slack tide we'd caught 1000lb of fish, every one of which was returned alive to the water. As a specialist fish photo-journalist I had shot four rolls of film, yet not killed a single fish for the photo.

With aching arms we broke down the rods and stowed them in the cabin. Everyone was silent, for only the anglers on the boat knew what happened that day. It was a memory that I can share with you now on paper, yet recall as vividly in my mind as though it were yesterday. Those tope had probably been travelling to that bay for thousands of years, undisturbed except by the odd commercial fisherman in his cockleshell craft. Having discovered one of the few remaining secrets of the oceans you will, I am sure, respect me for not mentioning the exact place on the chart. While this may at first appear to be selfish, there are those who would be tempted to take 1000lb of tope and kill them for crab-pot bait. This dignified, powerful adversary deserves better than that. It deserves the chance even if temporarily defeated, to find life again by being returned alive to the water.

* * *

When you come across a species of fish that seems to have been suspended for a million years in some evolutionary time warp, you will want as I did, to arrange an encounter with such a fish. The monkfish is related to the shark and also to the skate family; it eats almost anything and with its drab brown and dirty white colouring, its tiny pig-like eyes and jaws like a mantrap, it can hardly be considered one of the more attractive fish. But because it is something of a rarity around our shoreline it is of interest to anglers. Probably there are a lot more about than we imagine, but most anglers are unlikely to *see* one in their lifetime, let alone catch one.

While on my various tope fishing forays into the vast Blacksod Bay, I came across information that gave the possible location of a monkfish area. It was in extremely shallow water. No more than ten feet deep and no more than 150 yards from the westerly shoreline of the Belmullet peninsula. To get there, I requisitioned Vincent Sweeney and the famed *Girl Emer* and together with a couple of the

40

lads we set out to try the monkfish mark. This area is not fished commercially, and certainly has no rod and line pressure on it which in turn means there is no information on the how, where and why of fishing it. We were simply there to pioneer the rod and line aspect.

So it was with subdued excitement that I readied the tackle as I waited for the *Girl Emer's* anchor rope to pull tight in the flooding tide. Lowering a split-tail mackerel bait over the stern I fed out line slowly to avoid a tangle with the wire boom. At around ten feet it stopped, and I slipped the reel into free spool with a ratchet left on as an alarm. Apart from the odd big bull huss that intercepted the bait, all remained quiet. It was in complete contrast to the frantic sessions with the tope, and gave me time to contemplate the vast expanse of the surrounding bay. To the north, wisps of smoke from peat fires dissipated in the sea breeze, while the occasional car could be heard winding its way through the broad streets. To the west lay the shelter of the ten-mile-long Bellmullet peninsula the main buffer against the ravages of the Atlantic Ocean. The other side, Achill's twin peaks were silhouetted against the blue sky, while east of us lay Cleggan Point and the Gweesala River. For two hours nothing happened, so I replenished the bait. I have always been an exponent of the 'leave-it-until-they-find-it' school of thinking, working on the basis that bait left inside the boat is unlikely to find its way into a fish's mouth.

I started to wind up when the tip began to be dragged reluctantly seawards. I wound faster, struck, and found myself attached to some unseen adversary that was running slowly across the bottom. Line was gained easily and through the depth I made out a blotchy brown shape. 'IT'S A MONK!' came the shout from Vincent, excited at the prospect of a big fish aboard. Surprisingly the fish came easily — that is until it hit the bottom stern rudder of *Girl Emer*. Then it started to go haywire, thrashing and crashing until Vincent could stretch a gloved hand towards the leader. 'Jesus Christ, I wish you'd hold still!' he shouted to the fish, the leader twisted around his one hand, the sun flashing on the gaffhead in the other. The fish was big — certainly over 20lb — but it wasn't until it hit the deckboards and we could tag and weigh it that we realised it was nearer 30lb, and my first attempt as well! When we'd taken some photographs we slipped him back into the water.

After successfully catching this single fish — yes, you've guessed it — I returned the following year, determined to try again — first catching some tope, then finishing with a session after the elusive monkfish. One particularly foul day there was a southerly blowing horizontal rain that left us with no chance of getting at the pollock or coalfish, and little chance of even holding anchor in the bay channel. But having travelled hundreds of miles to get there I wasn't going to be so easily put off and we decided to go out to the monkfish mark.

I was experimenting with a form of mackerel meal groundbait, moulding it into balls and throwing it out uptide in the shallow water. I will never forget that day — it was the day I set a record for the most monkfish landed from the bay in one session. I caught three fish between 30 and 38lb, plus a 42 pounder.

Next day needless to say we returned, anxious to capitalise on our new-found success. I say 'our', but in fact I had been the only one to catch monkfish; Jerry had remained monkless. Perhaps the reason for my success was that I had been watching the angle of the boat at anchor and had placed my groundbait and hookbait at the extremity of each swing — so perhaps luck really had very little to do with it. Chris decided he didn't need another day of getting cold and soaked in the foul weather, and therefore stayed ashore. Only Jerry and myself left the pier with Vincent to go to the monk mark. By late afternoon Jerry remained fishless then I landed two big monkfish, another thirty pounder and a new Blacksod Bay record at 44lb. To cap his poor run of luck Jerry lost a very big monk that tore off the hook at the gaffing stage, despite being fought by him valiantly on just a 12-lb line. To be honest the gaff straightened out, followed by the hook.

On a windy June afternoon one year later, at exactly the same spot *Girl Emer* again swung at anchor on the monkfish mark. Aboard were myself, Jerry and Nigel. I had already landed six 30-lb tope in six drop downs at the channel, and the two lads had a tope apiece. We were finishing off the day with an experiment to see if there were any monks about this early in the year. We had a rubby-dubby sack tied on the anchor rope, but had a wind-against-tide situation. Instead of dropping a bait over the stern or boatcasting away from the boat's side, I elected to climb up on the bow and throw the split-tail mackerel bait up near the anchor rope! A strange procedure but a sixth sense made me stay up on the bow, clinging to the rail. Just before packing up time I had a slight tug on the rod and the line fell slack, indicating the grip lead had been broken out of its strong hold in the sand. Allowing a few seconds for the fish to move off I engaged the reel gears and wound fast to take up the slack. As it came taut I thumped the rod back, which in turn was wrenched back down towards the surface. 'FISH ON!' I shouted, 'A BIG MONK!'

Being up the bow in a gale of wind my words were whipped away and it was a few seconds before Vincent saw my predicament through the wheelhouse glass. Carefully I inched my way back, staying near the cabin roof rather than risk being tipped off. The fish was unseen but with the rod in maximum curve and the reel's clutch set properly I had no fear of loss, until I saw the size of the monk. It looked huge! Nearly three feet wide with jaws snapping like a trap, it crashed and careered around just out of gaffing range. There was now a very real chance I could lose this fish as it certainly had the power to make an unstoppable run to the anchor rope; and if it managed that it could entwine my line and snap it like cotton. As it circled for a third time I resolutely set in my mind that this was the place for 'hit-and-hold' tactics. I would not give one turn of the spool back to this monster monkfish. Screwing the drag up, and with the backup pressure of my thumb on the spool I heaved and pumped until that vast form swung nearer and nearer to Vincent's outstretched hands. Familiar with the excessive activity of a live monkfish in a confined space, Jerry had cleared the other rods away, and awaited events. With an extra heave the rod bent flat and the monk planed, jaws snapping and head shaking, towards the gloved hand of Vincent. In a flash he had the leader, the gaff was in and the three of us hauled the fish aboard. We had a set of Samson scales to 44lb but it clunked these down to the stop. A new record! We decided that here was an Irish specimen monkfish and thereon made the decision to bring it in for official weighing on land.

Under the silhouette of Blackrock lighthouse the needle swung on the scales to settle at 50lb 8oz! What a monster! A new record for the *Girl Emer* and a record for Blacksod Bay. With fish to over 50lb landed only 150 yards from shore, and from ten feet of water, this area offers the most exciting potential for monster monkfish, maybe topping the Irish record. Of course I hope to go back next year . . . and the next . . . and the next. After all, a 50-lb monk is a big old slab of fish — but there's always the chance of a sixty!

4

Blue and Porbeagle Sharks

THE SOUTH-WEST COAST OF
ENGLAND

A good many years ago — too many years ago now I start to
think about it — I had the craving that many anglers have,
to catch a shark. You know, one of those huge, evil creatures
that devour horses by the minute, and in war films, always
attack the war pilot whose plane ditches in the Pacific. In the
late fifties Cornwall was England's centre for blue shark
fishing, with the ancient port of Looe seeing thousands
brought in to be weighed at its quay-side scales. Not
unnaturally it received a great amount of publicity, which in
turn brought anglers from all over Britain — which in turn
led to the sharks being over-fished. I had already spent
several seasons down there, bottom fishing for bream,
conger and ling on the Hands Deeps and Hat Rock out from
Looe — each time listening with envy to the radio as the
other boats hooked up on the blues. In those days I was
paying £7.50 for a charter but the shark boats cost £10 a day
and I just couldn't get that extra £2.50 together to take a
crack at shark. Then one year my father decided to take a
week's fishing down there with me, and arranged to split the
cost of a shark boat. So we chartered the *Ganesha* skippered
by Ernie Curtis.

Meeting in the tackle shop on Looe's quay was always
something to be savoured. It was full of smoke, loud voices,
pound notes going over the counter, tackle and rods,
oilskins, and the usual complement of Cornish skippers. At
that time I would guess there were as many as twenty shark
boats going out from the harbour each day. We met Ernie on
the boat, clambering over the *Paula* to get aboard.

'Morning Ernie.'

"Ow do m'dears. We should have a bit of a bumpy ride
I'm afraid, the wind's a bit fresh, but the fish are out there
by the radar buoy.'

45

The *Ganesha* backed into the Looe River, and together with about eight others we ran downstream past Banjo pier and Hannafore rocks. Away in the distance, at staggered intervals, we could see the dancing mizzen masts of other boats that had left half an hour earlier. Each one was racing to get past the lee of its neighbour, and therefore get the best drift. After some two hours running, Ernie slowed the engines and swung the boat beam on to the wind. The engine cut and we were enveloped in that heady silence as the *Ganesha* took up the regulatory rolling motion. In a couple of minutes my stomach started complaining, only to be made worse when Ernie gingerly lifted out a mesh bag from a plastic dustbin, full of the most evil smelling mess any fisherman could wish to see or smell! Rubby-dubby as it's known to British anglers, is a concoction made up of minced mackerel or pilchards, some bran, and a liberal slop of neat, pure pilchard oil. The resultant mixture is left to mature for a couple of days in the dustbin. Strong sunshine throughout July definitely adds to the aroma so this was some of Ernie's top class rubby-dubby. Once in the water it left an oily slick, with rainbow-coloured bubbles popping to the surface every time the boat rolled.

'Let's get the gear out boys' said Ernie, taking consummate care not to get his hands covered in the mixture. Then the tackle came out. Real heavy shark gear of the day. An old, solid glass 80-lb rod, complete with those heavy ceramic guides that looked like the grandmother's glasses. To this was attached one of the old Hardy 'Fortuna' reels, and some 80-lb Searanger line. Then came the shark trace, with cable of un-nameable breaking strain, and a big 12/0 mustad hook onto which was attached a whole mackerel of about a pound. An old net cork acted as float, and regulated the depth at which the bait fished. Four rods were used, each set at a different depth and distance from the boat.

After three hours of pitching and rolling, we were both beginning to wonder what the fascination was in shark fishing. Ernie on the other hand was confident and assured us that the sharks would be along in about fifteen minutes! Twenty minutes later, sure enough, father was attached to something that was very definitely not a conger, ling or bream! The line had raced off, and Ernie ran out from the cabin to set the hook and allow the angler all the 'fun' of winding in what I now realise to be the equivalent of a sack full of wet cement. Of course the sheer weight of a 60-lb shark impressed us, and we watched with excitement as Ernie gaffed it aboard, and chased it across the deckboards of the pitching boat, clubbing it with a wooden mallet.

It was my turn next and I screwed up by striking too fast. Then father screwed up, and I screwed up again! Eventually father landed a 40 pounder, and I managed to get it right with a seventy-six pounder! Thus ended a terrific day's sport, and we were elated as we ran up the pennants signifying the number of sharks caught. That seventy-six pounder qualified me as a member of the Shark Club of Great Britain, the 'in' thing to join at the time — and so began my entry into the world of the Sharker. Though I have now landed hundreds and hundreds of sharks to nearly a quarter of a ton, they still hold that certain mystery for me and I hope that I never lose that *need* to go shark fishing.

I spent two weeks every year for the next five years catching blue sharks off Looe before I moved across to the Isles of Scilly after building up a file of the blue shark's movements in the Western approaches. One of my last trips out from Looe resulted in my catching one of my largest blue sharks from English waters. I was sharing a boat with a German ballistics researcher, and as far as I can remember we were in the *Paula* skippered by Dick Butters. The day was perfect. A clear blue July sky with just enough puffy cloud to add some atmosphere. It was around this time that line classes were beginning to make a showing in Britain, and I wanted to take a blue on the now defunct 6-lb test. I'd rigged up an old wooden Scarborough casting reel, something in the region of six inches in diameter, and filled it with around 400 yards of 6-lb line. I ran it on a carp rod that I had, and spent half the day arguing with the German, who complained bitterly that he would lose all 'his' sharks through my using the light line. He ran a pair of 80s himself, and short of a piscine confrontation with either Moby Dick or a Polaris sub on exercise, was determined to land just about everything and anything.

He fortunately had the first run, landing a forty pounder. I had a run on the six, which he screamed at me was going to take his bait as well, thus discounting any chance I would have of claiming a record. As he was not about to move his own bait I was forced to strike, and just as obviously broke

47

the fish off. This was greeted with Germanic glee, especially as he had another run straight away. He boated a thirty pounder, and I had another run on the 6-lb outfit. When I broke this off relations deteriorated even further. Apparently the ones I was breaking off were in the 200-lb range, and would have belonged to him if I wasn't on the boat! After this I put the light outfit away and used a 30-lb Vortex Goliath bottom-fishing rod, completely unbalanced with a Mitchell 624 reel and 55-lb Searanger line. I was just rigging up when he had another shark on, estimated by him to weigh at least 80lb. It turned out to be about 35lb and had gutted the bait.

While skipper and the German struggled to subdue the writhing fish, I looked over the side to see THREE big blues up round the rubby bag! I shouted aloud in my excitement, and the German whirled round, oblivious of the close proximity of his gut-hooked shark's jaws. 'Look out m'dear, 'ee'll 'ave your foot off else' shouted Dick, trying to hold the writhing fish on a short wire. Too late. The German saw the big blues in the water and immediately the biggest one on the right was his. Frantically, he yanked and tugged at the wire disappearing down his shark's throat, Dick levering with the T-bar disgorger in a vain effort to free that hook. By now I was rigged up, and I knew there was no chance of the German getting that hook back for several minutes. Calmly I picked up the head and guts of a mackerel, and delicately, slowly, and seductively put it on my hook. The German by now was almost apoplectic with rage: 'NO, NO, ZAT ISS MY FISH . . . HE IS AT MY END OFF DA BOAT . . . YOU MUST WAIT UNTIL I PUT MY BAIT IN DER VASSER! But with his line all over his legs, and Dick still trying to get his hook free I knew I had him. Slowly I lowered my rod over the side and put the reel lever in free spool. As the mackerel skeleton sank down so I lightly thumbed the reel, and smiled at the German. He was still jerking on the wire, Dick shouting back: 'Old on m'dear, 'ow can I get the hook free if'n you'm pullin' the wire?'

The blue hit gently, a slight bump, then the drag on the tip as he ran off the line. I flicked the reel in gear, and waited for the line to pull tight. The rod was wrenched below the surface and line screamed off the reel throwing spray in my face. This was bigger than I thought. Dick was still laughing, and had given up trying to retrieve the German's hook. 'Good for you boy,' he whispered. 'I'd just about 'ad enough of 'ee myself!' It took me a full twenty minutes to subdue that fish, and I was more than pleased when Dick sank the gaff in. The German refused to help us drag it aboard, and went off into the cabin to sulk. As it crashed onto the deckboards I realised it was my biggest blue to date, a fact confirmed when it weighed in at 100lb — the biggest blue shark taken that week.

The best ever day as far as numbers of blue shark are concerned was spent off Mevagissey in Cornwall. I'd spent a week catching fish up to about 70lb off St. Mary's, in the Scilly Isles, and decided to stop off on the return journey for a day's sharking from this port. I spent half an hour in old George Pierce's tackle shop, trying to get a place on a boat with three other guys. The boats from 'Mev' usually fished five rods, and I was happy to pay for the use of two rods to make up the numbers. This allowed me to use one rod set shallow and one deep, thereby covering more of the 'kill' zone.

Eventually we managed to get out, and the wind swung round to south west, about a force four, gusting five. The occasional top surfed off a wave, and it became obvious that even without the assistance of the mizzen mast, our drift would be a fast one. As far as I was concerned this was to the good as it meant the rubby-dubby trail would be strung out over a considerable distance. After an hour and a half we stopped, over went the rubby bag, and inside fifteen minutes I had a run — I hadn't even had time to get my second rod out! It was a fifty pounder, and heralded the start of an excellent trip. The other lads had run their lines out, and inside half an hour had lost three and landed two, both of similar size. I got both rods out and landed fish on both, a brace of blues going just over 70lb a piece. By mid-day the sea conditions were beginning to worsen, but seemed to whip the sharks into an even greater frenzy. At one stage we hooked up on five sharks at the same time and landed two. Most of mine came on the distant rod, indicating that the blues were hungry and taking the first bait they came to. I took full advantage of this and ran both baits at similar depths, and very close together, something not to be recommended if you want to avoid 'double-baiting'.

By two in the afternoon we were in the midst of a howling gale. Not cold, but a warm, strong south-westerly that you could stand out in all day clad only in a sweater. The skipper walked down the pitching deck to me. 'It's gettin a bit lumpy boy. You fellas feel as though you wanna stay out here?' I looked to the others and we were in agreement:

'We're OK. We'll stay out as long as you reckon it's safe to shark fish'.

'Well it seems as though the fish are here boy, we may as well stay!'

That's the sort of talk I loved to hear, so we worried less and less about the weather conditions, and more about converting the many shark runs into fish on the deckboards. Over the next hour we had a shark either on or running every ten minutes. It wasn't that the skipper was using a lot of rubby-dubby, far from it. It was just one of those days when the ocean is full of feeding sharks, and anything we cared to put in the water was taken. I even caught a blue on a small whiting I had brought out in the freezer, in case of a conger trip! As 3.30 pm and the end of our charter time neared, the wind rose, so we had to set about packing up. There wasn't a man aboard who wanted to put his rod away first, so I opted to pack mine up. The others, and taking this as a lead, followed suit, forgetting of course that I had paid to have two rods out. Just as the last line came in I had a take on my 50, and after a very hard tussle, boated another good blue.

It was a rough journey home, and taking the surf on the port side, meant we all had to hold on to something to avoid being rolled out of the boat. As we came under the lee of the mainland, so the skipper set about running up the pennants, signifying the number of sharks caught.

'I don't reckon I've got enough m'dears, it's a while since I had a catch like this!'

We'd taken a total of fourteen blue sharks, and my efficient two rod system had done me proud by giving me my best blue shark catch in British waters: 8 sharks, 5 of which were over the SACGB qualifying weight of 75lb, the largest being 89lb! I realise in retrospect that every single one of these sharks could have been returned, but in those years of abundance we just didn't think. Looking back though, it was a fantastic day, so typical of what the once famous Cornish blue shark fishing used to be like.

★ ★ ★

After several years' fishing on the productive south Cornish blue shark grounds, I become aware of another species of shark that was in the catchable category. In the early fifties a good many sharks were mistakenly listed as makos, and were subsequently found to be porbeagle sharks, otherwise known as mackerel sharks. Occasionally they would be caught while out on the offshore blue shark grounds, but many skippers thought they were a species that lurked closer to shore. This was borne out in later years, as the craggy north Cornish and Devon coastline began producing porbeagles for those few anglers prepared to brave the elements, and risk a blank session. I watched with interest, as most of my previous porbeagling had been concentrated around the Isle of Wight, off the central southern English coast. Here I had taken shark, but only in patches, and they were beginning to show a decline in numbers. After following reports in the press and listening to the word on the angling grapevine, I booked up one of the trawlers that was operating for these North Devon 'beagles', out from the port of Appledore.

Appledore is a quaint village, but quite a long way by boat (and around the dangerous headland of Hartland Point) from the grounds. This factor I took into account when booking the trawler, as I reasoned that a big boat would have more chance of returning with its full complement of crew and anglers, should the weather turn nasty. It's all very well getting out to a prime fishing mark, but one does like to return — if only to develop the photos! Companions for the trip were all strangers to me: a couple of Englishmen from the north, and three Welshmen from Cardiff. They were all on their first porbeagle trip, so we met in a bar in Appledore to discuss what the following day would bring in the shape of sharks. Although the fish were localised, they were notoriously difficult to catch, and there was no set pattern to follow, you could only try the 'hit and miss' procedure. It was possible, we were told, to catch three or more in one day, then catch nothing for the next week. That evening as I sat in the camper, looking through steamed up windows, I listened to the shipping forecast. When it got to Lundy Island and gave a westerly, force five, I knew it was time to take a nightcap of sea sick pills. It took a long time to get to sleep that night, as the wind whistled through the roof vent and buffeted the side of the van.

Next morning I was up at six. The wind was still blowing so it looked to be touch and go as to whether the trip was on or not. At seven I met up with the skipper and the others on the harbour wall, to discuss the day ahead. It looked far from good but the skipper, Chris Sylvester, decided it was certainly worth a trip outside to see what the race looked like. It meant an hour's run, but as the race was the barrier we had to cross, there was nothing else we could do. If he thought it looked too rough we'd just have to return. An hour and a half later the trawler was facing the lighthouse, Chris standing outside the cabin with a pair of binoculars, straining to see the height of the tide race.

'Here, take a look y'self Graeme . . . you can't miss it — and don't forget we're maybe three quarters of a mile away yet!' I fumbled with the binoculars until they picked up the walls of white water that marked the treacherous Hartland Point tide race. Huge waves, some five feet high surged and tumbled as far as the eye could see — from the finger of rock marked by the lighthouse, out towards Lundy Island.

'It'll be hours before that subsides' said Chris. 'We're going to have to make a decision pretty soon.'

For some ten minutes we waited, quietly trying to assess the chances of getting through, sizing up the height of each wave. The main problem with a tide race is the upredictability of the waves. They can come from any direction, at any size and any speed. A boat can get sucked into the main race in seconds, from where it is broken and smashed out through two miles of extremely rough water.

'I reckon us'll 'ave a go' said Chris, putting the boat in gear, and pointing the bow into the wind. 'Lash everything down now, and you lads better come into the cabin — just in case!'

Inside fifteen minutes we were into the race — a hissing, boiling maelstrom of confused waters churning past the hull. I defy any normal man not to have a sensation of gut fear in such a situation. One mistake, one tiny turn of the rudder in the wrong direction could have spelt disaster. We rolled and pitched, tossed and turned as the propellors fought to bite water. About halfway through it hit us. A wave, about five or six feet in height and coming straight from the starboard hit the trawler beam on, and rolled us deeper into the next wave. Green water burst over the side, slooshing from one side of the deck to the other. Ropes, buckets, anything that wasn't physically screwed down clattered over the decks.

'Hold on boys' shouted Chris, 'we've hit a wrong un!'

He fought to control the wheel and applied more power. You could see from the speed at which we were passing the headland rocks that we were being sucked out into the race, instead of the quieter water beyond the Point. The engine revs whined but nothing happened. Still we rolled and crashed with water breaking against the gunnel, and spray bursting into the air to be whipped away on the wind. Frantically, and I use the word in its truest context, Chris applied full revs, and slowly the trawler crashed her way through the maelstrom. In three minutes we were over the worst of it, yet I felt sure we had gone under, rather than over most of the waves. Once in the quieter water beyond, everyone relaxed . . . but all of us flashed an occasional glance back over the stern to the boiling race of Hartland Point. Hopefully by the time we had to make our return journey it would have subsided.

We motored down the coast until we were off the rough ground adjacent to the radar station. The engines were cut, and we were left to drift along the shoreline, about 900 to 1000 yards off. The rubby-dubby sack went over the side, and six sets of shark gear ran out, each baited with a dead mackerel. Inside ten minutes, and with barely enough time for the trail to get going, one of the northerners had a take directly under the boat. It was so soon that we found it hard to believe, yet he was tied to the distinctive up and down vertical fight of the porbeagle shark. It proved to be a small fish of some 60lb in weight, but being the first of the day, and following our safe journey through the race, it merited a huge cheer as Chris gaffed it aboard. Over the next hour we made two more drifts in close to the rocks, which gave us a couple more 60 to 70-lb sharks. Both these had also come to freeline tactics, suspending the bait directly beneath the hull.

We decided on a move further offshore, still keeping to a line off the radar station, as this was known as the general holding area. After half an hour of bottom fishing I had a few dogfish, so decided to have a doze in the comfort of the cabin. I remember waking to the shouts of the Welshmen, who had apparently hooked up on a good shark. The trawler was smothered in stanchions and struts, which meant any big shark that had to be walked round the boat, would present problems. Here indeed was such a problem. The poor guy, tied to what was obviously a good shark, was contorting himself around a stanchion, the rod half under the water, his pals holding him by the belt to avoid a verdict of misadventure on the coroner's report. Eventually it was brought under control and played to a standstill at the stern of the boat. It was well over 100lb and crashed onto the decks. Four sharks already, and we were still only half way through the day! One of the Welshmen then hooked another, but lost it when his line was cut across some pinnacle rock.

We motored up for another drift, and no sooner had I run my balloon back than it started bobbing furiously before 'plipping' beneath the surface. This fish continued to swim towards the boat, so I was forced to wind down on him and thump the hooks home. He gave me a bad time on the 50, and after twenty minutes we boated a hundred pounder. Five sharks aboard, and still time left for another! We ran the gear back, then sat on the deck to eat sandwiches, and recount the day's events. The wind had dropped appreciably, down to somewhere over a force three, and warm summer sunshine burst through the low scudding clouds. By keeping below the height of the gunnel, we sat in complete comfort. The drift extended for about a mile east of the hotspot, and nobody really gave much thought to a porbeagle working out of the area.

Suddenly a ratchet screamed and everyone leaped to wind their gear out of the way. I looked for my balloon but could see it nowhere. One of the Welshmen had line running off with a shark, yet mine was hanging limp by the gunnel. Maybe I'd been cut off. I stuffed a half eaten sandwich between my teeth and wound in slowly. The Welshman struck and was dragged to the bow as another 100-lb porbeagle powered away. Suddenly I found the line drawing tight vertically beneath me. Then the tip dragged down . . . it was a shark! I spat the sandwich into the sea, heaving back on the rod to set the steel. Two sharks on at once would surely pose problems. As the Welshman's appeared to be larger, and was running away from the boat, I decided to buckle down and really give mine some 'dingo' to get it in quickly. But all I succeeded in doing was to make the shark fight harder, and give myself some nasty turns as I tried to negotiate the stanchions. After fifteen minutes the wire came up and we gaffed over another 'beagle in the 100-lb range. This left the field clear for the Welshman who proceeded to boat a fish well over 120lb.

Seven sharks aboard, and half an hour to go! We lost two more: one cut off on the reef, the other spat the bait after a long fast run. I've always had a feeling these fast runs were small fish, or maybe even tope. All you ever got back was a mackerel full of puncture marks, and early strikes produced nothing. The other northerner, who had spent much of the time moving his gear to let others boat and play their sharks out, suddenly was being levered over the side. Somewhat despondently he had left his bait dangling over the side, reel in gear, and only a trace length deep. A shark had obviously bypassed all the other baits and sensing the increase in smell as it neared the rubby sack had risen in the water to investigate. On seeing this solitary mackerel lying suspended in the water, it promptly ate it and swam off. Our friend was now watching line drag reluctantly from his reel as he fumbled to release the drag pressure. After twenty minutes or so, we boated a short, fat porbeagle of maybe 140lb.

Eight sharks in the boat — boy, what a day! No sooner had we disposed of this than the Welshman at the bow slammed into another. This fish however proved to give a very different fight, preferring to stay away from the boat, and making longer, harder runs. 'Better pack your gear away now boys' said Chris, 'we'm all 'ave to be off 'ome soon anyways.' After half an hour we were still no nearer to going home. The porbeagle was beginning to come under the boat and was now on a fairly short line. Sweat ran from the angler, as he tried vainly to get some line on the reel. With only a butt pad, and the problem of the structure and stanchions on the boat to negotiate, I really felt for him. Twice the leader came up, and twice the leader was wrenched below the surface when anyone tried to touch it. I climbed up on top of the cabin, onto the trawling gantry in an effort to look down through the water to try and see him. Third time up and the wire came out from under the boat.

From my vantage point high up on the gantry I could see the pectorals fanned out as a massive porbeagle planed out from under the hull. I called to Chris to come and have a look. Chris reached out and closed a hand around the wire, gingerly easing it up. The fish just as calmly took it back again, and Chris ran to the other side of the boat to see where I was pointing.

'My God boys . . . 'tis a 'andsome fish an' that's for sure. I reckon 'e'll go over two fifty!'

'Nearer three hundred!' I shouted.

Just then I looked round to see a supposed 'helper' from a local club heaving on the wire leader. The Welshman was finished, jammed in the corner, legs and arms shaking like jelly. The wire came up some more, but before Chris could get across to take it, he'd taken a turn around a cleat post on the stern. At the precise moment the big shark made off on what most probably would have been its last run anyway. The guy took another turn around the cleat, and the wire parted with a sickening twang! Nobody said a thing, especially to the Welshmen.

The journey back in was very quiet, but everybody at least perked up when we went back through the race; now, at slack water, it could have been a farm pond. Only the occasional swirl gave an indication of the treacherous rocks below the surface.

There was a crowd gathered on Appledore quay as we tied up, the tourists' cameras clicking away furiously. The largest fish went around 140lb the others ranging from 90lb to 122lb.

We went out the next two days, and received Neptune's ultimate chastisement in the shape of two entirely fishless days. The weather was perfect, the gulls accompanied us down the coastline, but as soon as we neared the radar station hotspot, they veered off, as if indicating there were no fish. The sharks had moved on to pastures new, chasing the mackerel and bass shoals further up, or down, the rugged North Devon coast. We were happy though, myself, the two northerners, and the three Welshmen who gave vent to some staunch Welsh hymns on the last day as we crossed the Hartland Point race for the final time.

5

Mixed Bag

KENYA AND FLORIDA

For many years I had toyed with the idea of travelling to East Africa to sample some of her fishing. Having never been there before, it held that mystical quality of the unknown; the potential for adventure and excitement — something to take the mind off the more mundane pastime of surviving in the civilised world. I had a taste for Africa and its Indian Ocean after visiting Mauritius. Mauritius is in the Southern Indian Ocean, whereas East Africa — primarily Kenya — is much nearer the equator. Deciding that another dismal February in Britain was more than I could bear, I organised a couple of weeks out there.

Having decided on the country, I was left in something of a quandary as to where I should base myself! There are over 250 miles of accessible fishing waters off the Kenyan coast to choose from. From Shimoni, some fifty miles south of Mombasa, to the island of Lamu in the north, many hotels operated charter boats. January to March was apparently the optimum period to go there due to the regular summer weather not allowing the boats out (during the months of May, June and July, the *kusi*, the south-east wind blows very hard — which isn't very good if, like me, you're prone to sea sickness!). From January to March the sea is flat calm up to about noon when the monsoon (north easterly) picks up, blowing about a force five until about nine or ten in the evening. It then drops away to nothing. This pattern is so predictable the boats know exactly when to go out fishing, and from my travels all over the globe, I've never known anywhere else be as predictable as this.

I decided to get the cheapest flight but it proved to be a false economy when I arrived, some 36 hours later after four flight changes and overnight waits at loungeless airports. I had chosen to go to Watamu and to stay at the Seafarer's Hotel. I arrived jetlagged, yet excited which my host 'Muff'

Becker must have misinterpreted as still having some energy since he decided I needed a quick three-hour tour of the reef outside. Still half asleep I unpacked some trunks, grabbed a rod, and twenty minutes after pushing off from the beach, was fighting a double-figure dolphin! That fish hit a small konahead lure trolled through some diving birds, a mere three hundred yards from the outside barrier reef. What an introduction! Actually we thought we had hooked a plastic bag that was floating under the birds, but the dolphin was obviously underneath, waiting in the shade for some morsel to zip past. It's amazing how anything floating holds a fascination for this species. Back at the hotel I grabbed some grub and left to try and get some sleep. I had a 7 am start the next day.

The Seafarer's proved to be the ideal base in this modern angling paradise. Situated on the sandy beaches of the Natural Turtle Bay, some 12 miles south of Malindi, the boats are moored off the beach outside your door. Although I had taken a bonefishing flyrod, I was told there were none to be caught, besides which, the water from the beachline to the barrier reef was a Marine Reserve. I can assure you that Marine Park or not, I would have experienced great difficulty in not presenting a wig-wag minno to a passing bonefish! One just doesn't do such things. After a couple of days to become acclimatised I began to get a 'feel' for the coastline — this tropical haven that still retains links with the seafarers of yesteryear. Many of the old wooden dhows are still to be seen, sailing out on the wind in the morning, and returning from miles away after a day's fishing, with the north-easterly monsoon billowing out their ungainly sails. The principals of the dhow sail have always fascinated me, yet they have been used by merchant sailers from Arabia, India and the Persian Gulf since 4000 BC, to bring cotton cloth, axes, spearheads and knives to trade for ivory, rhino horn, slaves and spices. Today, the dhows still visit Mombasa, and other reminders of Kenya's past are still to be found all over the country. A regular companion of my fishing trips here was Carl Looman, a Dutchman who started farming in Kenya, then moved to the coast to help with the fishing. On about the third day out in *Ndege* (little bird), I had a blind strike on my 12-lb Graphite casting rod. I was dragging a small hexhead lure in the wake when the rod bent double with the line screaming from the reel. The boat was pitching and tossing in the heavy swell.

'Do you want the net Graeme?' asked Carl, pushing the morse control to neutral.

'No, I reckon this fish is a bit too big for the net, I must've lost a hundred and fifty yards of line in that first run.' Gradually the runs slowed and the line cut through the waves on the port quarter. Carl started the engine and idled it in gear as I slowly gained line.

'I reckon it's a wahoo or perhaps a big dolpin by the line angle Carl.'

'Yes, or maybe it's a tuna. We have some birds working about half a mile north of us. By the way they're breaking surface I'd say they were yellowfins.'

This was my first hard fighting fish of the trip, and I was gradually beginning to lock down with the Graphite rod. It's amazing how quickly you remember just how much to apply with a favourite rod, so gradually the line started to run deep, and the line-beating tail throb of a tuna started plugging on the rod top. Tuna are the hardest fighting fish in the ocean, and I remembered the fastest way to kill a tuna is always short, hard pumps. Even though I had that Graphite tip under the surface several times, it still took me a full twenty minutes to crank that fish up; it was a super yellowfin tuna of 21lb. A nice start to the day, but alas, that was to prove the highlight as we finished with only a few extra skipjacks.

The yellowfin however proved to beat the old Watamu record of 15lb, so that provoked me into looking into the local records list. Surprisingly enough, there were no Kenya records for fly-caught fish, so I decided to take a crack at landing one, purely as a technical exercise. Theoretically it should have been simple, as all you had to do was motor up to a school of bonito and cast a fly into their midst. This however, proved decidedly difficult. I had the ability to punch out a flyline shooting head forty-five yards on a calm day, but with a pitching boat, a constantly moving school of fish, and the wind to take into consideration, it took me a full *three* days before we came up with a working system. Carl would motor *Ndege* up parallel with the moving school, cut the engine and I'd fire the shooting head down into the school. Oh yes — and I also had to have the wind slightly up from the school, and blowing on my left shoulder and face.

The one time when everything came right, I found myself attached to a 3-lb rainbow runner. I unhooked that fish with shaking hands, as although it was no monster, I had received a lot of stick from the locals, who thought I was mad to make an attempt with a fly rod. Surely it was easier to use bait? Well, naturally, but I had set myself a task, and with the assistance of Carl as boat handler, we set another local record for runner on fly. Larger fish can easily be taken like this, as Kenya's coast has loads of yellowfin, skipjacks, kawakawa, tangueague and rainbow runner that drive bait to the surface. I'm sure, as in the States and Central Southern American venues that saltwater flyfishing will be the sport of the future for the Kenyan anglers. Even sailfish can be enticed up on teasers, allowing a flyrodder to drop back a fly into his mouth.

The days passed by, and Carl and I took *Ndege* out miles over the offshore banks and into deeper bluewater, returning around lunchtime each day to avoid the worst of the monsoon winds, and in time to enjoy afternoon tea and cakes on the verandah. A couple of our better catches proved to be a 140-lb haul of skipjack tuna in only a few hours. This included a double-figure fish which proved to be another Watamu light-tackle record. A further morning was spent off Whale rock, at the entrance to Mida creek, some three miles south of Watamu. We were trolling along in *Ndege,* scouring the skies for birds — our bonito lures streaming behind — when suddenly, the radio crackled with the news that one of the Seafarer's larger 'Hai' boats had landed three tanguegue. We changed rigs, and began trolling the same ground. There was a lot of surface weed about, lifted out of Mida creek by the high spring tides. As we slowed *Ndege* to clear the lures for the umpteenth time, there was a huge splash underneath one of the half beak baits. It was rigged to a 20-lb outfit which sprang tight as an unseen adversary ripped line from the reel. Ten minutes later and I had a big barracuda alongside, a lean, long fish that looked as though it would have eaten anything and which tipped the scales at 24lb. Over the next few hours we had fast and furious sport with light 12 and 20 outfits on the tangueague — a long fish closely related to the kingfish of the Atlantic, and recognised as a sportfish by the IGFA. We lost many lures and jigs to the jaws of these predators, but

60

not before we had boated seven of them well into double figures.

And so the days of tropical bliss passed by. I would come in off *Ndege* at 1 pm or later, have a swim then sunbathe under the rustling palms, as the monsoon wind blew away any early morning clouds. I'd write up my articles in an effort to keep pace with deadlines, or maybe mooch off along the beach looking for that 'special' photograph. I was hooked on Africa and its lazy pace where nothing is rushed, and what you don't get round to doing today, you put off until tomorrow, or even later. I found myself gorging on the superb pineapples here; the tinned variety will never again have the same taste. At night the warm air would throb to the drums of the Giriama dancers, while stars glimmered through the palm fronds. I quickly located Casseopia and Orion the Hunter, both higher in the sky as I was now on the equator. I always liked to see Orion, like most fishermen I'm superstitious, and believe in using all the luck that comes my way! This was also the first place in the world where I could see the Milky Way clearly. It was an enormous belt of pale white stars running from east to west, and displayed its true glory over the new moon period. High cirrus cloud would sometimes make it hazy — a sure portender of some rain showers. Another pleasing discovery was the lack of mosquitoes due to the north-easterly monsoon winds driving them inland, away from the coast. I thought that they would have been prolific, and had taken along some old net curtaining which I used to rig over my head with some coathanger wire. At Seafarer's, the twin beds had runners, along which a huge 'mozzy-proof' curtain could be drawn, and I was told I would have been glad of them had I been there during the rainy season when the situation is reversed and the winds blow off the land bringing down hordes of insects from the hills.

Over the next few days spent chasing the tuna schools in *Ndege,* Carl and I listened in on the radio to the increasing number of sailfish catches being made off Malindi. Malindi lies some 75 miles north of Mombasa, and some 15 miles by sea from Watamu. It is a picturesque Swahili town that dates back to before the twelfth century and which today is well known for its friendly and hospitable people. For some reason the sailfish only feed avidly off Malindi, gorging themselves on the huge prawns that move offshore. As the prawn season changes so the sails stay around, driving into schools of Malindi herring. The main run occurs in November and December, often with a further run of fish in February. Over the next few days we decided enough were being caught by the Malindi boats to warrant a full day's session. That evening Carl, Muff and myself discussed the possibilities of getting there. We couldn't take *Ndege* to the prawning grounds as that would mean a three-hour run from the base of Watamu, but Muff decided that if we set out at around 6 am, we could motor up in one of the Hai boats, fish for a few hours, and surf back to Watamu on the waves of the monsoon winds.

The biggest shock to my system was getting out of bed at 5.30 am; it took several minutes of 'Jambo Bwana' knocking on the door to evoke any sort of response from my frame. The dawn sun was just creeping over the horizon when the boat slipped her moorings and nosed cautiously through the Watamu reef opening — not the sort of place to be caught during the hours of darkness with a monsoon blowing! I wouldn't like to cash in my chips only three hundred yards from land. I remember a fellow angler called Dennis, who had this particular philosophy that always stuck in my mind: he told me he'd be happy to die with just three things — to owe the bank a million pounds, leave all his bills outstanding — and to have his ashes sent to the taxman with a note saying he could have the LOT!

The run down to the north of Malindi proved uneventful, although the monsoon wind unfortunately picked up early. We found the Malindi fleet way up by Mambui and as we neared the boats, I saw an angler with bent rod in the stern fighting a leaping sailfish. For the next hour we trolled around the Malindi boats, praying the fish wouldn't go down. By eleven o'clock they had disappeared, either moving farther north, or dropping down deep on the prawns. We changed baits and the wind increased, pushing the Malindi boats home, but leaving us, stubborn and determined, to catch a fish. By one o'clock it was surfing from the tops of the waves, and I knew that with a three-hour run home, we'd have no more than an hour left. Then Carl saw some birds and we crashed our way over to them. As we neared the wheeling terns a shout came from the mate. There was a shadow behind my teaser — a sailfish. We quickly tried to put flat lines in front of him, and I jerked the teaser as hard as I could. He just wouldn't take. He followed us for some six or eight minutes, switching to the outriggers — following a flat line, but always — *always* coming right back to that teaser. A couple of times he wrenched the teaser line from my fingers, shaking the wooden plug like a terrier would a rat. The captain was shouting, the mate stood in a tangle of lures and lines, Carl watched fascinated by it all — while I hurriedly racked my brains to think of a way to get that fish. I was so close to my fifth different species of billfish that I could taste it! Every time he came after that spume of bubbles laid by the teaser, but just wouldn't come on top for the fish baits. It was unheard of — and infuriating! Then I suddenly remembered my trusty old konoclone. Only a ten-inch job but it had caught me a lot of fish and threw out the bubbles. While the others dropped fish baits on the sail's nose, I cranked in and began re-rigging. As I dropped the 'clone in and spooled it back in the wake so the sail disappeared. 'Damn!' I knew he would take, I just knew it. I ran the 'clone way back in the hope that he was still tracking us. For a minute I held the rod, then, 'whop' — a distinct rap on the lure. It drew tight and I struck. 'ZZZZzzzzzzz'. Line was wrenched off the reel, but he came away. What a fighter! I ran the 'clone back even further, and by now was losing my cool.

I decided to lock down on that fish if it came again, and battened down on everything. The lever went up to the 'Stop' button, I put a couple of turns on the 'pre-set', dropped in the ratchet, and for good measure put my thumb on the spool. I pointed the rod at the fish, gripped it tightly and waited. I didn't have more than a minute to wait. With the line held across my finger I couldn't miss that 'whop-whop' as he hit the lure with his bill. Two seconds later he took it and I hit him very, very hard — about seven times, and burning my thumb in the process. Out he came, slashing, leaping, twisting. Then he took off on a fast flat run, buzzing line from the reel. I backed off the drag, and fell into the fighting chair. He must have cleared the sea around a dozen times, his speed leaving me with an incredible bow of line in the rough seas. The short, hard Bermuda pumps soon had him coming my way, and we billed him aboard. Only an average 45 pounder, but a fish that I could *positively* call my own.

On the way back home would you believe I lost another

three sails that threw the hook? I knew what the problem was because the hookpoint was like a hypodermic. I was getting too much stretch from the line as I was running the lure way, way back in the wake. Once I saw a sailfish leap and throw the lure, and it didn't even register on the reel. The rod top kicked once and that was it.

We got back at six o'clock surfing down the waves with an incredible variant in yaw when the skipper misjudged a wave. This is an exciting way of travelling in a boat, big swells with breaking tops hissing around your stern, the engine pitch whining as you surf down the crest, losing sight of land as you bottom out in a trough. It's also one of the easiest ways to get a boat into Davy Jones' locker. The first one that breaks into the stern fills it up, making the boat dig low. It can't rise to the second wave which just washes into the boat — after that it's all over. No bailing necessary as they say!

The next few days on *Ndege* seemed an anti climax after the sailfishing, but we came back to the beach with fish, every day bar one. Still the wahoo and dolphin packs failed to show on the banks. The sails were moving farther north off Malindi and were now being caught by the Lamu boats. Down at Shimoni in the Pemba Channel the odd striped marlin was beginning to show. Peter came in from a day out on one of the Hai boats with a bonito they'd dragged on an outrigger. A blue marlin had batted it twice with his bill, taken a squeeze with his jaws and somehow missed *both* hooks that Peter had carefully sewn inside. I had that feeling that the fishing was about to explode into life, and I had only one day left.

Someone mentioned the koli-koli (lowly trevally) that could sometimes be found just outside a reef south of the coloured water of Malindi, and I decided to use my last trip on *Ndege* to go after them. The run up to this area proved quiet, only a couple of skipjacks coming our way. The shoals of koli-koli also failed to materialise, though I did manage one fish, and lost another on the 6-lb test. They are a member of the 'jack family which makes them one of the dogged scrappers, never giving up until the net's under them. Both Carl and Pete landed a couple apiece on the 20s, but the 6 remained unlucky. On the journey home Peter spotted some birds offshore, and as the wind had failed to materialise we decided to drag through them. As we neared the diving birds my 6-lb outfit at last roared away and I backed the drag off. Whatever it was that had taken the lure sure wasn't going to be stopped in ten yards. He cleared about two hundred yards from the spool of the tiny multiplier and I set about getting some line back as he slowed. It took me fully twenty minutes to boat that fish, which turned out to be an 8-lb barega, a sub-species of the tangueague, and resembling a kingfish. Next run through I hit a 5-lb rainbow runner, one of the zippiest fish in the ocean on 6-lb test. He took me fifteen minutes. Then another took, a twenty-minute job of arm-crankingthe tiny rod, which was grossly overpowered by the 6-lb test, which would have made a great 2-lb outfit. He weighed 5lb 2oz, and was only 8oz below the All-Kenya Record for 6-lb test! I tried to be happy with coming so close, but nobody remembers second placers. However, by the pressure I had on that fish, I think it would have been no trouble getting the Kenya record up to around 9lb. The rainbows were obviously schooling on the surface, but my time was up. The same old thing — 'you should have been here last week/next week' etc.

Thus ended my first encounter with African fishing. I was captivated by this massive continent and its raw, still untamed environment, the blistering sun, the beauty of the life and death struggles of the insect and animal world. I was well pleased with my light tackle fishing, which had given me a total of fifteen records over eleven days. Yet still the potential for world records lie within easy grasp. The fact that immense shoals of baitfish are driven to the surface by unseen predators make the light tackle aspect exciting to say the least.

I hope sincerely that this wonderful country never sees too much western civilisation, and gives many more anglers the chance to enjoy fishing safari-style.

★ ★ ★

My *first* encounter with a sailfish was off Upper Matecumbe in the Florida Keys. I was sharing the *Marlin Too* charter boat with London anglers Cliff and Mark Johnson. It was a glorious day, as we nosed the big boat out between the flats, stopping only to chum up some bait. The sea was like a sheet of glass, reflecting the first of the sun's early morning rays.

It was going to be a hot one and that was for sure. By nine o'clock everyone was fully lubricated with sun oil and a breakfast of Budweiser beer. Bobby, the mate, began running back ballyhoo on 30s and 50s to dance and skip enticingly in our wake. On the centre flat line he ran a big double-hook konahead lure on a set of 80. For over an hour we dragged the baits along the edge of the blue-green drop-off that marked the edge of the reef. A solitary pelican wheeled behind us, investigating the curious action of the skipping ballyhoo. Cliff was lying on a bunk, Mark was standing on the bridge talking to the captain, David Day, and I were sitting on the gunnel watching the baits. Suddenly the 50 buckled over and line started screaming from the reel.

'STRIKE — HIT THE FISH!' shouted David.

Mark jumped into the fighting chair but there was no need to strike. That fish was well and truly 'on'. Line was still running from the International reel as Mark gradually pushed up the drag. After a give-and-take struggle a fine wahoo of 34lb was gaffed aboard, its tiger-striped flanks standing out clearly. The baits were re-rigged and we commenced trolling again. This time David decided to take up way offshore, in a straight run out from the reef. An hour passed and everyone had dropped into a relaxed doze, the burning sun lulling the senses. Suddenly I yelled out as a dolphin bounced out of the water off the port quarter. Another followed it, greyhounding after the first. 'School of dolphin — you'd better get ready!' shouted David.

No sooner had he spoken, than three rods buckled over simultaneously and we spent the next half hour landing beautiful fish to 20lb. As suddenly as they had arrived the school departed, and we stood laughing at the drumming of the fish down in the hold. Cans of beer were broken open and we celebrated a great start to the day.

Still the sea remained flat calm, an eerie feeling when you're twenty miles offshore, and out of sight of land. This time, when we resumed trolling, we ran a pair of big konaheads from the flat lines. An hour and a half later, there were still no fish. Bobby changed the lures and a slightly different action konahead gurgled and kicked in the wake behind. I watched it from my position on the gunnel, fascinated by the spume of bubbles that spiralled behind it as it churned beneath the surface. Something about it made me walk across to the fighting chair and sit in it, my hand resting lightly on the spool of the big 80. Ten minutes passed, and I relaxed slightly.

'Gimme a sandwich can you please Cliff?' I shouted.

He came beside me and handed it over. As I took a bite the ratchet screamed and the big rod bucked and kicked violently. I bit down so hard on the sandwich that mayonnaise spurted out from each end, covering my tee shirt like paint. Grabbing the rod I jammed the butt into the gimbal and struck three or four times. The line was still dragged from the spool even as the engines died.

'Could be a billfish' shouted Bobby as he cranked the other baits clear. 'Even a marlin maybe.'

I pulled back hard on the rod, trying to gauge the size of the fish.

'No, I don't reckon it's a billfish. Doesn't feel heavy enough. The way he stripped line on that first run, I reckon it could be a big wahoo.'

The runs grew shorter, but were very fast all the same. Up on the bridge, David stood shading his eyes, straining to see what I had hooked into. I gained line, and a fish boiled on the surface about forty yards back. Bobby looked up to David.

'You see him yet Davy?'

'Yeah, I think he's got himself a sailfish. If it is, it sure is a big mother!'

Cliff reappeared from the cabin and began shooting with the movie. Still the fish wouldn't jump, just making those short, jerky runs. I felt a head shaking down beneath the surface. Yes, it was a billfish; that familiar sensation as it batted its bill against the wire leader told me so. The double line showed, then the leader. Leaning out, Bobby's fingers closed around it and he eased the fish up.

'You wanna keep this one Graeme?'

'What is it, a white marlin or a sail?'

'It's a sailfish, and boy it surely is a HELLUVA sailfish. He's up near 80lb!' David shouted down from the bridge.

'That's a damn big Atlantic sail Graeme. I've taken a lot of guys out who would pay big bucks to get that fish mounted. We can take him in, but it's up to you now.'

I thought for a second of a huge sailfish mounted over the fireplace, thought of the cost of mounting, crating and shipping back to England. Strictly a 'no contest'!

67

'Put him back, but I want to get him in the boat first though, get a really accurate estimate.'

Bobby reached down and closed a gloved hand around the bill, dragging the flashing fish up and over the gunnel. The body pounded on the side as Bobby fought to unhook the lure. He opened up the massive sail and we all gasped at the pale bluish-grey vertical bars and rows of spots. David shinned down the ladder to help Bobby return the fish. He shook his head in disbelief as they lifted the fish over the gunnel and it crashed back into the water. 'How big?' asked Cliff. A broad grin spread over David's face as he pumped my hand. 'Nice fish Graeme, he'll go 75lb!'

Later that same year, in early October, I found myself in a big Hatteras gameboat, with fellow angling writer Joel Arrington. I had already spent three days sampling the superb shore fishing from North Carolina's famous Outer Banks. My guide was beach expert Joe Malat, who drove me many miles along the sand dunes in his four-wheel-drive jeep, trying to locate the bluefish and drum. The variety and excellence of North Carolina's sport fishing — both salt and freshwater — is unmatched in the eastern United States. That could not be counted as an empty boast. It is instead, a claim based on a variety of facts which endow North Carolina with a quality of angling that is unique. The level lands of the southern coastal plains extend eastwards from the fall line of the rivers to the tidewater section. Here, where the rivers flow large and slow, you'll find all of the southern warm-water species along with the annual salt-water to freshwater spawning runs of shad and striped bass. The tidewater section fringes the coastal sounds from Virginia to the South Carolina line. The Outer Banks, run in a sandy strip 175 miles long from the Virginia line south to Cape Lookout, and then curve back to the mainland. This barrier reef of open beach and sound-side woods varies in width from a few hundred feet to a mile or more, encompassing the great inland sounds, Currituck, Albemarle, Pamlico, Core and Bogue. The sea shore of the banks and the inlets which pierce this sandy reef provide world-famed surf fishing. These same inlets — Oregon, Hatteras, Ocracoke, and Beaufort, also provide the doors that open on the offshore fishing grounds. Because of another curious combination of physical facts, North Carolina's saltwater sport fishery is equally varied. Cape

Hatteras, the eastern most tip of the Outer Banks, is the place where the cold green waters of northern currents collide with the sapphire Gulfstream and force the northern-bound flow of tropical water away from the coast.

Besides being the nearest point — about twelve miles to the Gulfstream north of Florida — Hatteras and Oregon Inlet are known as 'Gamefish Junction', meeting place for northern and southern species. Here you can catch tautog and striped bass one day, then find yourself trolling for dolphin, barracuda and tuna the next! I had been advised to try North Carolina's offshore fishing by Alan and Andy Card, the brothers who run the highly successful Bermudan gameboat *Challenger*. Earlier in the day I had landed kingfish (king mackerel) to 25lb and now I sat next to Joel and the captain, discussing what other species we could try for. We were in the colder green-water taking the 'kings', and I had taken all the pictures I needed.

'We could take a run offshore and see if we can't locate a finger of blue-water' suggested Joel.

'What do you reckon on the chances,' I asked, 'not only of finding some blue, but of catching some fish as well?' Joel looked at the captain,

'Whaddya reckon? shall we try?'

'Sure, why not. Graeme has taken some big kingfish — let's take a shot at it.' The engines were started, and the rods brought in and stowed. An hour later and I was halfway through lunch when the engines slowed. Up on the bridge came the captain's voice: 'Bluewater up ahead — rig up some small Jetheads!' Inside half an hour we had eight yellowfin tuna in the boat, the largest about 20lb. Another half hour, and four good wahoo up to 35lb joined the tuna! What else could happen? The fishing was great, the sun was sparkling on the waves, and a strong breeze was lifting small whitecaps from the wave tops. As I ran back my lure into the wake again, Joel sidled up.

'The captain has just taken the water temperature. He says if we rig up fish baits, there's a good chance of a billfish.'

'Whites, or are we too late?'

'They usually last until about the second week in September, but way out here there still may be a chance. It's up to you. We can stay on the wahoo and tuna, or you can re-rig for bills.

I'd taken a good many fish so far, and I wanted to press my luck as far as possible. A cold front was forecast for the next day, and maybe we wouldn't get out. We were lucky to be in a finger of bluewater anyway, being the only boat this far out, the others working the 'kings' in the green water.

'OK. Let's try it!'

Forty minutes later and a pair of ballyhoo were skipping in our wake, a churning teaser tied near the stern spiralling away a spume of bubbles. I sat in the chair.

'BILLFISH BEHIND THE TEASER! GET IT OUT! GET IT OUT!' The captain's shout jolted me from the trollers doze, and I scanned the depths as the mate hand-stripped in the teaser.

'HE'S STILL ON IT! — GET IT OUT OF THE WATER DAMMIT!'

I looked behind the teaser but saw nothing. The captain's high vantage point cut down surface glare and allowed him to see more. The teaser clunked over the stern. 'OK. He's dropping back now — WATCH YOUR BAITS!'

In a second there was a welter of spray underneath Joel's ballyhoo — 'Look out, he's under yours Joel!' A split second later and my own fish bait disappeared in a vortex of saltwater and the rod kicked over. Instinctively, and with total disregard for the drop-back usually given to a baited sailfish — I struck. Too late — the captain cursed at me — but my run of luck was still holding; I actually had a hook-up! First the line ran off the 30-lb outfit, then the sail came out, wagging its bill in fury. I backed off the drag as it tore off on another searing run, equally as fast as any wahoo I've ever hooked. More jumps, then tail-walking, the spray whipping away on the freshening breeze. Another few minutes and he started to give — slowly at first — until I sneaked the drag pressure up and he began planing behind the boat, the beautiful sail erect like a banner from a crusade war.

'Hold him there' shouted Joel, his camera's motor drive whirring through twenty frames.

'Wanna keep him Graeme?' My heart was still pounding with excitement from the breathtaking leaps.

'No, but I want some photos inboard though.'

A gloved hand closed around the bill, and a thrashing form flailed on the deckboards. We both fell on top of it to stop the fish damaging itself further, and removed the hook.

It hadn't even gone in past the barb, and literally fell out from the roof of the bill. Lucky simply wasn't the word for it! I got some photos and posed with the mate holding the bill and myself holding the tail while Joel finished off the roll of film.

'He's a forty-five pounder Graeme. Nice fish. Especially for October!' We trolled for another two hours, and with typical angler's greed, I cherished the hope a white marlin would take hold. No such luck, and we returned to Oregon Inlet with wahoo to 30lb, yellowfin tuna to 20lb, kingfish to 25lb and a bonus 45-lb sailfish. Not a bad day at all.

Next day was cancelled as the cold front hit the Outer Banks and I considered my run of luck temporarily curtailed.

My next encounter with a big Atlantic sailfish was in May the following year. I had been lucky in catching billfish and wahoo with twelve-inch Jet lures that I had made up in England, and I had begun to believe that I could run one of these big 'beasts' in the boat's wake, at every opportunity. Billfish are so unpredictable you have to try to convince yourself that the sea is full of them, and that one is about to grab hold at any minute. I was going out to the 'Hump' off Islamorada, on Jim Taylor's gameboat *Ace*. The other three friends sharing the boat were using the regulatory ballyhoo baits for dolphin, but I had received a message the night previously that a couple of blue marlin had been brought up on big konaheads. I would miss out on the chance of some dolphin action, but a nice marlin would more than make up for that.

I ran one of these big jets from my 50 on the stern flatline. I usually run them close to the boat, almost as close as a teaser — but something made me run it way back in the wake, about two feet beneath the surface. I jacked the drag on the International up past the 'Strike' position, and hoped the new Ande line I had loaded it with, would take the impact of a hit. About three miles off the Hump, over went my 50, ratchet screaming.

'BILLFISH!' I shouted, obviously not knowing what the hell had grabbed the line. 'HIT THE ENGINES!'

Jim looked down from his vantage point high up on the flying bridge.

'HOLY CHRIST — HANG ON TO HIM G.J. — DON'T GIVE HIM NO SLACK!'

I struck, and cranked like a madman as the *Ace's* twin engines roared forward, setting the hook. Crewmate Davy yelled up to Jim — 'OK Jimbo — He's ON!' The engines slowed, and the fish changed down a gear and accelerated away. The Fenwick rod bent over, and suddenly I realised how tight I'd put the drag. I pulled the lever back gingerly and the line purred off smoothly.

'Whaddya reckon Davy? A blue? or maybe a white?'

The fish tore off on another thirty yard burst. 'I reckon it's a big wahoo Graeme, or it could be a white.'

I wound and pumped in an effort to keep that line tight. I well remembered how that hook had dropped from the bill of my North Carolina sailfish, and I surely didn't want a repeat of that. Still the fish didn't show — until a blue-grey shape began to materialise from the depths. Jim appeared beside me. 'How's that drag Graeme?' I pulled off two feet of line and he nodded his approval. He stood next to Davy who was pulling on his leader gloves as he stared at the shape. 'What the hell is that Davy? Is it a wahoo or what?' Before he could answer the fish rolled and came nearer the surface. 'It looks like a Mediterranean spearfish!'

The gaff appeared and both men hauled on the wire leader as it broke the surface.

'Keep him tight G.J. — and watch for any sudden runs!'

I watched — boy, how I watched. A Mediterranean spearfish was a fantastic capture, not for size, but for sheer rarity value. I wanted that fish in the boat so bad it hurt!

'No, it's a big sailfish' said Davy, and sank the gaff in. I was disappointed for a second as I thought of the fame attached to the capture of a spearfish, but this quickly vanished as I saw the size and quality of this fish. The bill was perfect, and the sail completely intact, no line tears, the mauve-purple colours shimmering under the Florida sunlight.

'Oh man is he a pretty fish' said Jim. 'Sure would make a super wall mount.'

I shook my head slowly and they laughed. This was the third big sailfish inside a year I'd landed and had not mounted. Back on the dock at Whale Harbour it topped the scales at 63lb, and was probably the most photographed fish that week. Me? I figured the only thing I'd like to have mounted is that twelve-inch Jet lure the sail took. How it ate it I'll never know!

6

Skinny Water Fishing

FLORIDA AND BERMUDA

I stood on the bow of the skiff, idly swishing the fly rod backwards and forwards. The sun beat down from a clear blue sky, the reflection from the mirror-like surface making me squint, even behind the polarising 'shades'. Our guide, Max Winters, spat a mouthful of tobacco juice into the water, where it coloured brown for a second before disappearing in the grasses below. In the stern lay Chris Dawn, my companion on this, my first trip after a fly-caught tarpon. The venue was Islamorada in the Florida Keys, a favourite stamping ground on my world travels, and where I had caught many a record fish.

My initial contact had been George Hommell Jnr, the proprietor of Worldwide Sportsman, Upper Matecumbe's fishing shop. George had suggested the venue, method and guide. All that remained was for the fish to co-operate! I'd read a lot about the 'Silver King', and longed to get one of their piscine scalps under my belt. I had chosen the most difficult way to start tarpon fishing. Casting a fly is an art in itself, and an art to be savoured on fishless days I hasten to add! It was mid May. The tarpon were supposed to be running, and we were anchored by push pole, only some forty yards from Indian Key. Off the port quarter lay the Keys, and Indian Key bridge, through which we were hoping these shallow-water leviathans would run.

Fishing for the past few days had been patchy, but with the enthusiasm all fishermen possess, we were hopeful of a hook-up. Chris and I had decided to take fifteen-minute spells standing up on the bow waiting for a tarpon. The flyline was coiled on the fibreglass deck, ready to be aerialised at a moment's notice by the big No 12 Graphite rod. Off our bow lay two more tarpon boats, exactly the same, with anglers standing on the bow, occasionally false casting to judge casting ability. This fly fishing can best be described as a dull game. You wait, sometimes for hours, mostly seeing nothing, then suddenly you have to cast to a fish in a matter of four or five seconds. You may get two shots before the fish moves out of range or if the Gods of sport fishing are smiling, three! That does not necessarily mean you hook a fish. Far from it. Tarpon are no less fickle creatures than any other fish. Usually getting a fish hooked initially is a minor problem. Getting them to stay on the hook is a different ball game altogether! Chris had already used up his quarter hour 'standing' session and was lying in the stern rubbing sun oil into his rapidly reddening English skin. A plug of tobacco juice stained the water again as Max watched Chris spill sun oil over the deck.

'No need to spread that stuff on the boat Chris — she don't burn up too easy till the afternoon! 'Sides, by the colour of your skin, your goin' t' have t' cover up pretty soon!'

'Don't worry Max. I won't burn. I'm used to the sun.'

Max's eyes swept the area down sun for sign of any approaching tarpon.

'Yeah. Ah ken see thet!'

I lifted the line in the air and threw the big fly rod in clean easy sweeps, trying to gauge the power hidden in the glass walls. It had taken me a while to get used to the faster action of the graphite rod, and I shot the line out about thirty yards. It was a good throw. Sssssssss . . . CLICK. It took all the slack, and pulled line off the Fin-Nor centre drag flyreel.

'You throw much fly in England Graeme?' enquired Max.

'Only for trout. We use lighter gear, and the fish don't make long runs. We have to scale down tackle to get any sort of real fight from them.'

'You put out a pretty good line. You ever hit tarpon before?'

'Nope.'

'Well ah'll tell ya. There's a better'n even chance as he'll either throw the hook or bust ya outa sight!'

I tried to look dignified at what I thought was a doubt cast on my angling ability.

'I've caught quite a lot of big fish before Max. Marlin, tuna, bones. I figure I stand as good a chance as the next man.'

'I don't doubt it Graeme, a'h jess trying to tell you the law

74

of averages out here. The tarpon has a real hard mouth. Don't matter how hard you strike, unless you're real lucky an' catch in some skin or gristle, your hook holds nothin'. On fly, out here, if you're really lucky, you'll land one in eight!'

'Rest assured I'll give it my best shot Max.' I stripped in the flyline, coiling it neatly at my feet. If a tarpon came I'd be ready in a second. Out to sea behind me the water was so flat I could make out the white specks that were the big gameboats trolling the weedlines in the bluewater for dolphin, wahoo and sailfish. A few puffy clouds had begun to develop on the horizon, and the humidity rose to an uncomfortable level. The water we were moored in was about five feet deep. Behind us, up to Indian Key, it shallowed to three feet. Directly in front and to the side lay two large flats: Areas of shallow foot-deep water, covered entirely by sea grasses. A lone skiff was being poled across one, its occupants looking for tailing bonefish. A huge stingray flapped its way lazily off the edge of the flat, into the deeper water to our starboard. It ran on for thirty feet, then changed course and headed directly for us. As it neared the boat Max banged the side of our skiff with his hand. The stingray quartered and rocketed off along the bottom, sending up clouds of mud. A small pod of 5-lb barracuda schooled in front of us, searching for any signs of shoaling needlefish, their primary diet. I cast the fly in front of them and stripped back fast. Two shapes rocketed behind it, jockeying for position as to who would grab first. Neither did, and they peeled off either side of the bow. I dabbled the fly in water below my feet, watching small four-inch pinfish pop up from the bottom to tug on the hackled streamer fly.

'WE GOT TARPON!' The yell from Max almost made me lose my balance, as I tried to make out where he was pointing. Suddenly I saw them, three fish looking to be about thirty pounds apiece, swimming about fifty yards away on the edge of the flats. As they came closer I realised they were moving faster than I had anticipated, so started to aerialise the line.

'Not yet' whispered Max, 'let them work closer. You make that first shot count boy. You mightn't git another!' The shapes moved closer, gliding effortlessly over the brown-green sea grasses. They looked maybe fifty pounds apiece now.

'OK fire out about ten feet in front of that lead fish Graeme!'

I shot the line which sailed out beautifully. As it started to unroll I realised it was a little too accurate. SPLASH! Right on the lead fish's head. Amazingly he didn't spook.

'OK now strip it boy, strip the fly in.' I began to work in back to the boat. 'Keep it comin', you've missed that first fish, but . . . Oh . . . Look at that third fish. Yes. Strip it! Keep it comin' he's going to take it . . . KEEP COMIN' MY BABY!' Max was almost outside of the boat in his excitement, and I waited for the pull. Then a cavernous jaw opened, not ten yards from the boat and took in my fly.

'NAIL HIM . . . HIT THE SONOFABITCH BOY!' I thumped the big flyrod up two, three times, trying to drive the hook into that bony jaw. As I did so I saw the massive scales glistening on the flanks as the fish started to climb in front of us. CRAAASSHHH! It fell back into the water . . . climbed again . . . and was GONE! Maybe four seconds at the very outside.

'Bad luck Graeme, you had a 70-lb fish on there. He jess threw the hook, that's all.'

Chris had risen from his slumbers in the stern. 'Hell, did you see that?'

'Yeah. I was hooked to it for awhile!'

Chris walked up the skiff. 'Here let me have a go.' He stood in the stern, trying to wipe his hands on the side of his trunks.

'I hope you ain't got sun oil on that rod butt Chris' said Max, in a sarcastic voice. Hastily Chris wiped his hands and the butt with a piece of rag. In half an hour exactly the same thing happened. Chris lost a fish. It leapt three times before dropping the hook. The tide was beginning to drop and I was standing up on the bow, dipping the rod tip in some floating weed.

'May have to move soon' said Max. 'Water's dropping. We could try out on Buchanan Bank.'

Even as he spoke, I looked off the stern and there, swimming as leisurely as you please were seven tarpon, no more than twenty yards from the boat!

'Look at those!' I yelled, frantically trying to drag the entire fly line round to cast backwards.

'Get a fly to 'em Graeme. One is sure to take.'

I smashed the entire leader, fly, and flyline down in a

crumpled heap, right in amongst the school. Max groaned in dismay. I stripped in and lifted the line out from way off in the water. The big fly whistled past me at knee level before I managed to regain momentum. I shot the line, which this time hissed out clean, and unrolled perfectly. I stripped back. A huge tarpon broke from the main school and followed the erratically moving fly. Only yards from the boat the jaws opened and I actually saw the grey fly disappear. 'HIT HIIIIIIM!' I struck. The first time I felt was too weak, so a split second later hit him hard, locked down the flyline against the butt, and held the slack in my left hand. The tarpon, in that split second decided he didn't rate the steel in his jaw too much and was moving in the *opposite* direction. Something had to give. Unfortunately it was the line class Tippet.

'Broke him off?' Max looked over his shoulder at me. I couldn't look him in the face, and said. 'Just tried to set it a little harder Max.'

We moved and raced at forty knots out under Indian Key bridge, weaving between the mangroves, on route for Buchanan Bank. These are located some five miles out, and are one of the hottest areas for 'standing' for tarpon. Two boats were already in position, so using our electric motor, we slipped in the space between. We were moored on a long bank, slightly curving, and about two feet deep. In front of us lay a lagoon-shaped piece of water averaging about five or six feet deep. We took it in turns waiting on the bow, while Max climbed up onto a small platform over the top of the big outboard engine. It was used mostly in tournament fishing, allowing the guide to spot the tarpon from his higher vantage point, thus giving his client more time to get ready. We waited for about an hour and a half, before one of the tarpon boats followed a hooked fish with their electric motor. It looked to be about sixty or seventy pounds, and the angler in the bow was clinging frantically to a doubled rod. Suddenly Max shouted. 'Hey look. The school of fish that guy hooked his from is still comin' our way!' Then 'Damn — they're too far out!'

I watched the approaching school, trying to gauge how far they were from the edge of the bank. I starting false casting the line in the air, listening to its hiss as it whipped past my shoulder.

'Don't waste your time Graeme', said Max, 'they ain't going to come any closer . . . they can't be reached.'

As the fish moved by, I started to heave that fly rod like a stage coach driver cracking the whip on his team of six. Something, maybe years of judging casts to trout in my home lakes, told me those fish were worth a throw. The line reached the maximum aerialisation before the 'shoot', and with a final heave I sent the lot sailing towards those tarpon. The line seemed to unroll in slow motion, taking ages to extend over the water. Suddenly it jerked taut, carried all the loose line at my feet out through the rings and jerked on the reel.

'Jesus Christ Boy . . . You're there. Hey! STRIP IT . . . STRIP IT!'

I stripped that fly with hands that shook like a leaf in a gale. I knew . . . Yes, I KNEW I was going to hook a fish. Slowly, majestically, a huge tarpon broke from the school. I must have still had thirty *yards* of line in the water when Max screamed at me: 'HIT HIM, GIVE HIM THE BUTT LAD!' I hadn't felt a thing at that distance, yet Max had actually seen that huge mouth engulf the fly. Maybe years of staring through the water at the fish of the flats gave him extra keen eyesight. Maybe he just sensed that the fish had eaten the fur and feather creation. As the graphite started to come up so the entire ocean seemed to erupt in front of me, and a silver *animal* — no fish could look that big, cleared the water in front of me. I actually heard the gill plates rattling, as it shook its head violently from side to side. I remember it running over and over through my mind: 'Dear God, let that hook stay in . . . please . . . just keep it *there*!' The fish sounded, starting to drag off line against the clutch.

'Is the drag OK Max?'

'Yeah, Don't touch it. It's set already.'

He bent down and eased the electric motor into the water. Chris scrambled frantically for the camera. 'Where's the camera Graeme? I gotta get those jumps . . . Where's the damned camera?'

I didn't even answer as the fish came out again. This time I was on the backing, and the fish sixty yards away. At first I thought it was a free jumper, not the one I hooked, as the line bellied out in front of me. Max slipped the pole mooring and we started after the fish, now heading back across the lagoon. A few more leaps, and Max shouted, 'Bow to him Graeme. You're not bowing to him.' Even as he spoke I saw the fish climb six feet in the air. When he re-entered . . . I was not connected. 'Damn!' I started to wind the line in.

'How big you reckon Max?' Max started to laugh. 'Oh, he wasn't too big — round the 90-lb mark!' I looked to see what Max was laughing at. Chris was scrabbling in a bag for a camera, oblivious to my trailing flyline. He emerged with the camera, a beam on his face. 'OK Graeme . . . where is he?'

Having experienced some of the power of this magnificent fish I decided to try a different part of the Keys. I've told you I'm superstitious, so as they say, 'a change is as good as a rest'. I had lost a nice 30-lb tarpon while night fishing from Tea Table Key, dapping a pilchard up and down between the bridge buttresses. They had been rolling all round me, and I was half dozing when one suddenly swallowed the pilchard and left for the power pilings that grow from the flats there. Luckily, and by pure fluke, I managed to stay connected to this one, yet although I had it entirely played out on 12-lb test, there remained the problem of getting it to the side. The current was pushing from the Gulf out to sea so I had to hold it away from the buttresses. I manoeuvered it past *seven* posts. As I neared the eighth the fish rolled, ducked round a buttress and the line cut without a sound. I don't believe I have used such filthy language since my lawyer told me how much my wife wanted for divorce settlement.

So here I was. My third attempt at catching a tarpon, in Key West, the tail island in the Florida Keys chain. Key West has long attracted people with its year-round tropical breezes, superb climate and gin-clear water. This Caribbean Island is part of a coral reef, the last living reef on the North American continent. Temperatures are moderate year round, a point which wives of anglers will want to take into consideration, with a summer average of about 82 degrees. Summer is also the rainy season, but the rain falls mostly during the evening hours, and days are, for the most part, sunny. I had chartered a boat from Garrison Bight Marina, the *Chaser* captained by Mike Wilbur, with his crew mate 'Red'. I never did learn Red's last name, but it's not important. I had done all the tourist attractions on a previous trip: Hemingway's house, a tour of Key West on the bone-shaking Conch Tour train, the reef trips, aquarium, dive shops, and of course stood with several hundred others on the western tip of the quay, waiting for one of this Key's famous sunsets. The time was 6 pm. I had finished with the sightseeing and wanted to go tarpon trolling.

We slipped the moorings and eased the tournament boat out under the bridge, and down the channel towards the open sea. Speedboats and yachts were coming, foaming past us as they sped for the sanctuary of a Key West bar. Sloppy Joe's would be busy again tonight.

'Wanna beer?' drawled Mike. 'Plenty in the cooler if you want one.'

'No thanks. You know what I need Mike.'

Mike stood his beer down with a shocked look on his face . . . 'God-Damn! Not another beautiful blonde Graeme. Boy I don't know how you English guys do it!' We both laughed and Red began rigging up the rods. We were trolling using two 30-lb outfits, both culminating with a short leader and big, deep running plug. We tried drifting with a live pinfish first, but although tarpon were rolling in the deeper sea channels, none were interested.

'I think it's still a little early' said Mike. 'They usually hit when the sun is just a smidgeon above the horizon.'

We tried trolling, the big deep runners throb-throbbing on the rod tops. Twilight came quickly, as it always does in the tropics, and suddenly I felt a distinct 'rap' on the rod. Mike had seen it too. 'Watch it' was all he said. 'BANG . . . ZZZZeeeeeeee!' The rod bowed over and I heaved back trying to set the hook on the fish. 'No! No!' screamed Mike. 'Shorter jabs, stick him with SHORTER jabs!' Astern, some eighty yards off, the water opened and a massive fish poked its head out, thrashing the surface to a foam. In an instant it was gone. I slowly wound the line in spreading it carefully to prevent any humping on the spool.

'That was a real big fish Graeme. You should've hit him harder.'

'A hundred pounds?' I queried.

Mike took a swig from his can of beer, and nodded his head as he swallowed . . . 'sure, getting on for that.'

We resumed trolling as the tide started to flood in through the channels. Red cleared weed from the line several times in the darkness, and I was starting to get bored with continually holding the rod. I reached down for my can of coke took a swig, then WHAM! The rod buckled, I dropped the coke, spilling most of it down my front. 'NAIL HIM GRAEME . . . TWO, THREE, FOUR . . . That's it. Alriiiight! Now you got him!'

The line screamed from the reel at a frightening rate, while crashes in the distance made the experience of playing this fish a weird experience. My only guide was how much, or rather how little line was left on the reel spool! I gained a little line, only to have it dragged off the reel again in a vicious burst. Red was at my side, swivelling the spotlight in an effort to locate exactly where the fish was heading. The *Chaser* was in slow reverse gear, trying to keep pace with the tarpon, and keep some line on my spool. Suddenly the piercing beam picked out a cone-shaped cage bobbing in the tide.

'Hey Mike, he's trying to get around that buoy. If the line so much as touches that, that fish will cut him off!'

'Graeme you're going to have to risk losing that fish when I back this on him. If he gits roun' that buoy you're gonna lose him anyway. Wanna try for it?'

I nodded in agreement and set about the task of cranking possibly 120 yards of 30-lb test block on the reel, *under* pressure! The first thirty yards were OK then things got harder. I could feel that giant tail throbbing beneath the surface, batting against the leader. This was the longest I had kept *any* tarpon on for, and didn't even pray that the hook hold would stay good. My concentration was entirely on turning that reel handle and spreading the line on the spool with my left fingers. Turn-spread-turn-spread-turn-spread. After several minutes Red picked out the glowing red eyes in the spotlight, 'Here he is!' Mike moved back to take a look.

'Nice fish Graeme . . . You wanna keep him . . . have him set up?' I gasped my reply. 'No . . . Thanks . . . Return him!' My chest was constricted from exertion and excitement. I could feel my heart pounding like a steam hammer, my head was painful, feeling as though it would burst. I felt ill . . . I thought for a second I would die. In fact, thinking about it now I seriously think that was the closest I have ever come to having a coronary. Wanting that fish so bad, I was quite prepared to drop dead at the tender age of twenty nine! Red hauled on the leader and breached the fish on the surface. It thrashed the water, thumping into the side of the boat. 'Hey Mike . . . take a look at this mother. He's real big.'

Mike ran to the stern. 'Hey boy. We're gonna take him in anyway. This is a real big fish!'

'I can't honestly remember much about the journey in. I know they made me fish again, and I lost a baby tarpon of about ten pounds. Most of it was a blur. What I can remember though is three men dragging that huge 'herring' up out of the boat and along the quay to the scales. Had I caught THAT! We hauled it up on a set of scales at one o'clock in the morning. People just appeared from nowhere. The scales maximum was 112lb. The tarpon took them down to the maximum with a bump!

'Probably go about 118lb' said Mike. 'A helluva nice fish Graeme.'

At 1.30 am I turned the Buick Regal out of the marina car park to head back for a few hours' sleep at the Howard Johnson's Motel. I stopped by the traffic lights there. My tarpon was still hanging on the scales, with a group of hippies dancing round it taking pictures. I'd lost a lot of tarpon, but that three-figure fish glistening in the moonlight meant more to me than winning a thousand dollars!

While plug fishing and fly fishing are successful ways of taking the big tarpon, there remained a method that was supposed to be the most exciting of all. Live-lining. It consisted of free-lining a live mullet between the buttresses of the Florida Keys Highway 1 roadbridge, at night, with the line crooked around your index finger from the rod top. Only 16-lb and 20-lb spin-cast outfits were to be used if you considered yourself a *real* sportsman! You could feel so they said, the mullet getting agitated as a big tarpon homed in on it. When the hit occurred, the line was literally ripped from your fingers and the surface around the bridge erupted in a welter of spray. After hearing accounts of this method, I just had to have a go.

I had been working with my girlfriend up in the state of Utah, fishing and reporting on the striped bass of Lake Powell and the big trout of Flaming Gorge Reservoir. Here was an ideal opportunity to try live-lining. I'd fly down to Miami, hire a car and drive down to the Florida Keys for a stay at Marathon, in the Faro Blanco resort, close to the famed seven-mile bridge. Our hosts, Ritchie and Tina, were already waiting aboard the 24-foot T-craft, *Reel Thing,* as we arrived. Fishing times were from 5 pm until about 10 pm, 'prime time' being the thirty minutes either side of the sun melting into the horizon. As Tina gunned the *Reel Thing* out into the Gulf of Mexico a chill wind chopped the spray from the bow. It was May, and coincided with the yearly run of big tarpon. When I say big we are taking 70lb as small. Twice that night we moved the boat, jockeying with the other boats to get the best position. There were probably a dozen others, several of which hooked fish that night and disappeared into the gathering gloom, only to return minutes or hours later with stories of popped lines and lost fish. Sometimes these tarpon would hit the mullet, keep coming straight for the boat, take a couple of turns around the anchor rope or one of the many pilings and disappear . . . crashing water as they left you with a fluttering line. It was over in seconds. Either your luck and the hookhold held, or it didn't. We didn't even get the chance to hook-up that night.

Both Hilary and myself sat in the chill air, holding that 20-lb line across the index finger, feeling the twittering movements of the live mullet. The following night we were back there, about ten spaces down Seven-Mile bridge from the Marathon side. The tide was an hour later so we had high hopes. Again, some of the other boats hooked up, slipped their anchor rope and motored after leaping fish. Most got away we later heard and we had no luck either; our only action for the night being when Hilary's mullet behaved erratically, frantically pulling and tugging before it got the chop from a barracuda. She told me the mullet went absolutely crazy trying to escape the 'cuda, and that I would have no trouble in detecting a patrolling tarpon, swinging across the current by the bridge buttresses, searching out mullet. Meanwhile, both Ritchie and Tina were astounded at our poor luck, usually they had at least four tarpon hits a night.

Came our last evening. It was superb. I had spent most of the day on the bridge catching grouper and houndfish from the top, and had actually seen several six-foot long fish cruise between the supports in the ebbing current. Slack water was later this particular night, but at least the early flood would coincide with the sinking of the sun below the horizon. Everyone was keen to go, and most of the boats were already in position by 6 pm. We were late, having taken aboard a fresh supply of mullet from the Faro Blanco marina. The first two hours saw only two fish hooked, one a sixty pounder, was released, the other was lost. By 7.45 Ritchie had changed live mullet half a dozen times in order to get the most action in the water, while Hilary and myself sat waiting for the bait to telegraph a signal of its impending doom to our cramped index fingers.

At eight o'clock things started to happen. The early flood began and two boats hooked up away to the right. They slipped anchor and slowly followed their fish, bent rods wagging against the skyline. We barely saw the next splash, but it was a fish on the boat next to us, only some twenty yards away hooking into one of these silver missiles. Suddenly Hilary was standing, arm outstretched and mouth open. 'Ouch my finger!' With a twang the line was wrenched from her hand and an 80-lb fish cleared water only ten yards away. 'Hit it!' shouted Ritchie, 'hit it hard!' She hit. But Mr. Tarpon was bouncing all over the ocean and going generally bananas! Thirty seconds later the hook pulled. As I passed her my rod, an unusual occurence in itself, and Ritchie rebaited another live mullet, another tarpon crashed at the stern of our boat. The second rod was passed to me, and there was an explosion of spray as the whole kit nearly left my hands! I was already slamming the rod back to set that hook in the bony jaws as Tina started the big Mercury outboard. I was actually still attached and had some sort of secure hookhold. The fish cleared water three times, each jump putting yards of space between us. There was little point in trying to turn the handle. That, I hoped would come later. The *Reel Thing* backed into the Atlantic tide, fortunately away from the bridge and into open water.

By now it was nearly dark and we argued about jump shots, with me holding the rod in one hand and changing lenses with the other. By the time I had any sort of control and regained line we were half a mile from our anchor buoy. The tarpon had still managed a couple of jumps, but had settled into steady deep runs. That suited me fine and I left the camera work to Hilary, and set about putting some hurt on the fish. He came. Grudgingly. The Penn 850s was a dream to work with on that ultra smooth drag. I was able to keep maximum pressure on for minutes at a go. 'He's close'

Above: After a day spent churning through the bluewater, a Mauritian big gameboat idles her way to the moorings in Black River. The evening sunset brings the prospect of good tuna sport the next day.
Below: Fantastic in the water . . . fantastic in the frying pan! The dolphin or dorado is an ocean wanderer pursued avidly by the light tackle enthusiast. With strong runs, acrobatics and the appetite of a tiger, it's small wonder they are among the more popular species.

The unusual tail of this Pacific thresher shark is used to harass the shoals of fish on which it feeds. The author took this 130-lb fish on just 30-lb tackle while livebaiting a mackerel for striped marlin.

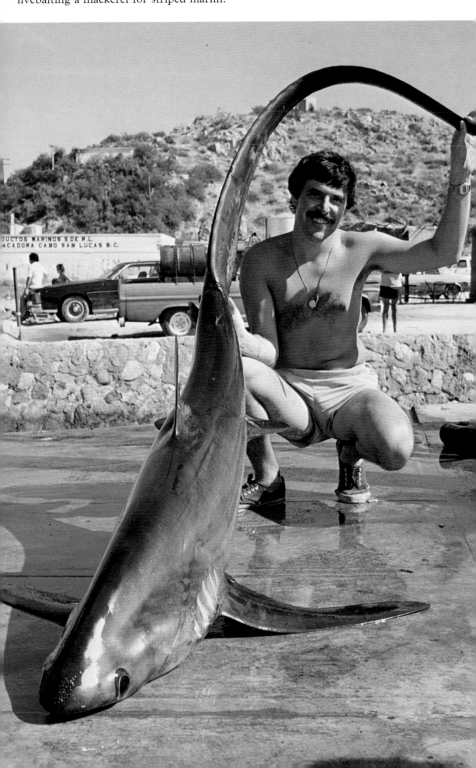

The strange anvil-like head easily identifies the hammerhead shark, one of the most efficient killing machines in the sea. This 378-lb fish was landed from the Indian Ocean.

ORGANISATION DE PECHE
DU NORD

BOAT	CORSAIRE II
ANGLER	G. PULLEN
SKIPPER	TRISTAN
FISH	HAMMER HEAD
WEIGHT	378 lbs
DATE	1.2.83
TROU AUX BICHES	

The copper-hued flanks of this deepwater fish hide a strength and stamina peculiar to all species of the 'jack family. This 70-lb amberjack was one of several landed by the author from a mark known as 'The Hump' off Islamorada in the States.

Three men strap the author's 561-lb Pacific blue marlin to the gunnel of *Flipper VI*. Many fish are simply too big or dangerous to be brought into the boat.

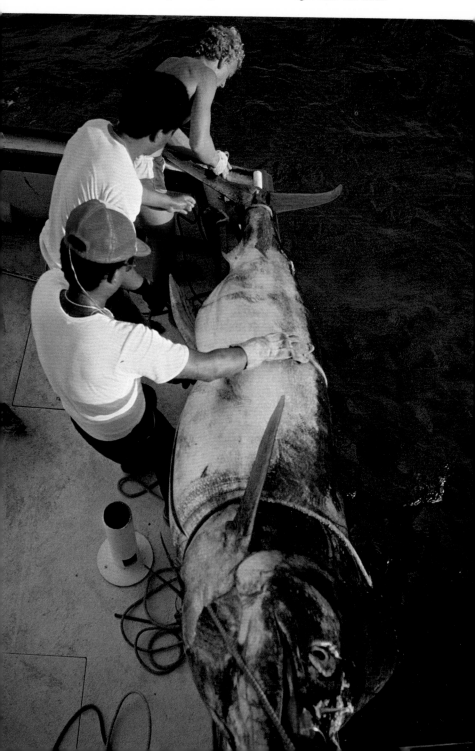

The east coast of Africa is largely unexplored by modern charter fishing techniques. The author has travelled several times to fish 'Muff' Becker's charter fleet out of Watamu on the Kenya coast and is holding one of his Pacific sailfish.

The physical side of big-game fishing is something most anglers fail to appreciate. If the reel seizes or locks up, the 130-lb line is capable of dragging a man over the stern. Watching the drag pressure on the big reel is most important.

Above left: The Cayman Islands in the Caribbean below Cuba offer superb shallow water sport with bonefish. Here the author's guide Denito plays a Little Cayman bonefish for the camera. All bonefish are returned to the water alive.
Above right: An aquine hunter of the highest efficiency, this 24-lb barracuda was taken by the author off the reefs of Kenya, only 200 yards from the hotel.
Below: This incredible array of dentistry belongs to a mako shark the author landed from Faial Island in the Azores. Unpredictable and dangerous this species can also turn up in British waters where it is known to reach 500lb in weight!

said Ritchie, keeping the stern to the fish. 'Keep him coming real smooth.' Tina leaned out in the darkness and grabbed the mono leader, bringing the massive silver head and shoulders of the fish out of the water.

'Release?' asked Ritchie.

'Sure. There's no way I can afford to mount something that large back in England.'

Hilary leaned over the stern. 'How big?' she asked.

Ritchie stretched over to the slab of muscled scales lying alongside the boat.

'Easy hundred, maybe more.'

I settled for the ton, and Tina jerked on the mono leader popping it and giving this magnificent fish his freedom. What a fight. And what a fish. Surely the finest inshore skinny water sport available, equal to, if not surpassing the acrobatics of the marlin. We had an hour left that night, but Hilary hooked and lost a second 100-lb tarpon; the hook as sharp as ever. But that's live-lining for three-figure tarpon. Some you win . . . some you lose. In the court of the Silver King . . . most times you lose.

★ ★ ★

I'm one of those people who undergo a Jekyll and Hyde transformation when let loose in a hire boat. In Florida, and especially down in the chain of Islands known as the Keys, there are nearly as many boats as people. The green reef water, and gin-clear shallows of the Gulf of Mexico's back country, is churned to a foam on weekends and Bank Holidays. This allows many anglers who cannot afford the cost of hiring a guide, to do their own thing in the shallow water fishing. Every year that I used to travel down the Keys, I always found myself taking a hire boat out from Bud 'n' Mary's Marina in Upper Matecumbe. For around a third of the cost of hiring a guide and skiff, I could get a day's fishing, and more to the point, I could do just what the hell I wanted when out on the water! If a bonnethead shark swam within casting distance, I wouldn't have to suffer the tongue of a guide who thought the only fish worth catching were tarpon and bonefish. Mind you, I only saw a fraction of the true population of the flats and shallows. Probably the main thing you're paying for in a guide is his eyes. I pride myself on being reasonable at fish spotting, but some of the

85

Florida guides have bionic bifocals or something. I would say I have hooked dozens of fish that my guide has said cast to, yet I've seen nothing.

Two particular days stick out in my mind as being typical of hire-boating on your own. It was late May and I'd had a few days offshore on the big stuff. I needed a rest so decided to go fishing for smaller species. I elected to try the barracuda off Indian Key, and succeeded in running the boat aground five times before I found the correct channels. I had taken some bran and pilchard oil with me, using it together with some boxed frozen chum to both attract fish, and smooth out the surface to aid fish spotting. I anchored on the favoured mark, about thirty yards off the Indian Key wooden jetty, in around two feet of water. It was a tarpon area, something I had taken into account when choosing this mark. Over the side went a small mesh bag of mushy fish mess, the oily particles popping to the surface and smoothing out the ripples. The quietly flooding tide was pushing the goo up onto a big flat opposite the road, and would I hoped, pull off something in the shape of stingray, 'cuda or bonnethead. I ran a couple of carp rods using pike floats and a single pilchard on the short wire trace. I then stood up on the bow with a pile of flyline coiled at my feet, and awaited a possible tarpon. Quite what I was going to do with a tarpon on my own I didn't know, as the outboard had to be dropped and started, plus the anchor had to come up. However when you're fishing on your own you also kind of figure to work the problems out as they come along.

My problem wasn't too long in coming. Slightly to the left of my slick came *three* tarpon. I worked the shooting head line out until I gauged I could shoot enough backing to reach them. They still headed towards me, and the line whipped past my ear, grey hackled fly 'feathering' as it went through. 'SSSSssssss!' the line shot through the guides and came up against the reel with a jerk. The leader unrolled and plipped into the surface about twelve feet in front of the fish. It couldn't have been sweeter, so waiting a couple of seconds for the fish to close, and the fly to sink, I started to strip back. A shape broke off and opened a huge maw to engulf the fly. I actually saw its mouth close and turn away as I struck. 'CRAAaaassshh!' Around eighty pounds of fish lunged into the air, crashed back in and powered away. The line whipped between the guides and the tip pointed straight at the fish. Too much drag saw him break off in those first few seconds. I couldn't do anything but laugh, both at the incredible power of the fish, and my own stupidity at attempting a solo feat. The fly rod was placed on the deck and I looked round to the other side to see both floats gone. I wound out the bow in the line of one, and nearly had the rod torn from my grasp. An unseen fish shot through the water so fast the hiss could be heard like an angry mamba. Then he came out, straight up and shaking his head like an angry Alsatian dog. It took me five minutes to boat that 8-lb barracuda, and another three to sort out the tangled lines, with another five pounder careering around the anchor rope.

After sorting the mess out I re-rigged and threw out the same baits — a pilchard on single hook suspended about a foot deep. They drifted round into the slick trail and disappeared almost as soon as they entered it. Even with the aid of polarising sunglasses I failed to see any fish in the slick, yet they were undoubtedly there. I took another six 'cuda up into double figures that afternoon, two falling to a fast cranked tube lure, while the others had less gourmet taste and opted for the suspended pilchard. The largest went fourteen.

The following day saw me out at the same spot, but thankfully I was now 'cuda minded and didn't bother to even try for tarpon. Again the fish came on the edge of the slick, and fell once more to the pilchard baits. They all gave me superb fights, their incredible build up of speed in the shallow two-feet deep water, making them an entirely different angling proposition to the ones cranked in on 50s and 80s offshore. Invariably, people who ridicule barracuda and claim they don't fight well, who have only taken them in deep water and on heavy tackle. Bonefish don't fight half as well when hooked in deep water, and only give a mediocre fight. I've caught stingray in deep and shallow water, and you would be forgiven for thinking the shallow water fish to be a completely different species. That afternoon I took another six 'cuda, superb specimens up to 19 and 21lb.

On a 6-lb test outfit I had a bonnethead shark, one of the hardest little scrappers to be had on the flats. Totally unlike the dull fight, if you could call it fight, that you get from the nurse sharks. The only other scrappy shark to be found on the flats is the blacktip which often clears the water acrobatically. The bigger barracuda seem to favour the slightly deeper water of the channels, and I have yet to take any double figures from the foot or so depths of bonefish flats. The worst fighting 'cuda I have found are the European variety. They're long, lean creatures that look half starved, and probably are. The ones I have caught came trolling close inshore to the rocks of Eastern Atlantic Isles like the Canaries. We would run Rapala Magnums in towards the rocks for bluefish, and obviously the odd barracuda would take a liking for the vibrating lure. On one particular occasion I unknowingly dragged a four pounder several hundred yards before deciding I did indeed have a fish attached and not a clump of weed as I had originally thought. They are a great species though, usually obliging in that they work on the assumption that if it moves — KILL IT! Their colossal speed from a standing start is also something to be admired.

My first experience of barracuda on the famed tube lure was several years ago on the Atlantic Isle of Bermuda. Pete Perinchief, his wife Eddy and myself were cruising the grassy area just in from the white sands of Whale Bay. We couldn't have been more than a hundred yards from shore, yet the water was only three feet deep. Pete wanted me to take one of the 'cuda known to frequent the area, on a pink tube lure. The day was a peach, just a few puffy clouds drifting off the land, making visibility excellent. Suddenly Eddy spotted some: 'Over there . . . see them!' A pod of about eight barracuda were lying, log-like over a clear sandy patch in the weed. My first cast went way past and attracted no attention.

'Drop it right in 'em' said Pete, 'then crank back like there's no tomorrow.' The lure crashed right in the middle of them and they dispersed in several directions. I started the lure back, skipping the tube lure through the surface. It zoomed past a single big fish and must have been twenty yards from it when that 'cuda took off after it. In a split second he had caught it, and jerked the tip of the rod round.

'HIT HIM, HIT HIM!' shouted Pete. Sixteen pounds of fury churned the surface to a foam as I tried to drive the hooks into that toothy mouth, then it took off on several hard runs. I was frankly amazed at its power, and it was several minutes before we lip gaffed, weighed, photographed and returned that fish.

In recent years this shallow water 'cuda fishing up at Whale Bay has been decimated by the greed of one commercial netsman, who seems hell bent on destroying the species completely. My last trip there saw only a few pods of 'cuda, and they weren't even into double figures. They are a ferocious species that are fearless when it comes to taking lures and baits. A twenty-four pounder I took off the mouth of Mida Creek on Kenya's African coast almost dragged me overboard with the power of that initial strike. Yet on the other hand I have been out wading flats for bonefish and turned to see six or eight big 'cuda tracking silently behind me, some as close as six feet. They seem to be fascinated or entranced by a pair of legs shuffling through the sand, and although initially quite terrifying, you soon realise that if you turn and wave your arms they rocket away like frightened sheep. Often they'll return minutes later, still looking evil, though I have learned to ignore them, and even quite like their companionship on wading trips! There's something exciting about fishing for them though, and I always get a minor case of the shakes when someone, after several hours of fruitless searching breaks the silence of the flats with that shout: 'CUDA!'

★ ★ ★

I stood on the flattened bow of the *Permit,* peaked cap shading my head from the worst of the sun. My fingers were looped over the bale of the Abu spinning reel, ready for action at a moment's notice. A gentle breeze tugged at the neckflap of my cap, fluttering it like a miniature flag. Overhead a pair of longtails wheeled and dived, revelling in the thermals thrown up from the nearby land mass. At the aft of the *Permit* sat Pete Perinchief, self-confessed bonefish addict, calmly pouring himself some iced tea. The water was some five feet deep, clear, over pure white sand, ringed only by a semi-circular bed of weed over which some garfish played. I shifted from one leg to the other in an effort to minimise cramp. I scanned the water in regulatory search pattern, using the polaroids to maximum effect as I strained to see any sign of life. There was nothing. There had been nothing for the last half hour. Pieces of wood drifted slowly by, indicating that the tide was starting to flood.

'Very often' said Pete, recorking the iced tea and gently

laying it in the cooler, 'you can spend a whole day, and not even see a bone.'

How reassuring, especially on my first bonefish trip!

'Yessir. I been out here many times and not seen a damn thing. You'd think the whole flats were devoid of fish!'

Forty yards down on the left a shape drifted onto the clear sand from one of the weedbeds. I straightened and hooked the line round my finger ready to cast.

'Relax' said Pete, barely looking up, 'it's only a small barracuda.'

I knew it was a fish, but I'd be damned if I knew what species it was. Another half hour passed, along with another five false alarms. Two were 'cuda, one was a trunkfish and the others a houndfish and bermuda chub. 'Yessir, catching bones is by no means easy. But mark you young Pullen, I *have* brought you to one of my easier marks!' By now boredom was taking hold. I wanted to cast at anything and everything. I wanted some action. Maybe these damn bones weren't all they're cracked up to be. Another houndfish hove into view, and instinctively I unclipped ready to cast. I looked round to see Pete looking the other way, so fired out the Wig-Wag minno lure and twitched it back. Feeling a tug as I watched it take, there was a splash and he was gone, snaking off through the water like a serpent.

'Lose your minno tail Graeme?' drawled Pete.

'Er . . . Yeah . . . but I don't know what took it, I thought it might be a bone.' Pete rummaged through his box and tossed a new rubber tail across the deck.

'Now you know Graeme that bones don't have any teeth.'

Caught in the act! Forty minutes passed and Pete turned his gaze from the water. 'I think we'll move back up to Shelly Bay. The tide will be well up there, and there may be a fish or two moving close to shore.'

As he turned to lower the outboard I saw a faint smudge of grey move across the sand in front of me, from left to right. Eight feet behind it was another. The first paused mid way across then moved towards the boat, stopping at intervals. Was it a fish? I couldn't make out. There was a slight ripple on the surface, and they could have been shadows from miniature clouds. I unclipped the lure, took a turn of line round my fingers and wrenched a couple of feet off the reel. Too stiff. I readjusted the clutch and tried again. Seemed OK now, so I opened the bale, took a back swing and let her fly. The lure went yards behind the 'cloud' and I wound frantically to catch up. The fish was still swimming towards me, so judging a locating point I slowed my retrieve and began tweaking the minno back in short, erratic jerks. The cloud stopped, then speeded up, stopping in jerks. Suddenly there was a tension on my line, I lifted slowly and felt the tip drag. Hammering the rod round I saw an enormous puff of sand, then felt every inch of stretch go out of the line. The rod hooped round, and I fumbled to ease off the pressure. The clutch groaned, I eased it, and listened as it rose to a crescendo in two seconds.

'PEEEEEETE! For Chrissakes what do I do?' He looked round.

'Whaddya got there? . . . Holy Christ, it's a bone, KEEP THAT ROD UP . . . WATCH THE DRAG . . . LET HIM RUN NOW!'

In three seconds the fish cleared fifty yards from the spool, then sixty, then seventy. It stopped somewhere an awful long way out and throbbed away with its tail, working across in front of us. Then I saw a glint of silver away to the right over a weedbed, but nowhere in the region of the line entering the water. There was an enormous belly of line between me and the fish, yet I couldn't crank down any more without risking something parting. Then it built up again. That awful pressure as the fish accelerated away on another run. This was another fifteen yards gone from the spool, and so far I hadn't got one turn on the reel handle.

'I'll pull up the anchor Graeme, we'll have to go with him, otherwise he's going to spool you.'

The fish swam back the other way, taking the belly out of the line and allowing me to regain forty yards. Then off it went, the line singing in the breeze, the fish's form flashing and twisting away in the distance. The runs gradually slowed and I saw the spool fill a little more respectably.

'Try putting some pressure on Graeme, we don't want to be here all day, those bones will probably be moving up at Shelly by now.'

Who is this guy? Here I am putting as much pressure on as possible and he wants more? I put more on, then more, then more. Amazingly the line didn't break. Lesson number one from Mr. Perinchief and after a further ten minutes I had the bonefish in the net. A beautiful sight . . . one solid bar of scaley silver, gasping away as Pete gently unhooked it.

'Nice fish Graeme . . . I guess he'll go five and a half, next time we'll get a bigger one.' Weighed, photographed and returned we commenced fishing. Within half an hour I landed another, slightly smaller, around 4³/₄lb. I was a bonefish fan in one afternoon!

During that first ever fateful trip to Bermuda, under Pete Perinchief's expert tuition I caught several more bonefish. I also lost them, spooked them, broke them off, straightened the steel on them, and cast a thousand times at shadows. I learned so much in one week that my somewhat limited cranial cavity began to expand. Was I not now a bonefish expert? The following year I was out on a tarpon boat captained by Max Register. The venue was Islamorada, Florida, and we were drifting over the big flat on the ocean side of Tea Table bridge. The tide was flooding well, and I shared the boat with Chris Dawn, my features editor at *Angling Times*. We were over in the Keys for the first crack at flats fishing there, having tangled with the tarpon on Max's boat a couple of days previously. It was a hot, comparatively still day, with the drone of traffic over the bridges for company. Rods were short 8-lb test outfits, spinning reels, single Eagle claw hook with a live shrimp nicked lightly through the tail as bait. My bonefishing expertise in Bermudan waters had suddenly been tossed out the window. Now I was confronted with trying to spot a fish over a weedbed, either tailing, or 'mudding' on the bottom. I couldn't see either, the only saviour to my despondency was the fact that Max hadn't seen any either. Both Chris and I are impatient anglers, both liking 'instant action' wherever possible. To spend hour after hour drifting over an apparently barren piece of weed-covered shallow water seemed a fruitless exercise.

We were maybe halfway through the day, and the optimum feeding period had passed. Max too, seemed to consign larger portions of tobacco juice into the water as he poled us slowly along. Suddenly, and maybe eighty yards off I saw this silver stick wagging in the water. I didn't shout out as I wasn't sure what it was. Then I saw another, and another, and another. I counted five and decided I'd better tell Max. 'Over there . . . see them Max . . . are they bones?'

'Yep . . . better get ready, but I'd let 'em get real close, those fish are tailing. Graeme you better make the first cast. Put it across the front of them, maybe ten, twelve feet ahead.' My heart started to accelerate as the fish grew closer, tails wagging like miniature striped marlin.

'OK. Fire out' whispered Max. My first cast went way past the school, and Chris had no shot on his line so showed us how to release high velocity live shrimp. 'Damn!' groaned Max. With one angler hooked in a weedbed, and the other twitching back a bare hook, he wasn't in the position to offer us any sort of advice. Suddenly my own shrimp came free from the grass, I cranked it over the heads of the bones, lifted it out and sent the next cast crashing into the midst of the school. I heard Max spitting tobacco juice like he had a mouthful of petrol . . . 'Holy Kerist, where do these guys come from?' I started tweaking the shrimp through the water, and felt a jolt on the tip. I struck, and not surprisingly broke the fish off in a flurry of spray and weed.

'You break him off or what Graeme?' asked Max.

'Yeah, he seemed like a nice fish Max.'

'What line is that on your reel?'

'Oh I swapped reels and used my own Cardinal with 5-lb Maxima line.'

I saw Max's mouth open in shock.

'Man you cai'nt mess with these critturs on no five poun' test. Jesus, some of the fish here *average* seven pounds apiece!'

I smiled weakly and offered the obvious remark: 'You reckon I should step it up a bit then Max?' Already his back was to me as he lowered the big outboard engine. By the time we reached the next flat I knew the day was doomed to disaster. By two o'clock the sun had gone round reducing the chances of seeing fish with the surface glare. We argued with Max about the chances of one of the many small stingray over this particular flat, taking a shrimp.

'Ah tell you guys they won't take shrimp. Only a fish bait. An' I don't have any. Besides the minute you start messin' aroun' with meat fish like them, you're gonna be sure to see the biggest bone of your life. I seen it happen dozens of times.'

By two thirty there was still no sign of bones, yet the boat seemed surrounded by flapping stingray. While Chris argued with Max, I sent a sly cast across the front of one of the fish. I saw it stop, hovering somewhere in the region of my bait, then tiny puffs of sand came up at the same instant I felt a sawing sensation on the line. WHAM! I heaved the rod up, there was an enormous splash and the ray stripped line from the reel diving straight under the skiff and out the other side. Max looked round almost unbelievingly: 'Oh no, dear God, not a damn ray!' Chris reeled round, startled by the sudden scream of the clutch. For fifteen minutes I had a wonderful battle with the fish, while Max just sat on the motor, back to the fish, chewing tobacco and spitting with disgust. After another five minutes I had the stinger near the boat, and the problem of what to do next became harshly apparent.

'Net him Graeme' said Chris. I looked at the barb, located just above tail.

'No . . . you net him Chris, you're closest.' Max stood up, picked the net from the decks, climbed round Chris and slid the net under a double figure stingray. As a parting gesture of our waning friendship the landing net broke in Max's hands, and he dumped the whole lot in the bottom of the boat. It was the fastest ride back to Bud 'n' Mary's Marina that I've ever had.

Next day, unfortunately for Max, he had the same two guys, so he kept well away from the stingray flats. He had similar problems with us however, when we discovered that the small bonnethead sharks also had a liking for live shrimp. By one in the afternoon we were boneless, but had seen several 'mudding' out of casting range. Despite frantic poling by Max he couldn't get us near enough to them. We re-anchored several times, and eventually found a mark that seemed to have several schools of fish moving over. Spooking several, Chris at last has a hook-up on his live shrimp. That fish stripped at least a hundred yards from a dead start, ploughed through a weedbed, and finally cut the line on a mangrove root.

'Did you see that' said Chris. 'I've never hooked anything so fast!'

Max laughed . . . 'sure you don't want to go back to the rays Chris?' Around two thirty I cast at what Max assured me were feeding fish. Personally I couldn't see a damn thing, but respected the man's ability enough to do whatever he told me. I had a take . . . struck . . . and saw the spool empty before my very eyes. After an incredibly long run the fish slowed, and spent the next ten minutes circling the boat, taking only the odd few yards from the reel. Away in the distance I could see his tail working as it throbbed mechanically into the tide. Another few minutes and he was near the boat. Max made ready with the net, and then, with a final scooping flourish he was mine. 'Thank God for that' said Max, 'I thought you guys were never going to get one.' It was a nice fish, maybe going seven pounds, deep bodied, but looking deceptively small in the water when we returned him. On the way back in we joked with Max, telling him the worst English jokes we could think of. After a sixth joke Max was nearly driving the skiff into a concrete stanchion, but it made the previous two days' escapades more enjoyable.

Although I have now managed to catch a few more bonefish, it's worth noting that they are a difficult fish requiring a different approach at each venue. One of my many trips to the Atlantic isle of Bermuda saw an interesting occurence, on what was my first day there. I decided to go down to Shelly Bay for swimming lessons. Naturally I had a bonefish rod strapped across my back, and the moped basket was full of lures and jigs. I stood the bike in the shade of a tree and wandered down to the beach. Several black guys were lounging in the shade, and dressed like a tourist, I became the butt of some humour.

'You goin' fishin' man?' I paused, trying to think to what other use I could put a fishing rod. Seemed a reasonable suggestion so I acknowledged: 'Sure, I'm going to catch a bonefish.' This was greeted with hoots of derision concerning the catchability of bonefish, their edible qualities, and what a fish was doing eating a lead-headed lure covered in plastic.

Placing my camera in the shade of a bush, I ran the line through the rod rings, glancing up occasionally at the swimmers and children splashing in the water some twenty yards to my right. What was that? A shadow of a fish moved from the swimmers, past the children, parallel to the beach, and . . . towards me. It seemed incredible . . . but . . . yes, it was indeed a bonefish. By this time the hands had started to go, looking like a bad case of the DTs. In fact had I not been teetotal I would have had doubts myself! I tried to tie a blood loop but the line wouldn't go through the hole. After three attempts I tied a uni-knot, wetted it, pulled and bit off the loose end. It was ragged but would have to do.

By now, as I crept down to the water's edge, I was definitely a case for the funny farm. The black guys thought

I had a screw loose, which of course I undoubtedly have, while the swimmers and children looked in amazement as a grown adult crept, apache-like, on his stomach, on a public beach! The fish was still there, moving slowly towards some rocks at the end of the beach. My first cast, as usual, zipped past the fish and exploded with a burst of spray in its path. The bone whirled round, as though trying to locate the source of the disturbance. Next cast was wide, but the third cast was a real peach. Forty-five degrees out and eight feet away from it, gently plipping into the water with minimum disturbance. Five twitches on the rod top and he nailed it, screaming away towards the children. I jumped up screaming for them to get out of the way, terrified that the fish might take a turn round one of their legs and part the 5-lb maxima line. It didn't cross my mind that 5-lb line under extreme tension and moving rapidly could act like cheese cutter wire and slice through several pairs of legs. However my screaming had the desired effect, and a mass of screaming, wailing children and adults ran from the water: 'He's got a shark!' 'LOOK OUT . . . It's a big BARRACUDA!' 'Is it a maneater?'

The black guys were behind me in the water, offering advice in high pitched voices. As the bone slowed some hundreds yards away I started laughing. It didn't matter whether he spat the hook, broke the line or I landed him. The present situation looked so ridiculous that I simply shook with laughter. If only Pete Perinchief had been there to see it. Eventually the pandemonium subsided, and after many shorter runs I decided to beach the fish in the shallows. Many and varied were the hands that wanted to grab that frail line and 'yank the crittur up the beach', but by introducing verbal abuse and threats of bodily harm to any individual who dared to suggest touching the line, I landed it. My bonefish mentor Pete Perinchief had always instilled into me the conservation aspect of bonefishing, but I still decided to retain this one for the taxidermist back in England. It tipped the scales at seven pounds, one and a half ounces, and now resides in a glass case with my fishing collection to retain some of the memories of that, somewhat eventful day.

One of my best catches was made about two years later, again fom Bermuda, again in the company of Pete Perinchief. We were drifting in some five feet of crystal clear water in the *Permit* up at Whale Bay, one of Pete's favourite marks. The clouds were drifting off the cliffs above in those tiresome patches that give you the 'now you see 'em now you don't' days. We'd seen a few bones, but nothing to shout home about. Suddenly there was a smudge of grey shuffling across the sandy bottom about thirty yards away. 'You take him' said Pete, 'lead him by a few feet and twitch it slowly, we're in deeper water here.' As I was behind Pete on the boat, and he was nearer the fish by some eighteen inches, it seemed the gentlemanly thing to allow him to cast for it. 'No, it's OK Pete, you're closest, you take him.'

'Now look Graeme, I can come out here any time and fish for 'em, now make your damn throw.' All this time the bonefish was getting closer and closer, somehow remaining unspooked by the figures on the boat. Eventually I cast out, covering the fish correctly and retrieving with little tweaks of the rod top. The smudge gained speed, followed by minno lure, and I felt the dull thump as he chomped on the hook. 'WHAM!' I hit him on a short line, and he took off for Cape Hatteras at a rate of knots. After maybe eighty yards he slowed, throbbing on the light rod. I increased pressure and gained line, turning the Cardinal handle as smoothly as possible. He ripped out some more, all in clear view of us, his form snaking over the beautiful sandy bottom. By watching the fish I could gauge when to pressure him when he rested and when to back off when he wound up for another run. After ten minutes he was circling the boat in that peculiar fashion, shaking his head at the curious pressure in his jaw.

'He'll go maybe six Graeme, nice fish, but he didn't run too hard did he?' I pumped some more, bringing him close to the boat.

'No, I reckon he's maybe five or so.' After another five minutes had passed he still wasn't too close to the boat. I cranked down and tried to lift him, then we saw his bulk as he rolled — sides flashing brilliant silver, fins spread, immense girth wallowing as he turned.

'Holy Christ' shouted Pete, 'that's a big bonefish . . . Take it steady Graeme. We don't want to lose this baby!'

I eased the drag, retaining finger pressure on the rim of the spool. 'How big Pete? Seven, eight?'

Pete shook his head. 'I really wouldn't like to say boy. That's the largest bone I've seen this year . . . You just take it easy . . . we've got all day if need be.' After another three minutes, and a couple of bungled netting attempts, it lay in the boat. A beautiful bar of silver bonefish, at nine pounds plus, my biggest on 5-lb test, but again I considered myself lucky. I was lucky to be in Bermuda in the first place. Lucky to have Pete Perinchief as an instructor. Lucky the bone didn't spook. Lucky it took my lure. Lucky it didn't run too hard . . . or too far. In fact that just about sums up what you need when out after bonefish. Even after days under the sun casting at shadows, you still need that vital element all anglers, both beginner and experienced alike treasure most . . . especially with bonefish . . . you need the luck.

7

The Speedsters

MAURITIUS AND BERMUDA

Everybody knows the worth of tuna. Commercial fishermen know their worth in terms of financial gain for their flesh, considered in Japan to be a delicacy. Anglers know their worth in terms of snapped lines, broken rods, seized reels, blistered fingers and aching backs. My own experience is limited to virtually every other species or sub species of tuna except the bluefin, but then I've never fished for one. Should I ever hook one, should I ever bring one to leader, I would have great difficulty in releasing it though. This shames me, for I realise they are an endangered species, but to catch one would, I think, cap all my other fishing exploits. I would only ever want one. A bluefin tuna of 200 or 1000 lb is enough fish for any fisherman's lifetime.

Until that happens there are plenty of other species of tuna that may not grow so big, yet put up a harder and possibly more satisfying fight on balanced tackle. Let me say right now that I rate the hardest fighting species of fish I have ever caught, anywhere in the world, in salt or freshwater, as the tiny little blackfin tuna. Seldom more than double figures, with a top weight around 40lb, I have never caught an 'easy' blackfin. Whether Neptune opens them up halfway through a fight and puts some new batteries in I'll never know, but I can assure you, you'll know they've been on the end of your rod. Fishing over the 'Hump' off Islamorada in the Florida Keys we dropped down 5lb blackfins for amberjack bait. We used ten pounders for drawing up big tigers and hammerheads; waste of a good fish unless you catch them on 6 and 12-lb test, instead of our 50-lb 'bait' rods!

My first big blackfin was a twenty pounder taken chumming over the challenger bank. I had freelined a single anchovy back into the chum lane, trying to get it to sink at the same rate as the loose feed. Already, after some fifteen

99

minutes of setting the anchor we had little tunny darting through the 'chovies chomping them up as fast as crewmate Andy Card could throw them in. I felt a tap as a tunny hit my pilchard, and ran with it, I spooled back, but the extra drag made him spit it out. He'd taken it deeper, where the others left it, and after a few seconds I felt the spool begin to whirr as a blackfin gobbled it up, and bombed down through the depths as I set the hook. That first run stripped yard after yard from the small International, and the fish bent the rod in a hoop. The seas were moderate, and my tackle good, yet I felt no shame in taking nearly fifteen minutes to bring that fish to leader. His head was always pointed down, that mechanical tail throb-throbbing and systematically driving the fish downwards. Only constant pressure from the rod eased him up by inches, until mate Andy could lead him up. Even then he led us a dance as the gaffhead was waved. I have been lucky and landed many blackfins now, but always I have that certain respect for a species that you wouldn't mind breaking away!

The next hardest are the yellowfins, a colourful tuna, with nearly as much guts as the black. A shoal fish up to about 60 or 80lb, the 100-lb plus beauties are mostly taken while blind trolling on lures. They come readily to chum fed from an anchored boat, especially in the vicinity of a bank or dropoff. The Atlantic island of Bermuda boasts some of the world's finest yellowfin tuna fishing and has probably held more records for this species on light tackle than anywhere else. I've had as many as twenty up to 30lb in a single day in rough weather, and have found choppy water brings them into a feeding mood easily. In complete contrast I have taken them on a glassy calm day, where even the merest zephyr of wind is welcomed by dry mouthed anglers. One such occasion a few years ago was on a trip with Jim Bashline, Associate Editor of *Field and Stream* magazine, and his wife Sylvia. Jim was out to try a yellowfin on a flyrod, Sylvia was on camera duty ready for the topwater action, and I was standing with a set of 20 and a pilchard-baited hook in case Jim saw a tuna that was too big for the flyrod! After half an hour of chumming, Andy Card spotted the bomb-shaped fuselages of yellowfins in the depths. They looked to be only five pounders through the clear water, but as they worked their way up the anchovies we could see they were 15 to 20lb a piece — an ideal size for the tippet strength Jim was using. However, despite being dished the most succulent 'chovies from the pack . . . they *would not* come up on top to where Jim could lay a fly onto them! It was infuriating to say the least. An hour went by and another batch came up. Maybe they were the same batch, but having eaten half our bucket of 'chovies they were BIGGER!

'Too big for the fly' said Jim. 'You better try one on the 30. See what size he is.' I moved to the stern and spooled the bait to twinkle down into the depths. Thirty feet below the surface and I could actually see a yellowfin home in and nail the bait. As he swam on by I set the hook. That was the last I got to turn the reel handle for around two minutes! I watched in amazement as the spool emptied, the rod tip bobbing rythmically with those distinctive tail beats. Even using a 30-lb class rod it took me at least fifteen minutes to get it back up to visible depths, and another five to bring him to the gaff. It was a nice fish from static boat, a forty-two pounder, that glistened and flashed as we admired the sun on its yellow finlets and silver blue flanks. Compact and tight fleshed, they not only fight hard but make terrific curry on the dinner table.

Later that day the same thing happened again. A pod of tuna worked their way up through the depths, chomping up the loose fed 'chovies. Again, there was no way that mate Andy could work them high enough in the water. Then he tried a few of the 'chovies from the surface of the bucket, that still retained sufficient ice to make them float. These did the trick, and the big tuna began rolling on the top. They were nice fish, ranging from forty up to around eighty pounds. Too big for the fly rod, and really a little too far out of range anyway. Jim allowed me the opportunity of trying for one on a 20-lb outfit, and I dropped down a bunch of 'chovies on the eagle claw hook to mingle with the loose feed. I lost sight of my own amongst the others, and dropped the reel in gear when I thought sufficient depth had been reached. A little tunny banged on the tip as it ripped off one of the baits, then a harder pull and the rod buckled over to the crash dive of a yellowfin. One thing with tuna is that they are so predictable you could almost set your watch by them. You know that first hard run will be blistering. You know that you couldn't stop it even if you wanted to, unless you wanted a popped line.

I waited, and waited, and waited. The spool emptied by about a quarter, and I had eased the drag back, allowing for the drag of line through the water to slow the fish down. Eventually it stopped and then began the back aching task of cranking it back up. I'd had a bad case of the Mexican two step the previous night, due to some spicy food disagreeing with my intestines. The need to boat this fish quickly became more than compelling, and I put pressure on the 17-lb line that I would not normally have done. To my utter surprise everything held together and didn't break. With renewed enthusiasm I took Andy's advice of short hard one-turn pumps, and kept the fish coming. In twenty minutes he was at the gaff, another three and he was in the fish box. A fish in excess of 50lb on 17-lb breaking strain line, and a satisfying achievement. I had been a little lucky in as far as the boat's tackle was immaculate and capable of taking maximum pressure for a considerable time. After landing the fish I needed no further encouragement to disappear down the cabin steps!

A species of tuna that I would rate as the third hardest fighting is the skipjack. From my own experience they may even be the fastest when initially hooked, but lack that little extra staying power of the black and yellowfin. They average around three to four pounds apiece, making them excellent trolling baits for marlin, or deep fished baits for big shark. I once took a twelve pounder on 30-lb gear off the Florida Keys that cleared line from the spool so fast I thought I was tied to a sailfish! That fish opened my eyes to the light tackle prospects of skipjacks, and enabled me to pick up a real monster from the Indian Ocean island of Mauritius. This area boasts the World All-Tackle record with a massive forty pounder, and twenty pounders don't even raise an eyebrow. However they are mostly taken on 50s which dulls the fight somewhat. One morning when trying for marlin bait I decided to run a set of 12. A spinning rod and reel in fact. I hooked a fish and spent twenty minutes easing him back to the stern, where it proved to be a skipjack weighing an even 19lb, a local Centre-de-Peche record on 12-lb class. The big rods landed skipjacks up to 33lb.

One last mention should be made of another tuna-like species. The Pacific and Oceanic bonitos don't grow to a large size, but hooking up five and six pound fish on 4-lb test line can give you a bonus days sport if the big fish aren't co-operating. They come well in the chum lanes as well, and take trolled lures or freelined baits. Light tackle tuna fishing was summed up in a few words by a Bermudan mate whose name evades me. I was tied to a yellowfin of over 30lb. I had been stuck on him for nearly half an hour, the 20-lb rod bent double. It was one of those lean ones that just wouldn't give up. As he neared the gaff the hook tore out. I cursed and stretched back, flexing cramped fingers. The verbally explosive situation was defused by the mate laughing. 'Yeah . . . they're spunky little critturs ain't they!'

★   ★   ★

Big yellowfins have never struck me as being the most spectacular lure takers. Nor for that matter are any species of the tuna family. What they lack in surface-to-air acrobatics they more than make up for with a reserve and determination to fight, second to none. In fact, size for size I don't think there is a single species that if tied by the tail to a tuna, wouldn't be dragged backwards all over the ocean! Also, the speed with which they hit an artificial is often faster than the eye can see. As a billfish tracks a bait or lure then attacks from behind, Mr Tuna takes aim from up to forty feet down, sets his tail into third gear and aims for a target. Occasionally they miss, and all you see is a pocket of boiling water, popping behind or to the side of the lure. Even when they do hit target, all you see is a boil of water where the lure was running. I would suggest that most anglers fail to see the take itself but get their first indication of a good tuna by an unhealthy curve in the rod and a rapidly emptying spool.

I was treated to a sample of this unbridled power, by a not overly large fish off the Indian Ocean island of Mauritius. I forget the name of the boat, but it was one operating from the Centre-de-Peche charter fleet. We were, as always, after Pacific blues, the month being February and a little early for the main yellowfin tuna run. However, as always when you start to run way offshore, you can never be really sure what is going to come up on the plastics. As it was, the billfishing had been slow on the usual Le Morne to Sugar Estate run, and I had asked the skipper to make a long run straight into the deep water. A gamble, but there was nothing to lose. I was running big konaheads, and the largest Murray Brothers lure I had. I needed as much action in the water as possible. By mid afternoon we had nothing. No signs. No strikes. Nothing. But then that's how many trips turn out, you only remember the good ones. We started the run back in and had not travelled more than a mile, when half asleep in the fighting chair, I watched three or four wheeling gulls, high, high up in the sky. Even as I thought of this sign as useful for the tuna fishing a month later when you spent the whole day scouring the ocean for signs of birds, so a screaming reel shattered my daydreaming.

Thinking marlin, the skipper slammed the boat into fast forward, sending clouds of black exhaust spuming into the air. I leapt to the rod which was secured by the traditional Mauritian lanyards to a fighting chair and began driving the hook home in hard thumping movements. At each strike line grunted from the tight drag, then built up into a searing, unstoppable run. Away off the stern we watched for the sign of a breaching billfish . . . none came. The fight began in earnest as I readied myself in the harness and settled into that familiar role. After ten minutes I was in control, had a little line back from that first run, yet the line was slanting downwards and across from the stern. Black marlin fight deep, could it be a black? Surely not out here, miles from sight of land, the black marlin are notorious for hugging the contours of any land mass. As I began the real tug of war in earnest and the stretch started to come out of the monofilament line, I felt that jag-jag-jag of the rod top that spelled tuna. On the huge sevenstrand konaheads it seemed amazing, but there was no doubt in my own mind as to what we had. The only other alternative was a very small marlin hooked in the tail, but the chances of that were so remote as to be barely worth thinking about. Gambling on my instincts being correct I pushed up the drag and tried to get the fish's head up towards me. Tuna always stand on their noses, tails to the surface and continually throb that tail fin to drive it deeper and deeper into the dark waters. You have little choice when they first hit. You can only give line or lose it. Broken line. Torn hook. Seized reel. If you keep their heads up each throb of that tail sends them a little higher in the water albeit in a circular motion, but at least you can get a turn on the reel. After another ten minutes the double line showed, I spooled it, stood up with both thumbs on the spool and levered that fish towards the mate's outstretched hand. The leader was grabbed, the gaff flashed home and a superb yellowfin tuna was heaved over the side to land on the deckboards, its bright yellow finlets shimmering in the sunlight. Back at the clubhouse it tipped the scales at 94lb, and non-anglers found difficulty in believing the amazing fight this tiny football-like fish had put up. But that's the yellowfin tuna. As the advert says. Probably the best fighter in the world!

★　★　★

This was a lucky capture. So lucky I am loathe to recount it for fear of disbelief, but as I have witnesses, authentication and photographs as I have for all my captures, I will explain how I came to catch one of the rarest species of tuna that swim. I had caught yellowfin tuna from Bermuda, skipjack tuna from America, longfin or albacore tuna from South Africa and Greece, plus all the different sub species of bonitos. The occasion was my first half day's fishing from one of my many trips to Mauritius.

Landing from an overnight Air Mauritius flight one March, I arrived and was greeted by Ram Aneerow and Jacques at the Centre-de-Peche Club on Black River. Did I want to rest and sleep? No, I had slept on the plane and wanted to fish. All the big marlin boats had gone, and all they could give me was the manager of the catamaran, Marc, as my skipper, a crewmate and a 15-foot dinghy. No scope for billfish, but it was fishing and that was good enough for me. My intention was to run Rapala Magnum lures for anything that came along, our operating area being parallel to the reef from Black River to Le Morne. I grabbed my rods, some lures, water and the cameras. Marc grabbed the outboard and a tank of fuel. The mate swam out to the mooring to collect the dinghy. An hour later we were trolling a line outside the breakers rolling on the coral reef that protected the island.

I had one small 3-lb fish aboard, and was rigging a dead bonito in case we saw a shark, the whitetips running close to shore here. Another hour of holding the rod and I felt my left forearm burning from the sun, and applied sun oil. An hour later and my arm was glowing red, as was my back a strip of which I had missed with the sun oil. Too late, I, who had travelled the world chasing all manner of fish, and had learned to respect the three influences of seamen, the wind, the sea and the sun, had got burnt. To this day I bear the scars of those few hours without sun oil. By afternoon the wind had risen and we were trying a drift for whitetip shark using the whole bonito with the hook stitched secretively inside. The wind rose considerably and Marc commented that we would have to leave soon; it could be a rough ride back.

I felt the sting of salt spray on my sunburn and nodded for him to start the engines. At sea, if you're sensible, there is always another day. As we recrossed the incoming troughs Marc stated that we couldn't make headway and would have to run a tiny gap in the barrier reef for sanctuary. It was also extremely dangerous as the shallow reef water would build up towering waves that could swamp and smash us. I tied everything down, covering my cases in plastic bags and stowing them in the bow. Suddenly the waves grew above us, and I confess to being truly scared, an emotion that builds thickness in the throat and constriction in the chest. This all happened so quickly that I realised seconds were of paramount importance. As Marc struggled to turn the bow of the open boat back out into the seas, the outboard coughed its last, and only the hissing surf surrounded us. By good fortune we had a spare motor and the mate quickly bolted it on the stern, as Marc fought to restart the first. I honestly thought my time had come, with the roaring reef coming closer each second. I made a mental count of all my rods and reels, and which friends would be most likely to move in on them first! They say your whole life flashes before you in a situation like this. Not me. All I saw flash past was my fishing tackle and marlin lures!

Suddenly an engine roared into life and we gained some steerage. A moment later, the second outboard smoked up and we clawed our way out to the deep water. It took ten minutes to reach deeper water and its even wave troughs as we made our way tenuously along the reef line, yet to my mind the wind was easing? In another ten it had dropped considerably, as it so often does in the tropics and Marc made the suggestion that as we were going home over good fishing ground, why waste the time? Why not put a bait out? I can tell you confidently that my knees were still knocking, but it did after all seem a logical suggestion. If you are going to go at least go down fighting. The dead bonito was retrieved from a box, re-rigged and trolled along the surface a few yards behind the boat for a possible whitetip. Thirty minutes after our near disaster I thought I had a hit. I was holding the rod as it was unsafe in such rough conditions to clip it even with lanyards, and a take was the last thing on my mind.

It was five minutes later when the fish hit again, screaming line out and burning my thumb in the process. To say it was the proverbial crash-take was an understatement and I had no idea what or how big this unseen fish was. For fifteen minutes I had a painfully horrendous struggle with it, losing line in seconds, regaining it agonisingly slowly. A big marlin boat on its way back in to the club stopped to offer the help of its fighting chair, but I wanted this fish on fair terms. I had started the fight by offering a bait, it was now my duty as a sportsman to finish it. We struggled on, no butt pad, no harness, no fighting chair, unable to back the open boat for fear of swamping the outboards. As I started to gain line, so I forgot the surrounding conditions and piled on the pressure. The fish came up as a dead weight, strange to me after the racing power of those first few runs.

'I can see it' shouted Marc. 'But it's no shark. I don't know what it is!' In five minutes a ball of tangled Stren line surfaced with the fish still twenty feet below. I wound the knots through the rings onto the reel and poured as much power into bending that blank as my lower abdomen could stand without damaging vital organs. Marc grabbed the leader, and as he pulled the fish to the surface the hook dropped out. Frantically I grabbed a gaff, the mate tore it from my grasp, leapt to the bow and gaffed it. I leaned over, clutched the wrist of its tail and manhandled it into the boat. At first I thought it was an amberjack with its colour, but those unmistakable finlets spelt tuna. It wasn't any old tuna either. It was a rare dogtooth tuna, and its weight? . . . 87lb!

★   ★   ★

There remains, and always will remain, a species of fish which is my favourite. It could be that it was this species that really impressed me initially with game fishing, or it may just be that I like fishing for them. I may even like the colours and symmetry of the fish . . . I don't know, but I do know I like them. Wahoo aren't exactly the hardest, most dogged of fighting fish in the ocean. But one thing's for sure, they're rated as the fastest thing on fins, and I can vouch for that fact. I've had the privilege of catching quite a few now, both on baits and lures, and they remain a fish that I'll never tire of. Long and slim, 'projectiles' is probably the word I'm looking for; they can swim through the water so fast you won't even see them.

My first experience with them was out on a rough day on the *Coral Sea* skippered by Boyd Gibbons and his brother Teddy. It was one of those days that captains refer to as 'a little choppy'. Take my word that it was BLOODY ROUGH! The wind was warm, and the rain had died away during the night, but the seas were still angry with a big swell running. By the time we had cleared the green reef water I was in a sorry state, and about to throw my kidneys over the side. Mate Teddy had run out four lines. Two flats run from stern-mounted downriggers, and a pair of baits run from the outriggers with egg sinkers on chin straps to keep the fish below the surface. Personally I couldn't have cared less whether Moby Dick himself swallowed me, the boat and half Bermuda. All I wanted to do was crawl in a corner and die, but I couldn't even do that in comfort because the damn boat wouldn't keep still.

Half an hour into the blue-water and I saw the port downrigger rod spring straight, then buckle over with reel screaming out its warning. I ran up, or rather staggered, and half-heartedly struck. A voice roared from up on the bridge . . . 'NAIL HIM GRAEME. JESUS! HIT HIM FOR CHRISSAKES!' That fish, not surprisingly came unbuttoned. Boyd swore, Teddy swore, I couldn't have cared less. A few minutes later I threw up, which made me feel slightly better. Both stern flat lines folded over simultaneously to a double strike and I screwed up both again. Man, those Bermudans were unhappy people! Half an hour later and after missing a fourth strike I became attached to something that physically ripped line from the 30-lb outfit. Up to that time I had never heard a reel shriek so loudly, and had certainly never heard line hiss through the water with such speed. The run slowed, was followed by a couple of shorter ones, then the fish was running parallel with *Coral Sea*, while doggedly shaking its head to try and dislodge the hook. As it surfaced near the boat I caught a glimpse of a purple-blue-barred flank, beak-like mouth and deep tail, almost vertical. 'Nice fish Graeme' shouted Teddy, gaffing aboard a big wahoo. 'He'll top 40lb!'

I looked at the beautiful long shape jerking in the fish hold, then went to the side and threw up again. Teddy grabbed the belt of my shorts to stop me falling overboard. 'C'mon boy we got more fish to catch' shouted Boyd from his perch on the bridge. Teddy re-rigged the baits, and ran back four new flying fish baits. In the next half hour I landed three more barred wahoo, a dolphin of 10lb and a bonus 30-lb yellowfin. Then I threw up again. My stomach ached from constantly heaving, and my back ached from the fights with the fish. My legs ached from the strain of trying to stay upright in the pitching boat, and my hips ached from being banged against the edge of the fighting chair. I was in a sorry state.

I landed another rip-roaring wahoo, and was by now beginning to get used to the searing first runs of this classic fish. I was also getting used to throwing up between fish, so did it again after this last one. As I hung over the side watching the white water churn past the hull, and spray slap me in the face, I wondered what the hell I was doing here. Fifteen miles offshore, in what must have been a near full gale, but the ocean was full of fish. Only two other boats were out, and neither had found the fish. By now I was soaked to the skin, but determined to hold together. I knew days like this were rare, fish were hitting well . . . if only the damn boat would stay still!

There was a break in sport and Teddy advised me to try and eat something. Feeling better I grabbed a Coke from the ice box and set about demolishing a ham and cheese sandwich. At that moment Boyd changed course to run across the wave troughs and the *Coral Sea* lurched more than ever. The Coke and sandwich tasted a lot sweeter going down than it did when it came back up. I wanted to die. The flat line buckled over and I staggered to the stern, teeth clenched, and struck about eight times

'OK Graeme you got him . . . you got him already!'

ZZZZzzeeee! The line ripped off the spool as another 30 to 40-lb wahoo pounded through the wave tops on its explosive run. I hung on and applied the pressure as the fish slowed down. Pump, wind, pump, wind . . . let him run again . . . then pump, wind, pump . . . He was at the back of the boat and Teddy grabbed the wire, Boyd beside him slipping in the gaff. I knew what was coming so set the rod in the holder and walked to the side. Boyd turned with the fish on the gaff. 'Hey . . . NICE FISH GRA . . . !' Graeme was over the side again, calling up 'HUGHIEEEEEeee!'

I finished that day with about seven wahoo, a yellowfin and a dolphin, and nearly ruptured my spleen in the process of throwing up. However, in more respects than one it was a day I'll never forget. NEVER. In retrospect I should probably have landed every one of those fish that took, but was not used to striking with short, hard jabs.

Another day, and I've had dozens of the wahoo now, but this one sticks out in my memory. It was off the outer banks of North Carolina. I was on a gameboat with Joel Arrington, and we were amongst the yellowfins of a finger of bluewater. I'd just landed a nice 45-lb sailfish, which we'd photographed and released. As far as I remember we were dragging four plugs, I was running a small jet, and Joel a wooden cedar plug. Suddenly three of the four rods folded, one sprang straight, then the other, leaving Joel to fight it out with his fish. By the searing first run it became apparent it was a wahoo, and as he pumped it nearer I saw some flashes of light beneath the surface of my own lure. The mate was winding in the other lines and I was slowly retrieving mine. Suddenly water was spouted behind my lure and several fish slashed at the mate's lure. Wahoo were everywhere, and we had three on at once! They were fought to gaff, boated and the lures run out again. We ended up with six or seven wahoo to 35lb from water that had seemed devoid of life.

The speed with which those fish hit was amazing, and brought back memories of one of my club members nursing a smashed rod butt from an extra fast hit from a 45-lb wahoo in Mexican waters. He'd obviously pushed up the drag too much thinking of a striped marlin, and this banded ocean racer had zipped in front of the billfish, nailed the lure and departed in some sort of a hurry, snapping the rod butt with its speed. Fortunately the rod was secured with a lanyard to the reel lug, otherwise it would have been an expensive trip! I've never had huge wahoo, but if you don't want things like snapped butts and burnt thumbs, you'd better make sure you back that drag on those first runs. A wahoo stops for neither man nor beast!

8

Odds 'n' Ends

MARATHON, MEXICO AND ENGLAND

I walked slowly along the quayside of the charter boat marina at Marathon's Key Colony, carefully scrutinising each vessel's price board. I was nearing the end of a trip along the Florida Keys, and had, apart from the bare essentials to get me back to Miami for my connecting flight, around a hundred and sixty bucks burning a hole in my pocket. Too much to waste on frivolities through the night, yet insufficient to charter a big boat for a whole day. My object, at this late morning hour of nine o'clock was to see which of the boats hadn't already left for a day's fishing, and find who was going to give me the most for my one and a half!

It was late May. Most of the boats were plying their trade amongst the bluewater weedlines in search of those elusive dolphin shoals. The wind was fresh, so I didn't envy the marlin anglers their bone-crunching journey miles out to sea in search of deep water. A voice wafted through the cabin of one of the boats. 'Hey man. How ya doin'? Look like you wanna go fishin'. I'll take ya offshore for two fifty.' The accent seemed to cut the air like a knife, so different from the usual Florida drawl. This was more clipped, and upstate — a long way up several States.

'Sure I'm interested in fishing, but you're from New York aren't you?'
A pair of feet lifted from the back of a chair and a burly figure covered in hair appeared in the bright sunlight. 'SAAAY. You must be from England. I'd recognise that cute accent anywheres!' He stepped up onto the gunnel and shoved out a massive hand. I grasped it and was treated to a handshake like a mechanical vice. I squeezed back as hard as I could. 'Yes, I'm from England. Just a stone's throw from Buckingham Palace in fact. You've heard of it?' He laughed

and released my hand, allowing the blood to surge through my crumpled veins again. 'Oh sure I heard of it. Turn right at New York ain't it?'

Already I could see I might be forced to have a day out with this character, and thus began the fencing to see what the final price would be. We discussed the weather, my trip so far, what I'd caught, the price of gas, and eventually, the price. He'd lowered to two hundred for three quarters of a day, and I could sense I might get a deal for a little less. He lit a cigarette and sat on his bait chest.

'Look Graeme, I just can't take you out in the big boat for less than two hundred. It burns too much gas. Tell you what I'll do though. I've got a Mako moored at the back of my house that I use for family fishing. For one seventy-five we'll go drag for some dolphin in that. It's brand new, bimini hood, rods, everything.'

I waited a second, so as not to offend Mike, as I had learned he was a New Yorker moved down with a view to finishing his days on a fishing boat. 'One fifty and we've got a deal Mike. I really just don't have any more spare cash.'

'One sixty and I'll guarantee you we'll hook up on something.'

I laughed and thrust out a hand . . . 'You're on Mike!'

It turned out that Mike had retired from his own electrical company, the proceeds of which had apparently gone into building a superb bungalow backing onto a waterway, with a smashing white Mako moored at the bottom of the lawn.

'Some kind of place you've got here Mike.'

'Yeah. It does me and the wife. I guess the kids'll soon move away though. Not too interested in fishing.' We slipped the moorings and burbled out through the waterways. Once over the reef water he opened the Mako's twin inboards and we planed out to the bluewater at over twenty knots. Suds whipped away from the bow on the wind, a rainbow of colours arcing to the surface. 'She sure moves Mike' I shouted. 'You bet she does boy.' With that he pushed up the morse and squeezed another couple of knots out. We both laughed as we planed and bounced out into the bluewater, spray hitting the plastic canopy like steel raindrops.

Half an hour later and the Mako was whispering quietly

along a weedline, dragging four ballyhoo in its wake. I already had taken two dolphin, both around 10lb but we hadn't hit the runs of 'chicken' dolphin of around 5lb. The sun danced on the wavetops, lancing through my camera lens as I tried to take a shot of another gameboat. The occupants waved a beer can at me, and held up eight fingers and a dolphin. At the same instant I saw one of their flat lines fold over, the dolphin and beercan were dropped as they fumbled to get the rod out of the holder.

Twenty yards off our stern a big dolphin cartwheeled in a blaze of yellow.

'Fish back of the right rigger!' shouted Mike. 'Watch him, he's a big one!'

I heard the distinctive snap as the line popped from the rigger clip, and grabbed the rod as the line came tight. Setting the hook was no problem as the fish roared directly away from us, so fast that I was forced to back off the drag. Then he came out. Leaping, twisting, frenziedly trying to throw the hook. More line left the reel, then he began to run up off our beam, forcing Mike to increase the engine speed. In a few seconds we were running fast, a quarter power just to keep pace with the fish. 'Just look at him move! Man he's really smokin'!'

'How big do you think Mike?' He shook his head, and drained the can of Budweiser before tossing it in the waste bin.

'Oh he's not too big. . . twenty pounder maybe. . . but he's a mean one. . . probably a bull.'

After ten minutes I had the fish at the back of the boat, its yellow colours fading to a mixture of greens and blues. To see these beautiful fish in the water is to experience colours that can never be put on canvas. They change before your eyes, and fade even faster when the fish is safely in the confines of the cockpit. This fish was no exception. It was indeed a bull dolphin as Mike suggested, and tipped the scales at 21$\frac{1}{2}$lb. A real scrapper in a rough sea, small boat, and on a 20-lb outfit. Two hours later and I managed to boat a couple of 15-lb wahoo. They'd taken the flatlines that Mike had rigged from the stern cleats, adding an egg sinker to each of the ballyhoo in an effort to get them to run deep in the wake. This paid dividends, but it became apparent from the radio conversations that the weedlines were breaking up, and the boats were losing touch with the shoals.

'We could try inshore,' said Mike. 'Along the edge of the greenwater. Maybe stick something in a sail or big ol' 'cuda maybe. It's up to you Graeme.' I saw no point in wasting time in a fishless area, so agreed. 'Sure Mike, let's give it a crack . . . you know I'll try for anything!'

As the line of Keys islands stood out pin sharp against the skyline to the west, so I had that feeling of well being that comes from a nice day's fishing with good company. You don't need a boat full of big fish. Just people you get on well with, good weather and conditions, the odd fish for excitement and someone who knows how you feel, and what you're thinking. This is the most important part of enjoying fishing. Knowing there's someone else who understands the feelings of the day. These thoughts and others filtered through my mind as I jammed myself against the rolling boat, watching the bubbles from the wake, looking as Mike ran down a pair of ballyhoo on big sinker weights. He cut the engines for slow trolling, and we traced the edge of the greenwater. To the left I could see the black of the coral heads while a hundred yards out to my right, the water darkened as the depth faded away to dark blue.

In half an hour I had three abortive takes, all of which Mike thought were small barracuda chopping the baits neatly behind the hook. I was in one of those troller's dozes when something creamed the starboard hoo. The rod was bent double with line leaving the spool at a steady rate. I beat Mike to the rod by a mere handgrip and jabbed the rod upwards to set the hook. Grudgingly the fish slowed and stayed deep, occasionally bouncing the rod tip.

'What the hell is this Mike . . . seems like a tuna?' The tip jabbed down fast and juddered some line from the reel.

'I dunno Graeme, fightin' too strange for a tuna, I don't even think it's a 'cuda.'

After ten minutes a pale orange glow came from the depths. 'Holy God it's a big mutton snapper. Don't lose him now, they taste *great*!' A beautifully marked grouper-like fish rolled on the surface and was gaffed aboard by Mike. 'Man, he's a nice one Graeme, go maybe 15lb I guess.'

Back on his lawn the scales registered 13lb 2oz, marking the end of a superb day. I had no doubts about what happened to the snapper, the wahoo and dolphin; the wahoo and dolphin were consigned to the commercial outlet, but seeing

Mike's eyes devour the snapper I knew exactly where that would end up.

★　★　★

'I told you you'd burn if you didn't put sun screen on your lips GJ.' The voice came from within the confines of the cabin of the Islamorada gameboat *Ace*. It belonged to crewmate Davy, who was watching with amusement as I struggled to control a diving amberjack and tend sore lips split from too much sun. I was out over the 'Hump' drifting above that fish-covered underwater mountain for big 'jacks, and had taken several to around 65lb. Most we had released, Davy puncturing the 'blown' air bladder by carefully inserting the knife behind the gill cover. With a slap of spray they dived down to regain their strength.

It was a rough day, clear blue sky and a few scuddy clouds on a fresh wind. But I'd managed to keep my pancakes down. I had the boat to myself, and was tiring of the back-breaking task of bringing in yet another amberjack. Deep jigging for 'jacks has that kind of effect on you. Every time Jim manoeuvred the boat so the *Ace* drifted across the back of the rock, and I knew, I just *knew* a huge 'jack was going to nail the feather-and-bait jig combo. I'd started with a set of 80, in the hope of one of the seemingly ever present tiger sharks biting, but as the day wore on, and nothing came in with just a head, or even half chewed, I had dropped to my 50. It was a newly acquired International reel, and I'd landed several dozen amberjack and a bonus sailfish on it during the past week's fishing.

'It's OK for you mates' I shouted, 'taking it easy in the confines of the cabin while we sweat it out doing the work!' I heard him come up the cabin steps. 'That's what you came for though isn't it GJ? that an' heavin' your kidneys over the side?' I pushed up the lever drag and hauled back on the Fenwick till the corks creaked. The leader came to the surface. 'LEADER UP!' I screamed, trying to inject some comedy into the situation. 'QUICK . . . GAFF IT . . . IT'S A MASSIVE BILLFISH!' Davy walked to the stern, leaned over, and placing his gloved hand carefully through the gill, hauled a 60-lb 'jack up onto the gunnel. 'Another nice one GJ.' He unhooked the fish and carefully piercing at the back of the pectoral fin, slid it back over the side. A

deluge of spray came over the stern soaking him. 'Damn!'
'Serves you right Davy, teach you to mess with the big
dudes!' He towelled himself off, and inspected the jig. I lay
back in the fighting chair, feet up on the footplate, letting
the sun beat down on my face. What a life!

'Wanna grab a beer GJ?' boomed Jim's voice from high
up on the flying bridge.

'No, I'm OK Jim thanks.'

'Well throw me one up while you're there will you!' I
dragged myself out of the chair, and trudged over to the ice
chest. Boy it was a hot one today. Even Jim rubbed some
sun oil on his brawny arms. I shouted up to Jim. 'Here
catch!' I hurled a can of Coke skywards and he caught it.
'Jesus. I ain't drinkin' that. Gimme a Bud.' I threw up the
Bud I had in reserve in my other hand.

'Hey GJ' shouted Davy, 'let's get with it man! Let's get
back on the 'jacks!' He flipped the ballyhoo baited jig over
the stern and I thumbed the reel as I spooled it back down.
Jim had given up trying to tell me when to lock up the spool
for jigging. I'd caught so many big 'jacks now I'd gauge how
much line was off the spool and start anyway. This time it
went deeper. I locked up and swept the rod skywards.
Nothing! Again. Nothing! Third time I swept the rod up
and still nothing.

'Hey Jim you missed the Hump that time. Wanna go
round again?'

'We ain't missed the Hump man, it's markin' here on the
sounder. Send it down some more.'

I ran off another thirty yards, locked up and jigged.
Nothing again. I ran off some more, this time way past any
depth I'd previously jigged at. The lure hit bottom and I
locked up.

'Crank her up GJ, we'll go round again.' As I wound the
handle for around the tenth time something grabbed it.
Even with a lot of line out, it was a distinctive hit. By the
time I'd cranked and struck a few times the Fenwick was
hooped in a semi circle. Davy looked up at Jim. 'It's not the
rock Jimbo. I see he was a way off the bottom when he went
solid.'

'Could be a blacktip Davy, I seen 'em nail fish baits at that
depth, but I never heard o' one eatin' a jig!' Line ran off the
spool at an increasing speed. 'Feels a nice fish Davy, you
reckon it might be a 100-lb 'jack or something?' Davy shook

his head. 'To be honest GJ I haven't any idea what that thing is!' For fifteen minutes I hauled on the rod, making little impression on the adversary below. I had a lot of pressure on the drag, so with the tremendous amount of line out I decided to take it easy, and avoid popping the line with the water pressure. Another five minutes and I had it halfway up, but still it ran off short hard bursts that had me halfway over the stern. 'Jesus this is a tough one Davy, it's making my arms ache!'

I noticed that Jim was starting to manoeuvre the boat, a sure sign that he thought this was something bigger, and I reverted to the short, one-handle-turn pumps that has given me so many good fish. Grudgingly he came, then for the last few yards he came easily. 'I see him Jimbo, it's a bomber of a jewfish. . . can't see any sign of the jig. . . he must have swallowed it whole!' Davy leaned over, grabbed the leader and hauled the fish within gaffing range. Jim shinned down the ladder, cut the *Ace* engines and hung over the side with the gaff. I saw his arm jerk and both men struggled to haul the fish over the side. What first confronted me as it hung on the gunnel was a mouth and head like a dragline bucket. It was massive! Tiny pig-like eyes and flaring gills glared as it finally crashed onto the deck. 'That's a big ol' jewfish GJ' said Jim. 'I only ever caught two before, but I reckon yours is gonna top 100lb.'

Back on Whale Harbour dock it provoked much interest amongst tourist and other charter skippers alike. As the beam scale steadied, it registered 112lb. It was probably the ugliest fish I have ever caught, but as it had given me a dogged scrap, and more important was into three figures, I was a happy man as I made my way up to the bar. As I passed a group of upstaters one of them pulled me aside. 'Hey man, congratulations . . . you just caught my old lady!'

'How do you know it's her?' I queried. He pulled a face as he stared at the jewfish.

'Oh yeah that's her OK . . . JUST LOOK AT THE SIZE OF THAT MOUTH!'

The gallery of onlookers collapsed with laughter, and I nearly broke an ankle falling over some skipjacks.

*   *   *

I stood in the bar of the Hotel Hacienda at Mexico's Cabo

San Lucas, luxuriating as a cold beer slid down my throat. I had just returned from a day out with members of the Sportfishing Club of the British Isles, dragging baits and lures for striped marlin. The moon phase was wrong and we were lucky to have even seen a few fins on the surface. They proved to be unresponsive, the only highlight of the day being an extremely close encounter with a marlin that lay sunning itself in the still waters about three miles off Cabo Falso. We went through the obligatory circling procedure, gradually dragging the Californian flying fish and konahead lures closer and closer to the static fish. Eventually, while running off some movie film from the flying bridge, I saw the reason for its disinterest. Hanging loosely from the jaw of the billfish was a red and white konahead! Someone had obviously lost what they would believe to be the fish of a lifetime. The skipper then dragged the lures straight across its back, causing it to sink slowly out of sight. That was all the activity we saw for that day so I was commiserating with my colleagues, prior to going out in a small guided skiff for an evening's trolling before dinner. This had become a regular procedure on our trip, nothing exciting ever happened, with only the odd bonito or sierra mackerel hammering the Millie's bucktail lures.

An hour later, myself, Don Warren and another angler were holding 20-lb spinning outfits, and chatting about — yes, fishing. The sun had set and we were making our way back past the Cape rock where several seals lay, eyeing us with the scrutiny of an out of work hooker. Just as we passed the Cape all three rods folded round, with squealing drags and yelling anglers. A sierra of some 5lb and a 3-lb bonito were swung aboard, while my own reel continued to see line departing at a steady rate of knots.

'What the hell have you hooked Pullen?' asked Don, 'come on and stop messing around with it . . . we want to get in for dinner!' The run slowed and I buckled the rod round to maximum pressure. 'This is a good fish lads . . . I've no idea what . . . but it sure is big!' Laughs of derision and doubts were cast as to my angling ability. I was, as usual, doing something different and had run a Rapala Magnum out in an effort to pick up a bigger yellowtail.

'Hey Pullen . . . the guide reckons you've hooked a big grouper . . . we reckon it's Cabo Falso . . . reckon we ought to cut your line before our dinner gets cold.' I shot them a glance that would have frozen the Sahara.

'Nobody cuts MY line except me!' I roared. 'This could be a record snapper, maybe a massive cubera!'

'Rubbish! you've hooked bottom and don't like to admit it!' Suddenly the line planed away, dragging more line from the reel.

'SEE! SEE! I told you it was a fish . . . it might even be an amberjack!' For several minutes I fought vainly to prevent more line going out but it was impossible, the pressure was too great.

'I've guessed what you've hooked Graeme' announced Don. 'I figured it out.'

'What?'

'You'll see in a minute, it's just about to surface.'

The line started to plane upwards, and I fully expected a Mexican striped marlin to climb into the half light, framed in a perfect silhouette, with the Cape as a backdrop. Instead, a gargantuan seal bobbed up to the surface just off from seal rock. Across its jaws was a 5-lb sierra, with my Rapala Magnum hanging loosely in the fish's mouth. Uproar broke out in the boat as the seal blinked at us, we blinked back and the guide nearly fell off the outboard cowling with laughter. Even as we watched, the seal crunched its jaws, twisted its head, and sank beneath the surface with half my sierra. I cranked in the head and shoulders, trying to swing the bloody mess into the guide's lap. Over dinner that night I had the utmost difficulty convincing the rest of our party that I nearly set a world record for seal on 20-lb test. You know they just wouldn't believe me. Said I bit the sierra in half myself because I had no packed lunch that day!

★　★　★

Although good old England can't boast much in the way of hard fighting gamefish, she does have a couple of popular IGFA rated fish on her books. Quite how they got there I don't know, but there they are, and will presumably stay. Pollack and cod are prime targets for bottom fishing and drifting, but down in the West Country you have the clear water opportunity of using lures. With the proliferation of sandeels down there, it's not entirely surprising to find the 'Redgill' artificial rubber sandeel as one of the most popular lures in the sea angler's armoury. I've used them abroad, and find them equally successful for bonito and barracuda. This is an account of probably my best catch using this wonderful lure.

It was mid July and more years ago than I care to remember. So long ago that I had hair down to my shoulders, and wore a pair of kaleidoscope coloured jeans! Everybody knew 'the fishing nut in the pyjamas', and I, quite rightly, received a lot of stick for wearing them. However, I was over that period on one of my hot streaks for using the Redgill. The man who showed me how to use this lure to devastating effect was probably one of Britain's finest pollack anglers, Alan Dingle. I was out with him on his famed boat the *Lady Betty*, along with two other anglers. I had been out with Alan for the past week, and had developed something of a rapport with him. He'd let me know when the *Lady* was drifting over the top of the pinnacle rock, what depth the fish were marking on the sounder, and when we dropped down over the back of the rock.

This particular day was a real cracker, one of those perfect July days that we never seem to get nowadays: blue sky, variable breeze, and pollack on every drift. I had the retrieve down to a fine art, coming up only twenty turns or so before spooling back down to the rock. This gave me maximum time in the 'kill' zone, and I was getting near to two fish per drift. For some reason Alan decided to try the eastern end of the rock with a small gully in between. I had no idea what went on beneath the surface of course, but respected Alan's experience enough to go along with it. He was by far and away the most successful bottom and reef fisherman in Looe. I took a 9-lb pollack, unhooked it, dropped it into the fish box and sent the tail-wiggling lure back down.

By now Al left me to look after myself while he gaffed and unhooked the other anglers' fish. I remember the lead hitting bottom, I flipped over the Mitchell's gear lever and cranked slowly surfacewards. At around fifteen the line got heavy as a fish took in the lure. I didn't strike but kept up a steady retrieve. Four more turns and the handle stopped, the rod hooping over as the fish surged away. The clutch was set for a crash dive, but this one seemed different. Not so fast in the build up as that of a pollack. Slower, more powerful . . . it knew where it was going. Alan looked round, and opened his mouth to speak, the ever present cigarette hanging from his mouth, cap askew on his head. He looked forever like the seasoned fisherman, as indeed he was. 'No pollack is he boy? Maybe a nice ling.' I looked at the curve in the rod, the tip running down to the surface. 'I dunno Al, it isn't a pollack that's for sure.'

Even as I finished speaking I saw Alan's own rod fold over. He was an ardent fisherman himself, and used a rod whenever he got the chance. I saw him grin at me, the smile cracking his weathered face. 'This is how you do it boy!' I hauled back, gaining a few yards of line. Al's fish was still off and running. After five minutes I had mine coming towards the boat, the pressure of depth beginning to take its toll. Alan's rod being lighter than mine was hooped over, and he gained line in two-turn pumps. The fish felt heavy, far too heavy for a ling which would probably have cut the 18-lb nylon trace with its teeth.

'I reckon 't is a cod young Graeme' shouted Al, the other two anglers oblivious to the fact that we had by now drifted off the rock and were over deep water. 'I've had the odd one from this gully some years ago, but they was big fish mind . . . around 20lb!'

Slowly a shape formed down in the depths, starting off as a white dot, then changing into a speckled cod of still unseen size. It flopped up on its side and I gasped at the size of its girth. 'This is some fish! It's well over twenty!' Alan stuffed his rod into one of the other angler's hands. 'Here boy 'old onto this for a minute.' In a flash he was next to me with the gaff, tentatively drawing the fish towards him on the long 18-foot trace. The gaff went into the shoulder with a sharp jerk and the fish was hauled over the gunnel.

'Tell you what boy' said Alan, spitting his cigarette over the side and pushing his cap back on his head, 'he'll be the best part of 25, maybe 28lb! A helluva nice fish.' He strode back, doffed his cap at the angler holding his cod and proceeded to boat another huge cod slightly larger than 20lb. ''Tis a pretty a brace o' fish as I've seen in a while lad, we did well there. Let's get back up and see if we can get another.'

The *Lady Betty* bobbed and yawed as he went back upwind to locate the gully, Alan's eyes never leaving his compass and sounder. After a couple of minutes he turned the boat and cut the engines, nodding to me at the same time. I dropped down. The first two retrieves came to nothing, then on the third I felt that strange sucking on the lure as fathoms below a fish opened its maw and engulfed it. The line tightened then zeeee'd off the reel throwing spray over my sunglasses. Ten minutes of grunt and groan pumping saw the fish belly up on the surface, another massive cod, well over 20lb. We went in again, and again I hooked up. Another massive cod, this time pushing 30lb. The lads on the other side of the boat watched open mouthed as the fish flopped down in the fish hold, a broad tail sticking out over the edge. We lost the gully and I had to content myself with more pollack, one of which made 12lb. Then towards the end of the afternoon Alan seemed to take longer circling the area with his sounder running. He cut the engine and nodded. 'Got 'er this time boy, watch the bottom, we're right on the edge, you may lose your gear.' Fifteen minutes later and a fourth cod surfaced, my arms aching from the constant wind and pump up through the depths. The radio crackled into life as Alan reported the catch to the *Paula*.

' 'ad a few nice fish Dick, nothing too special, few pollack. Mind you we 'ad a coupla cod.'

'Oh ar, any size Al?' Most of the Looe skippers knew that Alan always played down the size of his fish, but that was Britain's big fish man, taking the largest shark ever from our British waters . . . a 500-lb mako.

'Not bad Dick, you know the size, a bit too big for the frying pan! See you when we get in . . . Cheers and gone.'

A BIT TOO BIG FOR THE FRYING PAN? We'd taken five cod in excess of 20lb, without our haul of pollack, and all from a rock mark, not a wreck. My own personal tally was eleven pollack up to 12lb, and cod of 20lb, 22lb, $29^1/_2$lb and $30^1/_4$lb.

9

The Big Flats

THE CANARY ISLANDS AND
THE BAHAMAS

My first ever trip after big game was one October in the late seventies. Having read a report on the superb big-eye tuna fishing available from the Canary Islands, I decided an exploratory trip was in order. Some of these tuna were really huge, weighing up to 300lb or more, with a smattering of massive bluefins thrown in for added excitement. I researched the islands and found out as much information as letter writing would allow. There were runs through the southern half of the islands from March to April and again in October. The islands themselves are located just off the north-east corner of Africa, set far enough south to make for pleasant weather conditions. The best place for fishing was on the main central island in the group called Gran Canaria. The place where all the action took place was the small fishing port-cum-resort of Puerto Rico on the southerly tip of the island. A small charter fleet operated there, fairly efficiently, and brought in some superb fish. The resort itself is set in a small valley that has one of the most settled climates in the world. Any clouds that do appear in the dawn to mid morning hours quickly burn off with the hot sun.

On my first trip out there, I went in October. I'd been told the March/April run had been poor and found the October one little better. No big-eye tuna were caught, although we did see a few thresher sharks landed. The only sport I had was with small skipjack and dolphin that swam into our chum slick looking for pieces of mackerel. Using a light 6-lb test spinning outfit I had great fun, and learned enough respect for these smaller game species, to want some more with their bigger brothers. Assorted bottom-feeding species of a variety of colours finalised the trip, and I wasn't too disappointed. After all, you can't catch tuna that aren't there.

I travelled to other parts of the world and had much better luck, but found myself on a short four-day trip to Puerto Rico around May. This wasn't a particularly good time of year, but as I was there to report on holiday and hotel accommodation, fishing was to be something of a bonus. At this time there was a restriction of how far the Harbour Master would allow the boats to go out, due to some local problems with a Fisherman's Union. This meant we had to stay within two miles of the port — which wasn't helpful considering most of the billfish and tuna fishing is done about three to five miles out in deep waters. This reduced us to trolling for wahoo or bluefish, which we did with negative results. We also tried a drift for one day but with the pitiful chum trail we had going, I wasn't surprised we caught nothing.

Our last day left us with no choice. A session of good old bottom fishing was in order. Thirty and fifty pound outfits were rigged up with 200-lb heavy mono leaders, culminating in a small tuna hook. To this was attached a side of mackerel, and five ounces of lead consigned it to the bottom. I rigged a second rod and dropped down a set of English baited feathers. Within seconds I was into a pot-pourri of ground fish that would have graced the most meticulously kept aquarium. A veritable kaleidoscope of colours flipped around on the deckboards, including a leopard-marked moray eel. Two of our party hooked nice fish which put up a fair struggle, and which on surfacing proved to be stingrays in the 25 to 30-lb bracket. Hope at last. Then my own ratchet sounded and I struck into a big fish. At first I thought it to be the bottom, as for five whole minutes the rod stayed bent. If I hadn't seen the bite myself I would have taken it to be 'Gran Canaria' and pulled for a break! Eventually something huge wandered off and the nylon trace parted. On taking a closer inspection, it was seen to be a chafing cut, with the line ground through, as opposed to the clean cut of a shark. Thus ended that short Canarian trip, but enough had happened to show that this inside ground was worth another look.

I was there again the following July, with a party of anglers from my club, The Sportfishing Club of the British

Isles. We were hoping (tongue in cheek) for blue marlin, as one of our members, John Holmes, had been enjoying considerable success for a number of years from his own boat *White Striker*. I remember there were eleven of us, and while we had a great time socially, the billfishing proved rather less than productive. Two days from the end of the trip I told the others I was going to charter a boat to myself as a special treat. Actually I had one of those lucky feelings coming on, and just knew if I could get out on my own, and do my own thing, something would turn up. I chartered the *Felusi* from the agent, Mrs. Gay Oulton, for a day, loaded on my own rods and made sure the captain and crew knew what I wanted to do before the boat left harbour. Communications were always something of a problem for non-Canarians, and like most charter boats, the captain soon got into a regular rut. There were more charters than charter boats which meant they didn't have to work too hard for their 'Moocho peseta!'

For two hours we trolled the offshore bank. I ran a pair of big 'softheads' on 130s from stinger lines in the outriggers, and a large konahead and my favourite dolphin-coloured konaclone from the flatlines on a 50 and 80. From the corner cleat I ran my old teaser. I relaxed in the morning sun, feet up on the gunnel, eyes shaded towards the boiling water on the stern. The *Felusi* was a big catamaran hull, and sent forth twin spumes of white water to attract the attention of any passing billfish. The first hour produced nothing, and as I sat watching the port set of 130, I saw the tip kick down. It sprang straight and I leapt up, fully expecting it to pull over. For a few seconds nothing further happened, then it tugged over again and a couple of yards of line buzzed off the drag before it kicked straight. That was it. No more action, and I can only assume it was either a small white or even a small blue marlin hitting the outsize lures.

We trolled the area on a figure of eight course for a further half hour, but nothing came. I talked to the other boats in our party to let them know of the action. They too, had seen nothing, so I decided on a change. We ran in to one of the buoys of the cement factory works, some three miles off and tied up. The mate chopped up some Spanish mackerel into a fine chum, put the contents into a steel mesh box, weighted it with a piece of lead and dropped it to the bottom. Then he jigged it up and down to release the contents. I've always been a great believer in the powers of smell, and began to feel happier with the day's prospects. I ran down two baits to the bottom, one on my own 50-lb outfit, the other, a whole skipjack on the 130. Heavy mono marlin leaders were used for traces, and this time a pair of tuna hooks whipped in tandem, were placed in my fillet of tuna. The big cat barely rocked at all on the anchor rope, obviously one of the most stable craft one could wish to fish from.

The first hour passed uneventfully, with the exception of some short runs on the whole skipjack. We wound up, a procedure which took fifteen minutes in itself, checked the bait and dropped back down again.

Two hours passed and the afternoon looked to be a blank. A bite on my 50? Or was it just the lead bouncing on the bottom? No, there it was again. I struck and spent five minutes prising it off the bottom. Once clear of the bottom, I found I could gain line quickly, and the mate put the gaff to one side. Obviously a small fish. Down in the depths we could just make out the white dot of a fish's underside. It proved to be a stingray about 20lb in weight. At least the day wasn't a failure, and I dropped a fresh tuna fillet down for the last hour's fishing.

Within minutes of it hitting the bottom the tip kicked. Just as I was settling in for a snooze too. That's what I like about bottom fishing. No rush about anything, half the time you don't know what's going on below anyway! I picked the rod out of the holder and wound down. Tug-tug-tug. Something down there was definitely eating its way up my tuna fillet. I pulled off some slack line, only a couple of yards, watching as it tightened to the rod tip. If it was another stingray I would be in no hurry to strike. They often take a minute or two to get the hooks well inside the mouth. The reel started to revolve, the ratchet ticking over slowly. It gained speed, stopped for several seconds, then moved off again. I pushed the lever drag over onto the 'strike' position, placed the butt in a butt pad and waited for the line to pull tight. As it did so I wound like a demon, striking at the same time. After about the tenth strike I came down solid on the fish and the rod heeled over. I quickly backed the lever off a little and line purred from the clutch smoothly. This was one helluva stingray, if indeed it was a stingray at all. It wasn't fast enough for a shark, more a slow, lumbering over the rocky bottom. Fortunately it chose to move away from the stern of the boat, and thus the danger of the anchor rope. There was no way I could slow it, and line disappeared from the spool at a steady rate. I looked to see from where a curious grating noise was coming, vibrating through my wrist. To my utter dismay the 50lb line had run across the watch strap of my left hand, the sharp edge shaving the line down to half the thickness! I gently eased it off, but before it went through the rings I could feel how rough it had been shaved, and I backed off the pressure even more. With the water pressure on that amount of line out, it could part any time.

For half an hour I tried to get that five yards of damaged line back safely onto the spool, but somehow that great fish knew it had the advantage. Each time I got within a few feet the fish stopped dead. I applied as much pressure as I estimated the line would allow, then held, for as long as I dare. The captain suddenly had an idea. He would slacken the anchor rope to allow me to get a direct pull above the fish, and yet get those extra few feet of line on the spool. He threw several yards of rope overboard and the boat drifted downtide. I cranked furiously to get that damaged line on the spool. It snickered through the roller rings, until I had several more turns of good line over the top of it. Now we'd get down to some business! I buckled that Fenwick rod over to a curve I have never seen in it since. The corks creaked under the foregrip, and I pushed the lever drag up past the 'strike' position onto full drag. This big ol' fish was going nowhere, and I held that position for as long as I could. All I felt was the flap-flapping of wings on the line many fathoms below, and after ten minutes I thought I would need to call for the shoulder harness. Suddenly I felt the tip straighten, and I dropped down for two hard pumps. He moved — he actually moved! I dropped again, not letting one single inch of line leave the International. Drop – pump – wind. Drop – pump – wind. Drop – pump – wind. I soon got into that old rhythym that has been the downfall of so many big fish. Keep him moving I thought, and he should be yours. A couple of times on the way to the surface I simply had to back off the drag and let him take line. I don't think he would have broken the line, but he may have dragged me overboard! Then the mate shouted that he could see his shape in the blue water below. Another five minutes and it was up on surface off the stern, a huge flatfish, wings flapping in the water. I stared in disbelief — it was massive.

'My God' I shouted, 'it's like a bloody great barn door!'

The mate and skipper turned round at hearing what they obviously thought were English expletives, then laughing to themselves, set about gaffing the fish aboard. It took both of them to drag it up on the stern, where it was lashed down for the homeward journey. We dragged konaheads for any unsuspecting billfish on the way in, but I couldn't have cared less.

The few clouds that hung inland over the mountains of Gran Canaria looked picturesque — as though some artist had reached up in the sky and dabbed a water colour brush on a blue background. The tiny white dots that were apartments in Puerto Rico's valley grew closer. Inside an hour we had the fish hauled up on the scales at the dockside. Many holidaymakers gathered to see the ungainly fish, and posed beside it for their respective family albums. I was pleased to pose by it too when I saw what the scales read — a superb butterfly ray. Its weight? Ninety-four pounds! As our club members walked over from the harbour bar, the usual jokes flew around.

'Took a konahead did it?'

'I suppose you think that's a flat marlin?'

'Always were good at catching flounders Graeme!'

I took all this in the spirit in which it was intended i.e. *serious!*

'You had a few billfish then?' I queried. Straight faces all round.

'Not a dicky bird man.'

To cap the day the captain sauntered up, content that the *Felusi* had weighed in the biggest fish again.

'Forget the marleen' he said to them. 'Come weeth me and I catch you the bloddy barn doors!' He spread his arm out to the butterfly ray. At this everyone fell into hysterics. I wonder if the IGFA will ever have line class ratings for barn doors?!

★ ★ ★

When trying to assess the degree of personal achievement in capturing any fish you have to take into consideration not merely the size of the species, or the fight it may put up, but the conditions existing at the time, and the tackle used. In this way, catching a huge ray from a boat on 50-lb class tackle can be equated to the capture of a smaller sized ray on light tackle from the shoreline. Although I had taken small stingrays to double figures both from the Florida Keys bonefish flats, and from the Banjul river area of west Africa, a memorable fish came my way, largely by good fortune from the Bahama island of Great Exuma.

I had been on assignment through southern Florida and the Keys, leaving myself a week to cover Exuma's excellent bonefishing possibilities. The flight on the small Aero Coach aircraft was pleasant indeed, the clear weather affording me the opportunity of viewing the vast expanse of extremely shallow waters for which the Bahamas are famous. I was staying at the Peace 'n' Plenty hotel in George Town, working with one of the top guides from Out Island Inn, and had some wonderful half day trips from both the skiff and the shore. Not wanting to waste any time I fished and walked the shoreline of George Town at every opportunity. Although I saw several small barracuda in front of the hotel, it was around the wooden jetty and the attendant moorings that I found most activity. I enjoyed sport with the grunts and pinfish that found sanctuary in the jetty shade, and using them for bait managed some small barracuda and good sized houndfish, a species not unlike our native gar.

One day I spotted a big stingray cruising the bottom, working out from deep in a channel, around the small bay, until it flapped its way under the jetty and out the other side. Normally these fish can be quite difficult to cast a bait to; a couple of live shrimps are best. Not being circular in shape the stingrays can change direction quite quickly. They can also spook if you drop a bait on their head, thus making any casting placements difficult. For possibly once in my life I refrained from making an immediate cast, my only bait a fillet of small fish caught from under the jetty. Normally I fire a bait/lure at anything and everything, working on the principle that you may only get one shot anyway. Something made me sit and watch this stingray as it appeared confident in its movements and direction: I would lose sight of it, then some minutes later there it was again, flopping along, occasionally stopping to root out some morsel of food and sending plumes of coral sand up over its head. When it disappeared from view the next time, I dropped my fish fillet in exactly the spot he last rooted around in, and sat back to await events. Sure enough, he came round again, pausing as he flopped around trying to locate the source of the smell in the tide. He neared the area then suddenly stopped, puffing up huge clouds of sand that hung suspended for a few seconds over his flapping wings. As the fish moved on and the sand settled I noticed there was no bait in the position I had left it and the line was moving through the water following the path of the stingray. Although I had felt nothing there was no doubt he had taken it.

As his previous patrol routes travelled through the jetty I had no option but to wind down and strike. As I thumped the hook home the light 12-lb class graphite spinning rod hooped over, and a slowly increasing drag squealed as the 'stinger' went up through the gears. It was a few seconds before he realised something was amiss. A predicament which fortunately made him whirl around and race for the open water, away from the barnacle encrusted pilings that would spell doom for me if the taut line touched it. I had merely a 12-lb line and a spinning reel, an outfit which was to all intents and purposes my bait-catching outfit. By piling on the pressure at an early stage I managed to turn the fish at every obstacle: yacht, mooring rope, staging. All were avoided, but the realisation that I had a reasonable stinger on only dawned on me when I had him close. It was considerably larger than the 15lb or so I had first estimated. Locals gathered to watch the problems involved in getting one angry stingray hooked on just a spinning rod, up to the shallows where I could beach it. I was in the 'what-do-I-do-now-I've-got-this?' situation.

It was easily my biggest shore stingray and it was in just a foot of water. I knew it would flail its poisonous barb around to search out its aggressor, so I was in no mood to enter the water knee deep and hold the fish aloft victoriously! An Englishman in the midday sun I almost certainly was. But mad I wasn't. By careful use of the rod I jumped down on the beach, and using all the spring in the Graphite construction, laid the rod over and slowly inched the ray into shore. If only I could keep his head facing the shore, every flap of wing would bring him closer. After a couple of minutes he grounded in six inches of water, and stuck on the coral sand. I had him. Or did he have me? The locals screamed instructions regarding the disposal and parentage of this 'Devil' fish, but I noticed they were safely ensconced on the jetty, and not on the beach with the fish. We are all brave *outside* the dentist's window! Seizing a piece of four by two timber I set about persuading Mr. Stingray to calm down, much to the delight of the crowd. Once despatched, I was still a little wary of a sudden lunge driving that poisonous barb into my calf, so I hauled the fish up onto the hot sand using a nail in the timber.

Not a lengthy or spectacular battle perhaps, but all the pitfalls that could so easily have meant the fish winning, had been avoided. It was nice for everything to go right for a change, an unusual catch like this one invariably comes when you least expect it. The scales told their own story with a weight of 34lb — and the stingray? Well it tasted beautiful that night aboard a yacht with some American friends, marinated with lemon and toasted with white wine.

10

Striped Marlin

MEXICO

In February 1979 I found myself on a plane bound for Mexico. I had organised a trip for English anglers to sample their first marlin fishing, and the venue was Cabo San Lucas, in Mexico. To get there from London we flew across Greenland, dropping down over the Rockies to Los Angeles where we stayed overnight, before catching an Aeromexico plane down to San Jose del Cabo, an airport some 32 miles from the tip of the Baja peninsula. At Cabo San Lucas we booked in to the Hotel Hacienda, which has one of the best views overlooking the sea out from the Cape, any budding marlin fisherman could wish for. Marlin action is commonplace in these warm and fertile waters which are situated some 900 miles directly south from the U.S. border. Renowned as the year-round home of this species, expert or amateur alike, you can practically guarantee yourself a billfish from this unique coastline. The area boasts a clean, dry air, free from humidity, and all the hotels are geographically located where the desert and the mountains meet the sea, providing a summer climate all year round. In the winter it is sheltered from the cold north-easterly winds by the Sierra de la Laguna mountains, and in the summer it is blessed by the cool breezes of the Pacific. From November until the end of May, the days are 70 to 80 degrees, although the evenings are cool. From June through to October, temperatures range in the low eighties.

After checking in, and depositing our luggage in the room, we did what most fishermen do, which is we rushed down to the beach to make sure the water was still there and to look for fish. About a hundred yards down the beach, near some boat moorings, I saw a splinter of small fry breaking on the surface. I waited a few seconds . . . yes, there they were again. Rushing back to the room I hastily unpacked my rod tube, and threw together a 6-foot casting outfit. Small groups of fry were still jumping out when I got back, harassed by some unseen adversary below. I tied on the first lure that came out of my pocket, hooks entangled with other plugs, spinners and spoons. I untangled one, a small one-ounce lead-headed jig, and with shaking hands tied it on with a very uncertain knot. A splinter of fry exploded to my right, and to my amazement I threw that jig about *eighty yards!* Unfortunately I wasn't attached to it as the knot untied, so on went another one and I began random casting, following the breaking fry along the surf-line. The others all went back to get ready for dinner, but I decided to stay on until darkness . . . just in case.

As dusk fell, I latched into a fish that made the clutch squeal, and the line start to disappear from the spool. After about thirty yards had gone and the fish looked set to criss-cross through some mooring ropes, I decided to start clamping down. It took several seconds to wind in the line until the broken end hung fluttering in the breeze. Whatever it was had bitten clean through a 15-lb mono trace mono.

After dinner we went to bed early, hoping for an early start to go for striped marlin offshore. I couldn't sleep due to jet lag, and spent a fitful night dozing, and listening to the tiny man-eating mosquitoes that buzzed incessantly. At six o'clock Pete Higgins woke me from a doze. The sky was still dark, but a roseate finger of colour pierced the horizon to herald the dawn. As I stood outside on the balcony, it was hard to believe that I was so far from home. I could still make out the constellations of Orion the hunter, and the Plough, which allowed me to locate the Pole Star. The sea in front of the hotel was like a sheet of glass, the reflections of the moored boats' lights, glittering on the surface. After breakfast we grabbed our tackle, loaded up with beer and Cokes, and walked down the beach to meet the boats. An old rowing boat was used to ferry us out to the waiting gameboats, small 28-foot vessels with a gantry on the cabin roof to allow the mate to look for marlin.

'*Buenos Dias, Capitan.*' I offered my hand to a short dark-haired man of about forty-five.

'*Buenos Dias, Senor.*' We shook hands, and he fingered our International reels and Fenwick rods approvingly.

The engines were fired up and we motored across the harbour to collect our live bait. These were small scad-like

133

fish called caballito, meaning 'little horse.' Apparently they swam strongly as a marlin bait, hence the name. We began trolling as soon as we cleared the headland of Cabo Falso or 'False Cape.' The water dropped away dramatically to 200 fathoms, so fish were found very close to shore. We fished with 50-lb class outfits, two on outriggers and two as flat lines. The lures were small lead-headed plastic jigs, or Ferro jets, designed to spend much of their time under the surface. The lures were streamed back by the mate, drags set and we were fishing. After only a mile we had strikes on three rods, one of which came off, the other two were small oceanic bonito. These were kept as possible bait, and we resumed trolling for another half hour. Suddenly the mate shouted from up on top of the cabin: 'Marlin. *Cabie la carnada!*' (Change the bait). We quickly wound in the lures, by which time the mate had clambered down from his perch, and began clipping new leaders on the swivels.

Within minutes we were running two dead flying fish, one from each outrigger, and a pair of konahead lures on the flat lines. I put out my own teaser from the corner cleat and it churned along in the wake, kicking up great spumes of spiralling water. Suddenly the engines raced and the gameboat veered over. The captain had seen something better than a striped marlin. About half a mile away, standing out on the glassy surface like two triangular pennants were the dorsal and tail fins of a basking broadbill *swordfish*.

We circled, and the fish looked to be massive between the fins, somewhere in the region of 400 to 600lb! We jabbered excitedly amongst ourselves as the mate took out a fifth rod, and baited a live caballito on the hook. Our second pass dragged the lures and flying fish ridiculously close to the fish. There was no question that he couldn't see them, he just didn't move. Then slowly, the great tail fin wagged from side to side and slid beneath the surface. The captain cut the engine, and the mate threw the livebait off the stern, spooling line back as the boat lost momentum. The lures were feverishly cranked in, but we left the flying fish hanging in the water. For ten minutes we waited patiently, but saw no further sign of that great fish. What we had seen was a rarity indeed, and I received due chastisement as chief photographer for not taking pictures of those fins on the surface. The mate wound the livebait in, and we resumed trolling. The only further excitement came when a 10-lb dolphin seized a whole Californian flying fish and made off with it. As Pete Higgins cranked it in quickly on the 80-lb tackle, the mate spent fully thirty seconds waving the gaff, trying to get it aboard. Always be careful of relatively small fish that you bring in on the big tackle. Very often they're a whole lot fresher than they appear!

We returned to port with no further action, and the next day saw us again trolling for billfish. We drew a complete blank, with the exception of a few small bonito secured on the jets on the way out. The day after was more promising. A light breeze had begun to ripple the surface, and way offshore I spotted some breaking water. We steered towards it to find a truly massive school of dolphins running parallel with the coast. We took off the big lures and flying fish, and re-rigged with six to eight-inch jet lures. The boat raced along, half as fast again as the usual trolling speed. Swimming along underneath the dolphin were tunas and a school of yellowfins that ran from five pounds up to about forty. When four rods folded over simultaneously with screaming reels, there were suddenly four very happy Englishmen on board that boat!

After catching several of these yellowfins I decided to leave out a green ten-inch konaclone, one of my favourite marlin lures. Maybe a bigger tuna would see it, and attach itself. After five minutes watching the action of the lure I turned to walk to the cabin. As I did so, my 50-lb rod buckled over, a marlin departed one way, and a ten-knot boat the other. By the time I had got the rod out of the holder, the fish had long gone. That was the end of the fish for that day. We continued to troll around, sometimes racing through the dolphin for school tuna, other times trolling more slowly along the edge of the school in the hope of a billfish.

Next day was windy, a cool breeze coming down the coast in fits and starts, making for a bumpy journey. We dragged the lures across the noses of several striped marlin, and had got over the usual excitement when the boat is raced over to a basking billfish. We all stood by our rods watching intently as the captain slowed the engines and circled the boat, putting the lures and baits as near to the marlin as he dare. The mate hadn't even bothered to take out a caballito for livebait. He just stood near the stern watching the fish's reaction. Suddenly it was gone, I can't even remember seeing it go. One minute it was there, stationary on the surface, then nothing. I scanned the ocean in case he came up again. Suddenly Cliff Johnson shouted out, 'He's got mine, he took my flying fish!'

He stood at the stern letting the line spill from the spool, then to everybody's amazement struck — *with his thumb on the spool!* It took a couple of seconds for the marlin to wake up, realising it was hooked, and another two for Cliff to put the lever drag on the reel up to strike. Unfortunately that was a total of two seconds too late, and he blistered the skin on his thumb as the monofilament line tore off.

When he was safely in the fishing chair and the rod butt was in the gimbal he struck twice more, just to make sure the hook was in well. Then the most majestic sight that four English guys thousands of miles from home could have wished for: the marlin came straight up, wagging its head from side to side as it tried to throw the hook. We all shouted, as the colours in its flanked stripes lit up, and the sun flashed silver on its flanks. We'd got a hook-up at long last! The fish sounded and Cliff hung on while it raced line from his Everol reel. Gradually the fish slowed and we watched the angle of the line rise in the water. He was coming up for sure, and there he was, leaping and crashing only forty yards from the boat. Cliff took the advantage and gained yards of line back until he was tight on that fish. I was up on the cabin shooting it all in 8-mm movie, and we later counted *seventeen* jumps! The fish was brought alongside, the mate despatched it with a wooden club, and we dragged it aboard. Everyone touched it, marvelling at how all the fins folded down into body slits, giving that billfish the ultimate in streamlining. Congratulations all round, and the beer cans got a hammering. The day was a success anyway, and we could want no more.

We re-rigged the lures and resumed fishing, running the boat in closer to the coastline. So close in fact that we could see people walking along the beach in front of the Hotel Solmar. After half an hour, we were all stretched out talking about billfish, the sun beating down, reflecting off the deckboards, when ZZZZZZzzzzzz! The line started to pour from my reel. Leaping up, I wrenched the rod from the rod holder, jumped in the fishing chair and placed the butt in the gimbal. I let the line run out for twenty or thirty yards as the captain stopped the boat. The line fell slack, floating on top of the water. Had he gone? Maybe it was just a dolphin banging at the big Californian flying fish bait? Maybe the line had just broken free from the outrigger clip? All these things raced through my mind, my heart pumping like a steam engine.

'Reckon he's dropped the bait' said Pete, when suddenly the line shot tight and the spool started to run again. I threw in the big lever and waited for the line to tighten. As it did so, the captain gunned the engines and the boat roared forward, helping to set the hook as I struck three . . . four . . . five times! ZZZZzzzzzzz! More line was wrenched off the spool, and my arms extended in front of me as I tried to keep the rod tip up. This fish jumped once, not a leap, more of a wallow. It was a flat running fish that tore line from me with consummate ease, more like a huge wahoo than a billfish. It took me fully twenty minutes to subdue that fish, and I can't remember a harder scrapping fish for a long time. Not much of a leaper as it only came out about five times, but boy, what a slugger! The mate wired it to the side and the captain sank the gaff in. There was great jubilation aboard the boat as we returned to port with *two* striped marlin to weigh.

Cliff's fish tipped the scales at an even 100lb and mine scaled 107lb. That night in the bar above the restaurant, the subject of conversation was marlin. We discussed tackle and tactics with an ex-Hawaiian skipper and his wife, Rick and Kella Bodinus. They were test running a 22-foot blackfin boat, and trying for billfish at the same time. Apparently the lack of success aboard our boat for the first few days was due to the moon phase, and nothing we were doing wrong. When the moon is full, or a few phases either side of full, the marlin can silhouette their food against the sky. They can therefore hammer schools of caballito or squid all night long, and simply rest on the surface during the daylight hours, driving anglers like ourselves, wild with their apparent lack of enthusiasm for our baits and lures. Occasionally, Rick will run very fast, trolling high-speed jet lures so that the marlin say to themselves! 'Jesus. Was that a bird . . . plane . . . or was it a fish? We'd better eat it and find out.' Using this principle Rick has picked up the odd fish when other boats return to port fishless. I had a day out with Rick and Kella, covering dozens of miles in the high powered blackfin, but only one dolphin obliged.

The next day saw the weather change drastically. The wind had backed round to north and was hustling the wave crests from the tops of the Pacific swell. Several boats were out, trolling down the wave troughs in search of sickle-shaped fins. Our captain plugged into the waves for nearly an hour and a half, running up the coast in the direction of Ensenada. Thankfully he decided to come back, but turning beam on to the huge Pacific swells to turn round was an experience indeed. I was glad I'd had the foresight to take a couple of Sealegs before breakfast, having first viewed the offshore whitecaps with binoculars from the balcony. Even so, I grew tired of the constant buffeting by the sea. You know the sort of things; wherever you sit, lay or stand you just can't get comfortable, all not helped by the fact that Sealegs make you tired (I now use the brand called Stugeron, which seem a lot better, and don't cause any drowsiness).

On the return journey I went below to lay on the bunk as the Sealegs had virtually wiped me out. I lay on the bunk, crunching on an apple, jamming a foot against the bulkhead in an effort to stay horizontal. Suddenly there were shouts from up on deck.

'Quick Pullen, you lazy sod. There's something grabbing your flying fish!'

I fell up the stairs, hitting my head on the top of the cabin door. I couldn't believe the size of the enormous seas following — and I was expected to see if I had a run or not! Some friends they were! I took the rod out of the holder, genuinely believing it to be the false alarm of rough seas knocking the line from the outrigger clip. Sighing, I plonked myself into the fishing chair and felt the line for any sign of life. Line was running off at asteady even speed, a sure fire indication of a false alarm. I turned to shake my head to the others when it whipped through my fingers, and disappeared into the boiling wake. I waited a few seconds, locked the reel up, and shouted for the captain to gun the engines. As the line came taut I struck back hard, each time, and the line left the spool in a buzz. Somewhere in amongst the maelstrom of white water a form broke surface only to be lost in the confusion of wind and sea spray. The boat slowed and I started to work that fish hard to keep a tight line. I've always had a personal phobia about allowing fish slack, and this was one that wasn't going to get any.

After ten minutes it became apparent that I was getting nowhere. With the rough seas pitching the boat about, I would gain ten yards and lose nine. The captain decided to back the boat into the seas, a hazardous operation in a following sea, yet it looked the only possible way for me to gain line. We couldn't turn beam on for fear of getting swamped, so I had to contend with being deluged with spray as waves pounded into the stern. Slowly, surely, I gained line. In inches, then in feet, as the billfish started to move. The leader came up through the white water and a ghostly shape twisted beneath the stern. Witha final few hard pumps I brought the leader within reach of the mate, who grabbed it and eased the fish in to the stern. Getting it aboard proved to be another problem, and only with everyone getting a soaking from the spray did we manage to manhandle it over the side.

We decided that was enough sport for one day, it was three o'clock anyway so we began the exhilerating run back to port, surfing down the combers that ran, unstopped, in from the Pacific. On the scales the billfish weighed 112lb and coughed up a dozen fresh squid and a couple of caballito.

A super trip, our party finished up taking 20 marlin to 150lb, many, the first billfish ever caught by what were now, Mexico-mad Englishmen!

II

Salmo Apache

ARIZONA

In the autumn of 1982 I was working on a TWA Press trip based on Lake Powell on the Arizona–Utah border. A massive 180-mile long body of water, it was producing some of the finest striped bass fishing of the year. The State of Arizona has always held a total fascination for me. Coming from the cool climes of our chilly shores to the sublime luxury of ninety-degrees heat in Phoenix, is like a door in Heaven opening. Phoenix certainly is the place to go if you're a sun-searcher. It shines a staggering 86 per cent of all possible hours in this, the Valley of the Sun. Phoenix's climate, with its warm temperatures and low humidity, make it one of the most desirable spots for vacationing in the United States. With an average of just seven and a half inches of rain per year, there is just enough rainfall for the beautiful summer desert plants yet it is ideal for sun lovers too. You want sports? Even with the incredible July *average* temperatures of 105 degrees there are still over 1000 tennis courts and 68 golf courses to choose from. Swimming, horseback riding and mountain climbing are available to those with an over abundance of energy.

But not all of the State has been tamed — in fact most of it is wild and rugged and away from 'civilisation' it can be a harsh environment. Tucked away in the hills and mountains is a rich heritage of Indian and Mexican architecture. Having a traditional cowboy flavour all its own — you feel right at home in an old pair of jeans and a favourite fishing shirt!

It was 5.30 am. Still dark. We were seated round a campfire on a small sandy beach in Gunsight Canyon on Lake Powell. The coffee pot bubbled on glowing embers on the fire's edge. I was talking, with four or five others, to Rome journalist Joan Nickels, discussing the ways and problems of the world — social disorders, children, marriage, relationships — even the odd tale of fishing was regaled to her as we sat shivering, cameras at the ready, waiting for the sun to rise over the Grand Canyon at Lake Powell. I had talked with Joan to around two o' clock the previous night. There are few women I've ever been able to hold a deep, emotional conversation with, and Joan was one. As I looked at her in the half light of dawn, her dark smouldering looks reminded me of a Navajo squaw, and as she sat crouched by the fire, I could imagine her waiting for her husband to return from a hunting trip. Arizona does that to you. Sets you thinking about what might have happened there hundreds of years ago. It's only somewhere like this, where the shadows from the massive canyon walls belittle anything you've ever done in the world that your imagination can take flight. How simple life must have been. Harsh, surely, but with such a basic level for enjoyment, for survival, that it's not hard to see how this country impressed the writer of the best fishing stories ever — Zane Grey.

As the morning sun glows over a mile-wide canyon, a New World is born. Perspectives shift by the hour as light and shadow play off the canyon's myriad colours and rock formations and you find yourself looking at one of the world's foremost natural wonders. Forests of stately ponderosa pine sweep southward from the canyon's edge towards the 12,000-foot San Francisco peaks where Hopi and Navajo Gods are said to dwell. Thousands of browsing deer add to the enchantment of placid meadows and lakes. Farther south, the spectacular scenery of Red Rock Creek Canyon reminds you of famous movie locations. Yes, this deserted area of Arizona is surely an impressive and even humbling, place to stay.

'Going fishing again Graeme?' asked Joan.

'I looked across to Harold Johnson, the Del Webb's company resident fishing expert. We had landed several striped bass to about 9lb, and some small catfish.

'What do you say Harold? Do we go catch the lady some more fish?'

Before I could answer, attractive blonde, Susan Rooney seated herself beside us.

'Why don't you go catch us a trout for breakfast Graeme? Those other things are too big!' Other things? things? Striped bass are a prized catch amongst even the most highly aspiring sport fishermen. One just doesn't refer to them as things!

'Susan, do you mean to tell me that a beautiful gal like you, don't know you cain't ketch trout here? The water's too damn hot for a start, besides which as head of P.R. it should be you who tells me where to go catch a trout.'

'Well I don't know anything about fishing, maybe we should talk with Bob Hirsch about it. Maybe we can organise something for you'.

Bob Hirsch is an American's American. Big. Like twenty minutes round the shoulders. Mature, with a voice like a V8 engine blowing with no exhaust. If ever a man looked like a man, it's Bob Hirsch. He's the Arizona fishing expert, and had already helped me sort out some of the striped bass. I left the matter with Sue to sort out when we returned to Phoenix. I thought no more about it until over dinner one evening in a Scottsdale restaurant (I had been talking fishing with Vito Zappala and Frank Crawford of Italian publications), in walked Sue Rooney and Bob Hirsch.

'What's cooking kids?' Bob's voice boomed across the restaurant floor.

'Nothin' much, grab a chair and tell me what trout fishing you've lined up for me, and remember it's got to be good. I've got the cream of trout fishing back home in England!'

Bob seated himself beside me, and Sue poured the drinks.

'How would you like to have the chance to catch a species of trout that very few white men in the world have ever had the chance to catch? Sounds good eh? Well, how about trying to catch that trout in a sacred Apache Indian area of the White Mountains, part of their Reservation. AND in amongst the most beautiful forested rim country you'll ever want to see? Yeah, kinda caught your imagination I guess.'

I was silent for a moment, trying to decide whether this was an Anglo-American wind-up. A good old Phoenix practical joke.

The following morning I found myself with Sue in the Phoenix airport terminal trying to book a hire car. When all the relevant forms had been signed and provisions in the shape of beer and sandwiches, plus of course all my photographic equipment loaded, Sue thrust a map into my hand.

'You're going to be on your own Graeme, just follow the route we've marked, and once you get up into the mountain country, if you get lost phone John Caid. He'll try to get out to you.'

My vacant, open-mouthed expression obviously had the desired effect. What the hell was I letting myself in for? I mean, surely all of America is covered by an arterial force of tarmac highways so that nobody can get lost. Just look across the next hill for a MacDonald's and you're home.

'Are you sure you're going to be OK Graeme? Gee, I wish I was going with you, I've never been up to the White Mountains, they say it's really beautiful up there.'

And I thought it was my animal magnetism that attracted them! Such is the world of the dreamer! It was still dark, so departing from the airport I left for the mountains. I wound my way up Highway 87 across the Mazatzal mountains where the big saguaro cactus started to thin out, and smaller shrubs suddenly appear. Within an hour the whole environment had changed. The cactus were fast disappearing, and were replaced by shrubs, small bushes and *trees*. I passed through sunflower and rye fields, reaching Payson in good time. I hadn't noticed any steep climbs, but suddenly realised I was able to look down onto things. The elevation was marked at 6000 feet! I stopped at a fast-food drive-in, grabbed a cheeseburger, fries and milk, then hit the pedal along Highway 260 towards Show Low. The change in temperature was enormous. I'd left Phoenix in ninety-degree temperatures, and it was now down a mind-blowing twenty-five degrees. I put the car heater fan on. In another two hours I reached my destination of Pinetop, and walked into a coffee bar to find John. He was seated by the door, and we quickly introduced ourselves. He wasn't a big man, probably around my own height, but he had that shrewd facial expression that let you know he was tuned in to everything going on around him.

'We should have no trouble catching one of those trout you know Graeme. If you can handle a fly rod OK that is.'

No problem there, so we decided on a tour of other waters before we began the long drive into the Reservation. John was the fishery biologist for the White Mountain Apache tribe, and these trout were confined to this one lake in the world. Nobody was allowed to fish there, with the exception of a three-day fishing tournament for a few specially invited people. Even then, the rarity of this unique species demanded that they were all returned alive. Conservation of

143

the highest order and rightly so. The latin name for this fish is *salmo apache,* or Arizona trout as they are known locally. The lake in which they reside is Christmas Tree lake, set deep in the heart of the forest, and only attainable by four-wheel drive.

After meeting two of the Apache game wardens and discussing everything from magnum 45s (that hung ominously from their hips) to the problems they experience with poachers, we began the drive. Our vehicle was locked into four-wheel-drive as we turned off onto a side track, between the most beautiful aspen glades I have ever seen in my entire life. I mentioned this to John, who replied, with a laugh . . . 'Hell, it's still early yet. Once we get some real cold weather those aspens will turn the most deep glowing gold you have ever seen. I've lived here years, and nobody, but nobody, has ever managed to capture that beauty on canvas. It's unreal up here in these mountains. No people this time of year, which is a real shame as it's got to be the most beautiful part of the year.'

The Reservation itself was a massive two *million* acres, smothered in lakes, pine forests and wildlife. The name White Mountains is derived from the large amount of snow that falls once December arrives. We drove through gravel tracks to view some of the prettiest lakes I have ever had the good fortune to see. Horseshoe Lake, Sunrise Lake, Holly Lake, A1 Lake; names that conjure up pictures in the mind. Off to our left lay a side track, wired and posted off. It was as close as I was allowed to go to the sacred mountain, the place where the 'Crown Dancers', the Mountain Gods, are supposed to come down from. This sacred area covers around 30,000 acres and no white man is allowed in. We bounced on, over boulders, through deep ruts, the engine moaning and wailing as rubber struggled to find a grip on the dirt. Several times John would stop the vehicle, just on the edge of the woods where it opened out into a clearing of pasture, his eyes slicing through the timberline for even the slightest movement. He recounted the big game he had guided hunters to at each clearing, his description painting such a vivid picture that I felt as if I had been there myself.

Onward down tracks that no ordinary vehicle could follow. Along the way were huge pines, blown down by high winds, sawn in two and dragged to the trackside by the game wardens. After half an hour of watching the sunlight dance and flicker through the treetops, we started a descent down a bluff. Through the uprights I could see the magical twinkling of sunlight on water, a sight which will remain with me for ever. John stopped and killed the engine. Dust clouds still swirled about us, the taste of the earth was still in our mouth. A heady silence enveloped us, the transformation to yesteryear complete. Christmas Tree Lake, dressed in beauty, a garland of firs and aspens around its neck. Its name came from the fact that the national Christmas tree was taken from here, back in the 1960s, to reside in Washington D.C.

In these dark, inviting waters lay the species of trout found only up here, in the majestic White Mountain territory of Arizona. *Salmo Apache,* believed to be related to a rainbow or even cut-throat trout grow to a world record size of nineteen inches, the average size being around 3/4lb. The deepest spot on the lake would run to around forty feet, thus minimising the overkill in the freeze up of winter. The water is fed by two ancient creeks called Sun Creek and Moon Creek, an assimilation so unique and typical of the ancient Apache. The White Mountain Apache tribe have no less than eight wardens constantly patrolling the surrounding forests, thus minimising any intentions on the trout and game stocks any poachers may have. We stepped out, and I tried to close the jeep door quietly to avoiding shattering the peace.

'What flies do you reckon John?'

'Oh, in the spring we use the Dry Spruce fly, and the Peacock fly work real good. The Woolly Worms and Warden's Worries work real good too.' He threaded up a fly rod that looked to carry around a number six double taper flyline.

'In the summer black ants and muddler minnows bring the fish on. Remember too, that the fish aren't exactly fly-shy around here!' While John rigged up the fly rods I walked a few yards down the bank, took some deep breaths, and felt that crisp cold air surge down into my lungs. What a place! Was I really here? It was hard to believe that it was way back in the 1800s that the Reservation was started. I reached down and swished a hand through the crystal clear water.

'Hell — this is cold John.'

'You bet. You're at 8000 feet, that water is probably only

in the low to mid forties. It's colder still up at Paradise Creek.'

I shook my head in wonderment. Such beautiful names for fishermen to conjure with. A certain mystery and intrigue held within the realms of that name itself. I walked back to John, and we sat on a tree stump, just listening to the sound of the silence. We were at peace with each other — with the animals — the world. Wars, famine and strife seemed too far away. Or maybe, if you lived up here in the mountains of the Gods, not far enough!

'You lived here long John?'

'Yeah, I guess. Good old Arizona has been my home for as long as I can remember. I was born down in Tucson, below Phoenix. My Dad came down from Oregon about 1960, my Mom came out here as a college student from Missouri. I moved up here for this job. Back in the 1700s people in my family were coming over from England from the east coast of the States, and they were attacked by indians with three or four killed.'

'None around here that don't like fisherman is there?' We laughed and walked to the waterside.

'I'm gonna try up yonder, you can stay here, or come up whichever you please. Don't make too much difference, I don't know any place better!'

'I'll stay here awhile and see what happens.'

I started working a line out, taking care not to snag any of the trees behind me. The water was shallow, no more than a couple or three feet, with a bank of drying algal bloom lying on the surface and drifting into the side. Looked ideal ambush territory for Apache trout so I punched the line out. It landed, like most of my first casts, in a crumpled heap. I started to strip the line back in for another cast when I saw a bulge where the fly had landed. Several hundred English trout fishing sessions had taught me to respect that sort of movement as a lined fish i.e. one that has been scared by a line, or shadow of a line falling across its field of vision. I slowed my retrieve in case he was following. Suddenly there was a tug, I lifted too fast, and a pricked fish rolled and flashed away. 'Damn!' How could I be so amateurish? That could have been my one and only chance at this rare species.

On the third cast I had a take. No, it was more than a take — a savage pull, and I found myself attached to a twisting turning trout that put up a tremendous struggle. Again, I had no landing net, and marvelled at its superb markings as it thrashed in the shallows. It had to come off, or break the leader — My GOD — I hadn't even asked John what leader strength I was using! Thankfully everything held, and I cupped a hand around the trout, scooping him onto a grassy mount. I fell on him, with shaking hands, to subdue the struggles and remove the hook from his scissors. What a great fish, not large, around the pound mark, but I felt a warmth inside to know that I was one of the few white men to ever catch this species of fish. I shouted to John who was already running up.

'Got one. Took on my fourth cast. I even lost one on my first cast!'

He knelt down beside me, out of breath.

'Boy he's a nice fish. What do you reckon on your first *salmo apache* Graeme?' My smile said it all, and I gently slipped the fish back. It wallowed for a few seconds, regaining its breath, then righting itself, shot off into the deeps, leaving a silty cloud of mud subsiding in the aquine shallows.

'Let's go get another one,' said John, and strode down the bank to his waiting rod. I spent the next hour catching another four trout, releasing them all as John had requested. Another weedbed was located near the bank, and within easy casting distance, so I departed for it. The grass is always greener, and never more true than in an angler's case! This bed was in slightly deeper water, but the trees at my back made a long throw next to impossible. I managed to get some twenty yards by using a steeple-cast thrown back high between the branches. The line fell in a heap but at least it was out near the weedbed. I twitched the fly a few inches, in an effort to gauge the 'pull' on the line and a bow wave headed from the weedbed towards the fly. I kept the fly moving, inching it through the ripples. The distance between the bow wave and where I thought the fly to be, narrowed, then suddenly a flash as he took. SPLAAASSH. A silvery form cleared the water, and brought John down the bank to watch the action. Twisting, turning, jumping, that fish fought like a brown, a sea-trout and a rainbow all rolled into one. In several minutes it was thrashing the shallows to a foam, then lying exhausted on its flank, I lifted it from the water. At around $1\frac{1}{2}$lb, it was in superb

147

condition, the strange markings seeming more pronounced as it lay on the wet grass. I reeled off colour and black-and-white photos from all angles, before slipping it gently back. My day was complete. I need not catch another trout as long as I lived, such was the sense of satisfaction. Needless to say I did. I watched John land two fish around the 1lb mark, and went back to my own rod and landed another! This time I felt I really had caught enough and walked off leaving to John, the entire population of Christmas Tree Lake trout!

Walking back along the wooded track I suddenly looked round to see no sign of the vehicle or John. Geographically, I was no more than 700 yards away, yet simply being out of sight of civilisation had given me that sense of being transported back a hundred years. Those clearings across the creek. Surely those shapes on the timberline were Apaches? Or huge elk, intently watching my movements to determine whether I was a danger or not. No. They were just tree stumps, the long shadows thrown by the westering sun, making human forms on the leaves. I tried to cross the creek and get a shot of the sun filtering through a particularly well-placed group of golden aspen. The ground proved too soft though and my boots quickly filled with ice cold water. All around in the soft earth were impressions of deer, and their heavier brethren, elk. Tiny flowers stood bravely amongst the grasses, and looking far down the lake I saw a figure walking round a bay. It was John, no doubt searching for another trout.

Near the edge of the creek stood a huge tree, a broken branch trailing along the ground. Thinking it would make a superb hide from which to photograph animals coming down for their evening drink I ensconced myself in its branches, tucking down until the leaves ceased rustling. After five minutes I noticed several birds alighting on bushes a lot closer to me than they had done before when I stood out in the open. Tops of trees rasped and whickered with the fading evening breeze, the sun grew lower in the sky, sending a dazzling display of liquid fireworks across the ripples to me. Overhead, a stately buzzard wheeling stiff-winged, used the failing thermal currents for some last hunting trip before the sun dropped. I must have sat like this for twenty minutes, drinking in the beauty of my surroundings, like a desert man slaking his thirst in a saloon.

Soon the shadows became longer. Too long in fact, and centuries old Stone Age instincts told me that now was not the time to be abroad in a strange forest. John had mentioned black bear, a species normally tolerant of man, but also known to be aggressive when provoked. I was seated on what potentially might be his territory, and would certainly not be doing any provoking. I got up and left, walking briskly to the waiting jeep where John was untackling his rod.

'Did you get any more John?'

'Yes, I got one more. He was a good fighter, 'bout a pound or so. Boy, I really love it up here. So quiet, away from everything. Gives a man a chance to think. Get priorities right, you know?'

I knew. I still had to drive back to Phoenix, but had no fear of falling asleep on the four-hour journey with the jumble of thoughts I had in my mind. On the way back I spotted some shapes on the edge of a clearing.

'Elk,' I shouted. I had never up to that time ever seen an elk in my entire life, yet I knew what those huge forms were. John ground the jeep to a halt and swung up his field glasses.

'They're elk OK. Three bulls, only young though. Here, take a look.'

The glasses revealed three massive figures in statuesque pose, some three hundred yards away, looking back at us. In a flash they galloped across the clearing into the lush undergrowth. The hunter in me longed for a gun, and yet, up here, it would seem almost sacrilege to raise a barrel and pull a trigger. Further on another elk, this time a cow, stood straight in the roadway as we rounded a bend. With a laugh, John blew the car horn and it cantered away.

'Now watch this Graeme' he said, taking a bugle calling horn from the gun rack. The elk was still cantering away from us when John put the horn to his lips and blew. The elk stopped and wheeled round, head and ears erect, looking straight back at us.

'BANG!' said John, laughing. 'That's how we get 'em.'

By the time we got back to the main track I was beaten black and blue by the four-wheel-drive's axles. As we pulled out onto the main track a form darted across in front of us. Jamming on the brakes John leapt out, grabbing the .22

from the gun rack. Crack–crack–crack. He watched for a second, then replaced the gun in the holder.

'What was that?' I asked nervously.

'A wild cat, but I missed him in the half light. Nice big bobcat.'

Somehow, the TV name 'Apache' will never be quite the same!

12

Tiger Shark
ISLAMORADA

There comes a time in your fishing career when you wonder just what the hell it must be like to catch one of the dangerous sharks. From my own research I could see that there were only three really 'unsuitable' species of sharks to go swimming with. Of the rest, the limited number of shark attacks reported around the world illustrated the fact that chances of being attacked were minimal. Unless of course you happened to be in the right place at the right time, and were stimulating the shark into a feeding frenzy by the addition of vibration and/or smell into the water. Looking at sharks in a glossy book, and catching them in their own environment are two completely different things. The shark, on a pound for pound basis is stronger in the water than a man on land. They possess incredible strength, more likened to a swimming muscle than anything else. With some species imparting up to 2000lb per square inch pressure onto anything on which they clamped, the average person would be well advised to leave them alone.

However, I didn't come into the category of the average person as being a fanatical fisherman, I had a mental instability all of my own. In my teens, I had cut my teeth on the blue shark fishing off Looe in the south-west of England — *the* venue of the time, where many British records were broken — until the over-fishing of mackerel, and an increase in the hire of charter boats made their numbers decline. I caught several hundred sharks, including porbeagles, blues and threshers. On my foreign adventures I have caught many others: bulls, dusky, blacktips, nurse, bonnetheads and others. They hold a total fascination for me, more so than the tarpon, bonefish, marlin and tuna, which are accepted worldwide as being the cult fish. Now I wanted to catch something substantially larger, more difficult, more dangerous.

One of the three species most likely to do damage is the great white, the absolute ultimate in sportfishing sharks and the greatest man-eater of modern times. They are huge fearless machines that home-in on their quarry like a heat-seeking missile. Nothing will stop them killing what they want. But, they are elusive at the best of times. Only a few venues throughout the world can boast any sort of chance of even seeing one, although they are an ocean roaming shark that can turn up anywhere. But for me, the great white was ruled out because the cost of getting to a good place and chartering a top boat that could do the job was prohibitive, besides which, I wasn't too sure if I could go the full distance with the 'White Death'.

The second most dangerous shark is the tiger. Growing to 1000lb it boasts a man-trap of a mouth that can bite a man in two with consummate ease. A brother to the white, they are at least a little more abundant and represent a better angling proposition.

Finally there is the mako. Possibly the greatest fighting shark that is notorious for its leaps when hooked, and a high risk of bodily damage when they get near the boat. Again related to the great white, it is an elusive fish at the best of times, and one with which I had already had a couple of encounters. The first contact I had with a mako was out from Looe one Easter. It was clear weather, but with a hard blue sky and cutting wind. We were out over the Hands Deeps drifting for pollock, hands in mittens, gently winding the fluttering rubber eel through the water. We had already taken a boxful of reef-sized fish up to about 10lb when a fish I was playing suddenly grew heavy. So much so that my 20-lb rod was finally bent double, the line dragging off slowly. The skipper of the *Lisanne*, a young Cornishman named Richard Butters, was of the same opinion as myself. Makos showed up over the reefs as early as May, now it was April but obviously fish don't need a calendar to tell them that the water is beginning to warm up and the food is abundant.

It was agreed that I was now attached to a mako shark that was swimming around the reef feeding on the pollock. He had followed the pollock up towards the boat, grabbed hold and set about eating it on the spot. It was more than likely unaware that I was even exerting any pressure with my 20-lb class rod. The outcome of such an event is a foregone conclusion, eventually the line came free and I cranked up the remains of a 9-lb pollock. It had been completely ripped in half, the ragged tears in the flesh indicating beyond doubt that the jumble of crooked teeth from the jaws of a mako shark had done the damage.

The following Easter I was again out off Looe in quest of the reef pollock. Same reef, same time of year. The angler next to me was into a very good pollock, probably up around the 12 to 14-lb mark. The fish had 'blown', that is the pressure of depth had blown the fish's swim bladder up and it was, to all intents and purposes, incapacitated. About thirty feet from the surface the 'dead' pollock came to life and his rod tip dragged beneath the surface, with its owner screaming and shouting. Phil Dingle was the skipper, and mouthed 'mako' at the same instant as I. I had a set of 50 ready rigged up, in case of such a problem, and we looked over the side to see a 200-lb mako eating on the double-figure pollock. It ripped a chunk out and the angler surfaced what was left of his fish. Meanwhile Phil and I raced against time to get a set of shark gear in the water. With no smell to attract the fish it would soon swim back down to the reef and our chance would be gone. Catching a mako would mean a great increase in business for Phil, and was the ultimate catch for a British angler. Sometimes only one a year is recorded; many years none show up. Yet here I was, with my second chance in exactly a year!

Phil impaled a 4-lb pollock on the 12/0 and dropped it over the side. It spiralled and flashed as it sank through the depths. 'Hold her there boy' motioned Phil, and I thumbed the spool to a standstill. We waited, like all shark anglers wait, for whatever may happen. With sharks you never know where they are, what they're thinking, or what they intend to do. After two minutes Phil motioned for me to bring the pollock up. Just as I reached over to flip the reel in gear, line was whipped away from my thumb. The mako had hit! Line melted from the spool, and for some unknown reason I flipped the reel in gear, wound down and thumped the rod back. Incredible, but I did it. Phil cursed, and I simply wound back a bare hook. Striking too soon had lost me my second chance of a mako, albeit I had blown my chances by excitement. The big three species can do that to the most seasoned shark angler, reducing you to a jelly of anticipation. Cool, calm actions go straight out the window, as too does the chance of the fish!

Five years later and I was drifting along for amberjack with three other members of the Sportfishing Club of the British Isles. The boat was the *Ace*, captained by Jim Taylor, a shark fanatic himself. The venue was Islamorada in the Florida Keys, one of my luckiest places, and somewhere I knew to hold tiger sharks. Jim knew it too, and he knew also that you didn't need to chum for these man-eaters. They were feeding on the resident population of amberjack over the pinnacle rock known as the 'Hump', a sort of sawn off volcano about twelve miles off Whale Harbour marina, slap bang in the main flow of the Gulf Stream. The amberjack fishing was superb sport anyway, and we had landed several up to 70lb in weight. We deep jigged with Japanese feathers tipped with a fillet of tuna and worked a pair of rods from fishing chairs in the stern, taking it in turns to hook up, and hopefully land one of the big 'jacks.

Crewman Davy stood by the standard gunnel watching the tip of a set of 130-class tackle onto which was attached a slab side of one of the amberjacks. It was dragging through the water as we drifted along, about halfway down to the Hump. The idea was to have a bait ready and waiting should one of the big tiger sharks follow to attack a hooked amberjack. Halfway through the afternoon, one of my companions had an abortive run on the slab of 'jack. A mangled bait came back, a fresh one put on, and the fishing resumed. 'Probably a small blacktip' said Davy, 'they can be a nuisance when we rig with small slabs.' I must point out that this small slab, weighed in the region of 15lb on its own!

We were rotating on the shark rod, taking a turn to sit in the chair as we alternated hooking the 'jacks. Fortune being what it is, I happened to be in the chair when the line went away on the shark rod. I dropped the gimbal in, jabbed up the drag, and the boat engines roared in to life as we tried to set the hook. Davy waved his hand, 'OK Jim, back her off, we got a hook-up'. Line was dragging off the spool at a steady rate, and Davy clipped the harness on, to ease the strain of holding the heavy outfit. I was aware of a moaning from the other chair, and we suddenly realised that poor Ken Wheeler had been trying to play a big 'jack on his 50 when the shark hit. As Jim had started the engines to set the hook, so Ken had to watch in disbelief as about sixty yards of hard-earned line went screaming from his reel. Now, with so much line out and a tiger shark fighting beneath the surface the odds were very much in favour of the amberjack breaking away! We laughed as Jim said 'Sonofabitch Ken, that sure is a helluva fight that 'jack's givin' you. Ah b'leeve he's gonna keep you thar awhile!'

While I heaved and cranked on the big 12/0, so Ken tried to gain line by half turns, fighting more against the tremendous stretch of monofilament line out, than the fish itself. The 'jack was probably swimming around over the Hump, still feeding! After half an hour had passed, I had the shark nearer to the boat, than Ken had his 'jack. Wagers were taken amongst the crew and fellow anglers as to whether a tiger shark could be landed on a set of 130, faster than an amberjack on 50!

With renewed fervour I launched into a new offensive on the shark, thumbing the sideplates of the reel as I pumped line in. Forty minutes and Ken had regained the lost line, and began to start off where he had been three quarters of an hour previously. My own double line came up, then I watched as Davy's fingers closed around the wire. Jim put the engines into neutral, reached for the twelve-gauge, and leaped up on the stern. 'Pull him up Davy, I gotta get a clean shot!'

'He's coming now Jim, hang on, I'll try to get his head up.' As the shark thrashed on the surface so the gun boomed as two shells tore through the spine, hopefully incapacitating the shark.

'Wire him up Davy, and we'll get a rope on him.' All the time Ken had been oblivious to the fact that his skipper was levelling a twelve-gauge only a couple of feet from his ears, being intent on whether my shark would cut his 'jack off, so the look of terror as the gun boomed was a picture, and we fell about laughing. I'll never forget that look of gut fear as Ken's eardrums were treated to both barrels of heavy powder. The tiger was swung aboard on the gimble and we finished the day without further incidents, save more amberjacks. Back at Whale Harbour marina the fish tipped the scales at 220lb. A nice tiger shark, but not as large as I wanted.

The following day, we were again out over the Hump, and

this time Davy sent down a whole 30lb amberjack to entice a big tiger. The 'jacks were not so thick, something that to me indicated the sharks were on the feed down below in the depths, and everything else was just trying to stay out of their way. We had a run on the 'jack and lost the lot. Hooks, trace, everything. All that remained was a swivel and six inches of wire. Either another shark had bitten through the wire or there was a kink in it to weaken it. I opted for the latter, a common problem when using single-strand wire. An hour later and Keith Priestley was puffing and blowing as he tried to hold some line on a good tiger shark. An hour later and he had gained little line.

'Cain't figger this one' said Jim. 'He's sure fightin' peculiar. I think he's wrapped up in the trace or sump'n.' Fifteen minutes later and we glimpsed the shape of a white belly. 'He's comin' in upside down Jim, must've took a turn round a pectoral or maybe he's fouled!'

As the shark neared the surface we could see it was foulhooked in the pectoral fin. It was a big fish, up around the 350-lb mark, and poor old Keith had spent over an hour dragging a big shark *sideways* through the water. Well that fish turned out to be the meanest 'crittur' this side of the badlands. First Jim gave it a single barrel in the spine. This enraged it so much it wrenched the wire from Davy's gloved hands, and Keith spent another fifteen minutes bringing it back. The wire went away again and this time ten minutes lapsed before we had it back. By now Jim's temper was on the wane and he again leaped up on the gunnel trying to sight up the fish.

'C'mon Davy, get him on top this time!'

As the head broke surface it suddenly rolled on its belly and headed away.

'I can't hold him no more Jim, he's tearin' ma arms out by the roots' screamed Davy.

I saw the set in Jim's jaw as he drew a bead on the shark. CRRAAAAAASSHHHH! He let both barrels go at once, straight into the guts of the tiger. It writhed and thrashed, then dragged Davy towards the stern where he had to let go of the wire. Jim lowered the barrels, and said in amazement. 'Holy Christ, y'know we ain't gonna get that mother. He's just one of those that'll never die!' Slowly, in jerks, the line dragged from the reel as the shark swam back into the depths. Keith was powerless to stop it, and after forty yards had left the reel, the line parted. Nobody said a thing. There was in fact nothing to say. The fish had won, and illustrated just what it takes to kill one of these eating machines.

We motored back to the Hump from where we had drifted several miles during the battle, and dropped the jigs again for amberjack. Nobody spoke, and nobody had the slightest idea what might happen next. As far as we were concerned we had seen the highlight of the day, and that was it. I hooked a big amberjack of 40lb, and Davy rigged it up on a new set of shark gear. 'Bit on the big side isn't it Davy?' I enquired. 'Naw, if there's a good-sized fish down there, he'll chew his way up a 70-lb 'jack if he gets the chance.' Two of the other lads hooked 'jacks as I sat on the gunnel by the shark rod. The first was a 60 pounder the other maybe larger. I watched the rod top of the big rod. It seemed to me to be quivering, almost like a rod does when there's a livebait on the other end, yet I was using a very dead 40-lb 'jack. Then it kicked hard once and I knew we had company.

'Davy, we got a tiger sniffin' here. The tip just kicked.'

He stood beside me, watching the motionless rod.

'You sure Graeme? Wasn't just the swell?'

'No, it was a shark OK. I think he's down there eating the 'jack.'

'Hey Jim, Graeme thinks we may have some company. Should I spool it back to him just in case?'

Jim looked at the rod top from high up on the flying bridge.

'No, leave it there, let him eat it good.' Even as he spoke the tip kicked two, three times then dragged over as the shark moved off.

'WHOOOOOEEEEE! We're in business Jimbo!'

I slid into the chair, struggling with the heavy rod as the shark pulled downwards. With the gimble and butt located, the harness was clipped on and the signal given to Jim to gun the engines.

'Sorry Tony, you're going to have to lose that 'jack' said Davy. Tony looked in amazement.

'Lose it, HOW am I gonna lose it?' Davy reached forward, drew out his knife and with one stroke sliced through the 50-lb mono, the tip springing straight and Tony falling back in the chair.

'Just like that' said Davy. 'Sorry, but this could be a real big shark.'

The engines raced and I felt the *Ace* surge forward as the props bit water, dragging the stretch out of the line, and putting fantastic pressure on my arms. I heaved backwards, hopefully driving the hooks in.

'We got a hook-up Jim, ease her off.'

For the next half hour I seemed to lose more line than I gained, this time in faster bursts so we knew the shark wasn't foul-hooked. Every time Davy walked back to talk to Jim I'd twist up the drag a turn or two. Every time Davy walked back he'd feel the drag and pulling a yard of line off, unturn it! By thumbing the sideplates and dropping down for quick hard pumps I found I could gain line. After fifty minutes of very hard pressure I felt the pain barrier approaching. In a few minutes I wanted to give the rod away, my back ached that much. Maybe if I offered Davy dollars he'd cut my line like he'd done with Tony's. All these things raced through my mind while I fought both mentally and physically with myself as well as the shark. In a few more minutes I would be through, the pain would ease, and I'd hate that fish so much a thousand dollar cheque wouldn't prise my fingers from the butt. It's what it's all about on big fish. The purely physical feeling when you know that it's possible this fish can kill you. Frightening to non-fishermen. Absolute heaven to devotees of the sport. Suddenly I was through. I felt that fish give. Found I could get two and a half pumps to the reel handle every time I dropped, instead of the previous one.

'Fish is comin', shouted Davy. 'Push her forward a little, he's going underneath.'

I watched the angle of the line change as the *Ace* burbled forward, felt that awful pressure, and saw the line start to drag from the spool. I knew it wasn't the shark taking the line, he was probably swimming slowly behind us, but just the thought of seeing my hard-earned line go back through the water was soul destroying. Suddenly the double line popped above the surface, small droplets of water shaking from it as it pinged under pressure. With a couple of turns of double on my reel I increased the pressure until the shoulder harness creaked. Slowly, oh so slowly the leader came up. One of the most tantalising sights to a big-game fisherman, the 'so near and yet so far' syndrome. A gloved hand closed round the wire, and then Jim was hanging over the side, pounding with the head of the flying gaff as he tried to drive it through the jaws. Water flew everywhere, with Davy hanging on like grim death to the lurching wire.

'Do it quick Jim. Can't hold on much longer.'

Then Jim straightened, his tee shirt spattered with shark blood. 'Rope him off Davy. He ain't goin' nowhere.' I saw the grin of relief on Jim's face as he pumped my hand furiously. 'Nice work G.J. you whipped him OK.'

'Kind of makes up for that last one Keith lost doesn't it?'

Jim turned, hand increasing the throttle of the *Ace*. 'Well it would have done G.J. except for one thing.' I frowned. 'What's that?' 'That's the third pair of glasses I've lost over the side this year. I reckon we'll catch a big ol' tiger one day with a pair of my glasses on!'

The journey back to Islamorada saw several small 'chicken' dolphin landed, but I didn't even bother to fish. I just sat in the sun, staring at the huge fish strapped to the side. I knew he was big by the length of time I'd taken to boat him, but he didn't carry that girth that a big bull shark I landed the previous year did. Davy came up beside me, coiling up a wire leader. He cocked his head on one side, judging the size of the fish. 'I reckon he's gonna be pushin' the four-hundred mark Graeme, maybe a little less 'cos he don't have much girth.'

'As big as that Davy? I thought maybe three hundred and a quarter.'

Davy shook his head and tossed the coiled leader on a seat. 'No man, he's a four-hundred pounder for sure. I seen a few big ones, and he's up there with 'em!'

Back on dock a crowd had gathered, anxious to see the fish landed from the boats. When I heard them 'Oooooing' and 'Aaaaaing' at the 50-lb 'jacks from the other boats I wondered what they'd say when they saw the tiger. As we tied up, Davy tossed the 'jacks and dolphin up onto the quayside, and the crowd moved round to us. Suddenly a tourist with an ice cream and a camera round his neck spotted the tail sticking over the stern of the *Ace*. He spilled his ice cream as he pushed past the others to get his snapshots. 'Holy God, Look at the size of the shark! Hey everybody this guy's got a mother of a shark here!' After that comment it took us fully ten minutes to drag the fish to the scales.

In fact when we finally winched the tiger up on the scales I was surprised there weren't half a dozen tourists hanging on its tail trying to get jaw shots. A hush fell over the crowd as the needle hovered in the wind. As it settled and the weighmaster squinted to get an accurate reading, you could have heard the proverbial pin drop. 'FOUR HUNDRED AND SEVEN POUNDS' he shouted, and a roar of congratulation went up from the throng. I'd caught what I'd come for. A big tiger shark. A known killer, probably the second most dangerous shark in the ocean. Only now I had a severe problem to contend with. I wanted another!

As I have said previously, the Florida Keys have always held a fascination for me, so it was not surprising that exactly twelve months later I was again out on Jim Taylor's gameboat. This time I was sharing with three other SCBI members: Bill Webb, and father-and-son duo, Cliff and Mark Johnson. As we finished breakfast across the bridge at Howard Johnson's, I watched the tops come off the waves by the bridge. As this is normally glassy calm, it was with some trepidation that we trooped over the bridge to see Jim. He appeared from inside the cabin, and I knew from the look on his face that we would be going. 'Look you guys it's not going to be choppy out there, it's going to be rough! If you want to go, I'll take you, but if you want to stay in, that's OK too. Most of the other boats have cancelled anyway.'

We decided to go. Three hours later, and we were hanging over the side doing the technicolour yawn, while only Cliff retained the contents of his Howard Johnson's breakfast. The boat rolled so badly in the massive swells that at one stage one of the outriggers hit the surface. Now measure an outrigger in degrees and you'll see that's pretty damn rough. We returned home by one o'clock, and had landed around eighty chicken dolphin before *mal-de-mer* made fishing of any description impossible.

Next day was still windy but to my mind, not as windy as the previous day. Bill Webb wanted nothing to do with another day pumping his kidneys, and Mark felt the same. I looked at the sea, the sky, the *Ace*, Jim, Davy. and the fish on the photo plaques. I decided I wanted to take a crack at it, reasoning that the best thing to do after falling off a bike is to get straight back on and overcome the fear. Cliff didn't want to go unless Mark went, no matter how hard I tried to convince him. It meant they would all lose their cost of the charter, so I told Cliff that if I went out on my own and hooked a shark I'd pay for half the boat — a not unreasonable gesture considering I was one of the worst 'yawners' from the previous day!

We left — just Davy, Jim and myself. I'd taken a breakfast of Sealegs tablets and felt my stomach roll as the *Ace* hit the larger swells outside the reef. I've got to crack this I thought, otherwise I'll never overcome it. I had a few small tuna trolling over the 'Hump', so we decided to drop for big amberjack. In fact it turned out that the wind was well down on the previous day, although there was indeed a heavy swell running. Well, to say we hit 'jacks as thick as bugs on a bumper is an understatement. You'd hook-up, lose the fish when the hooks jumped, another would take, you'd hook it, lose, then hook another. After the fourth drift I was on my third 'jack when Jim screamed at Davy from the flying bridge. From up high he could see much farther down through the surface glare and had obviously seen something huge.

'Get the slab, get the slab Davy, THERE'S A HUGE TIGER BEHIND GRAEME'S 'JACK!'

From the fighting chair I could see nothing, but saw Davy's frown as he looked in the water and gasped 'JEEEEEESSSUSS — Will you look at the size of this!'

'How big Davy' I shouted, 'how big?' The words were whipped away on the wind, and I was only aware of Jim beside me, hacking a great slab of flesh from the side of a 60-lb amberjack. He cursed as both he and Davy tried to rig up a leader for the bait.

'Stand up Graeme' shouted Jim 'screw your 'jack, take a look at that fish in the water. That's your big tiger man!'

I looked over the stern but only saw a faint smudge of colour beneath the surface. It didn't even look fish-like in appearance.

'See him!, See him!' I was tentative about confirming this colouring in the water to be a fish, and agreed that it did indeed look like something.

'Get this 'jack outa' the water Davy, I'm ready with the slab!'

As Davy gaffed aboard a forty pounder so Jim dropped the side of fish back over the stern, and spooled the big 12/0 as it disappeared through the water. For fifteen minutes we waited, the rod top of the 130 static.

'He's gone back to the Hump, Jim,' said Davy, 'he can

161

smell those other 'jacks and he's gonna eat 'em right up if we don't get there.'

The *Ace* powered and crashed through the swell, Jim watching for signs of diving terns to indicate the location of this undersea mountain. After several minutes searching he found it, and within minutes of dropping a baited jig, I was fast into another fish. After the seventh amberjack I was exhausted and needed to take a breather. Every single drift I had hooked a fish, bearing in mind some of the bigger amberjacks were taking twenty minutes with a harness to beat. The seas crashed and rolled the *Ace* about, but somehow I didn't even think of the seasickness from the previous day. I secretly wished that Cliff and Mark were out with me to sample such fishing, I knew they would be wondering what I was doing as the day wore on.

'Are you day dreaming again Pullen? Get that jig down — we're here to catch FISH!'

It was worse than being in the army, but then both Davy and Jim were bigger than me so I spooled the jig down. For some unknown reason I missed the 'jacks and felt the jig hit bottom. I hadn't raised the rod far when it went solid. I cranked out the stretch, struck, and saw the line peel from the spool. Then the tip jumped back and I knew I'd been bitten off. 'Tiger' was all Davy said. I caught my eighth amberjack, then my ninth until the last drift of the day arrived. Jim was standing beside me, hand on the line of the shark rod. The slab of 'jack was still dragging through the water.

'It's nearly three, G.J., make this you're last drop, we're gonna have to head home soon.'

I dropped down, locked the reel up and cranked like fury until the slowing handle indicated the jig had been swallowed. It was my tenth amberjack and weighed 67lb. As it crashed inboard, Davy set about unhooking it and I leaned back in the chair.

'Boy, what a day Davy, I'm finally and completely shattered. Can I get a beer from the cooler?'

'Sure, I'll get one for . . .' his voice trailed off and I followed his eyes. He was staring at Jim who was staring at the motionless 130 rod tip.

'Get back in the chair G.J.' said Jim, in a voice almost frighteningly calm.

'What?'

162

'I said get back in the chair, that big tiger's here — he's chewin' on the slab.'

It took me a few seconds to evaluate the situation. Here I was, having successfully landed ten amberjacks from forty odd pounds up to nearly seventy and the man was telling me now we'll go shark fishing?

'I said get in the chair G.J. This mother's about ready to go!' I slid into the chair, and felt Davy's hands around me trying to clip the snaps from the shoulder harness onto the reel lugs. I noticed his hands quiver slightly, and a sense of urgency not before noticeable. What the hell was going on? They passed me the 130 and I dropped the butt into the gimbal with three pairs of eyes watching the motionless rod tip.

'Hey are you guys having me on?' I asked.

'No it's for real G.J. you've got a big tiger shark about ready to pop.' Davy moved the fighting chair slightly so the tip pointed directly to this invisible fish. Then I felt the tip dip. It sent a shiver down my spine. It wasn't what could be termed a nibble for we were using a fillet from the flank of a 40-lb fish. It would take a really big fish to eat that. The tip dipped and this time stayed dipped. I was in. Jim, as usual, was right. It dipped, and dipped and dipped. I straightened my legs out and braced myself as the fish moved off.

'HIT THE ENGINES!' shouted Davy. 'Lets stick the mother!'

The *Ace* roared as Jim rammed over the morse controls and spray kicked up from the flared bow as we steamed into the sea.

'HIT HIM G.J. HIT NOW!' screamed Jim. I struck, trying to sink the steel into the jaws of this unseen adversary, conscious of a floating feeling as I was lifted bodily from the chair. The drag plates started to creak as inertia was overcome and they started to spin, the line crackling as it was wrenched from the spool. SEVEN, EIGHT, NINE times I struck, then I felt the *Ace* sink lower in the water as the engines were slowed.

'We got him Jim' shouted Davy. 'G.J. is on THE MAN!'

The big tiger lumbered off, completely unstoppable, even had I used a chain and rope. 130-lb class tackle is normally deemed as the heaviest sporting tackle that a fisherman can use, yet with this incredible unstoppable power it seemed like cotton. The first twenty minutes were the worse. I was already shattered from the exertions of catching over 700lb of amberjacks, and after my muscles had grown used to the dull aching, I seemed almost comatose.

'C'mon G.J. you're going to have to get to work on that shark. If he goes down and dies, we'll never get him up, he's too big. Plus we gotta think about it getting dark. I don't want to take the bottom out of the *Ace* on one of the inshore reefs at night. Certainly not with critturs like that sonofabitch swimming around!'

We all laughed, but I never felt unfunnier. Thirty minutes passed and I was on maximum pressure as far as my five-foot-eight-inch frame was concerned. The pain barrier was approaching, it came, I went through it and started on the tiger again. After forty-five minutes he felt close, but *very, very* heavy. I could only take him in single-turn pumps. At one stage everything went solid. I might just as well have been on the bottom with an anchor. Davy was moving the fighting chair all the time, and bent down to whisper in my ear.

'Graeme, now I know you're hurtin' bad but you gotta take him soon, he's gettin' his breath back quicker than you.'

'But it's all gone solid Davy' I gasped. 'Can't-seem-to-do-anythin'!' Davy sighed and whispered again.

'Graeme if you don't start makin' out you can land that fish ol' Jimbo is gonna cut the line!'

The HELL HE WAS! It wasn't the thought of losing the fish through the line being cut, but more the embarrassment of others thinking I was physically too weak to catch the fish that it had to be cut off. I took a quarter turn and felt the forebutt of the 130 start to creak. It was solid. I dropped the tip, took another quarter turn and heaved. This time the tip started to jag down as the tiger shook his head in anger. I'd woken him up. I couldn't hold this much pressure for more than a few seconds, so dropped again took a quarter turn and held him. He kicked and thrashed, the jars going right up through the rod butt into my very bones. He was MOVING! An hour came and went, then suddenly the double showed.

'Double showing Jim' shouted Davy. A few seconds later; LEADER UP JIM, PUT HER IN FORWARD!'

The boat rolled and pitched, and I watched agonisingly as Davy's outstretched fingers groped for the wire. IT

LOOKED SO CLOSE! Then they closed and I saw him pull hard, the veins in his neck bulging as he pulled on the fish.

'Damn it Jim . . . He's a big one!' Jim cut the engines and ran back, grabbing the flying gaff head en route. He was, as always in crisis situations, impassive. The wire pulled slowly from Davy's grasp, the force so great he had to let go, or go with it. As it twanged back to the rod tip he wrung his gloved hand and shook his head. 'He's hooked OK Graeme, but man Oh MAN . . . He's a good fish!'

Five minutes later and everyone was again in the same positions. Davy was holding the wire, Jim virtually over the side in an effort to make his first strike with the flying gaff the vital one. Again the wire was torn from his grasp, Davy swore, Jim swore and I swore. I shouted while half twisted out of the chair in an effort to ease the fantastic strain on my shoulders, back and legs. The abuse seemed so strange spoken with an exaggerated English country squire accent, that we all laughed. I knew then that it would be alright if I lost this shark.

'OK everybody' said Jim, 'we'll take him next time — he's gettin' tired.'

The wire came up after another five minutes, Davy grabbed it, wired the fish up and Jim drove the flying gaff into the jaw and out through the gill. So easy it wasn't true. He was ours! It took another half hour before we got him up on the gimble to swing him aboard, and only then could I see how massive he looked. Certainly the fattest, biggest jawed fish I had ever caught, making the 60-lb amberjack that it lay amongst look small.

Back on the Whale Harbour dock a crowd had already gathered, and I remembered Cliff and the lads when I saw them on the quay. As we tied up and started to off-load the big 'jacks I shouted out to their smiling faces 'Not a bad day boys, look at the size of these amberjacks'. To my utter amazement they looked straight past me.

'Where's the shark?' shouted Cliff.

'How'd you know I'd got a shark?'

'Jim radioed in here, when we came to ask why you hadn't got back, they said you were tied to a big tiger shark.' With my surprise element gone, they watched with envy as the massive form was dragged to the scales. It took four men to haul it up and four men to hold the crowd back so we could get some photos. Bets were shouted from the bar above as to the weight of the fish, and a hush fell over them as the pounds and ounces balanced out.

'FIVE HUNDRED AND SEVENTEEN AND A HALF POUNDS!'

The crowd cheered then above it all came a drunk's cry from the balcony — 'DON'T FORGET THE HALF!' he slurred 'DON'T FORGET THE HALF!'

I slept well for the next two days . . .

13

Billfish

BERMUDA, MEXICO AND MAURITIUS

My first encounter with an Atlantic blue marlin was through the 50mm lens of my Minolta camera. It was off the colourful island of Bermuda, aboard the famed gameboat *Challenger*. I was a guest photographer with Peter Perinchief, and wildlife artist Maynard Reece. Maynard's son was seated in the fighting chair when the blue snapped the line from the outrigger as it batted a rigged tuna bait. Mate Andy Card, brother of Alan, raced to the stern and placed the rod in the gimbal, feathering the spool with his finger to prevent an overrun. I was seated up on the bridge talking to Maynard, when this happened, and automatically swung my camera up to a point where I thought the line would come up. Maynard was using a lens like an astronomer's telescope, mounted on a tripod. On the deck Pete was metering his own camera in expectation of that 'front cover' shot of a blue marlin framed against a blue sky as a background. Marlin fishing is like that. You wait for interminably long periods of inactivity, then, without warning, the fish crashes a bait or lure, and hopefully launches its massive and impeccable frame into the air. I remember seeing Andy slap Maynard's boy on the shoulder as an indication to strike. Up on the bridge Alan gunned the big boat's engines and the rod pounded upwards, three, four, five times. A hundred and thirty yards away this fish pounded the sea to a foam, shaking its head as the steel bit home. Motor drives and manuals clicked away like a press gathering, as the Lord of the Sea began his majestic leaps. After some fifteen minutes he was wired up to the boat, where I switched to a wide angle lens. Fortunately he came out so close that spray spattered my face. Never has my old manual Minolta spooled off so many frames. I think I got two good shots on that first jump at the boat, the rest were those proverbial holes in the water, that all fish photographers seem to excel in getting.

The tuna bait had long since been thrown but with the hook lodged neatly in the scissors this fish was a classic candidate for a release. As Andy shook out the hook the fish slowly righted itself, then it sank back into the depths of azure blue and was gone. Everyone was satisfied, we had obtained what we came for, a marlin around a hundred and forty pounds, and some good jump pictures. However, I'm more of an angler than a photographer and I wanted to be on the receiving end of a blue. Two days later, and Andy phoned me to say one of the lures I had left with Maynard's party had raised one marlin and hooked another.

The following day I was due out on the *Challenger* with Leo Callaghan, a writer, and his wife and son. The weather was awful, even by Bermuda's standards; it was one of those mornings when I felt the bile rise even standing on the quayside. 'Gonna be a little choppy today folks' said Alan. When captains state they think it may be a little choppy you can bet your last lure its going to be damn rough. However, spurred on by the success of the previous day, and reckoning I might as well get soaked at sea as on shore, I went. Once clear of land and off from the short reef waters it got 'pretty choppy'. Andy ran out four lines, two on the flats and two on the outriggers. He was billfish orientated and decided to forego the chance of dolphin, skipjacks or wahoo and rigged up for marlin. A pair of little tunny were close-bridle rigged as deadbaits to skip way back on the outside of the wake. From the two centre flats he ran my lures: konaclone on one and a big 'geepee' jet lure on the other.

Leo and family retired to the sanctuary of the cabin, while I tried to talk to Andy as the *Challenger* lurched and rolled through the troughs. Squally showers drove rain horizontally across a grey sea, making it seem forever like a cod trip off the south coast of England in January. After half an hour of being battered, several hands were pumping up their breakfasts. I felt that familiar sweeping nausea and stared at the rolling horizon, fighting to keep control. I started to yawn, a sure sign of instability so jammed myself in the fighting chair and thought of good old England. I closed my eyes, the pallor of my face matching the deck of the boat. I kept swallowing and trying to doze. Inside the cabin I could hear someone retching, the smell of bile carried downwind to mix with the diesel from the exhaust. I caught a glance of Andy looking at me as he staggered from one side of the deck to the other reading an old out of date IGFA book. Jesus, how I hated captains and mates on days like this. Why couldn't they feel seasick like we mere mortals? Alan changed direction to port, running between the troughs as he tried to locate the dropoff of the *Challenger* tuna bank. I didn't need to look up to know that. I knew from a glance at my watch what the running time to the banks were and, if he changed direction it meant he had the sounder on and was running the edge. Cold rain mingled with spray to slap me in the face, and I huddled lower, my stomach rolling with the pitch of the boat. I knew in a couple of minutes I'd have to run for the side; I could feel it rising in my throat. Oh God, please let the boat stay still. I heard that piercing yell as though Andy was screaming in my ear with a bullhorn: 'LOOK OUT! HERE HE COMES!'

I looked up through half closed eyes, the following events slipping into slow motion where everything is clear and yet muddled. Out there in the boiling cauldron of prop turbulence and clashing waves was a sickle-shaped tail. It lunged and twisted, driving the body beneath the surface to keep pace with the motoring gameboat. Alan's cry was snatched away on the wailing wind: 'RIGHT RIGGER! . . . HE'S ON THE TUNA! . . . WATCH HIM! Alan jumped to the other corner, hand poised over the butt of the Fenwick rod. I dragged myself upright in the chair, the feeling of nausea vanishing instantly. It was here. The fish I wanted. I wanted to feel him. Feel his unstoppable power, being more powerful than I.

'LEFT RIGGER . . . HE'S ON THE OTHER TUNA!' I saw an indistinct shape surge down a wavetop, that sickle tail pumping mechanically. It dipped beneath the surface into that boiling wake.

'DAMN! HE'S GONE!' shouted Alan. 'ANDY KEEP AN EYE ON THAT LEFT RIGGER!' By now I was fully awake, and staring at the tuna bait bouncing over, under and through the wave tops. The big jet lure churned in the boat's prop turbulence, but I barely noticed.

'HE'S ON THE LURE . . . GRAEME WATCH THAT EIGHTY!' Andy's shout came at the same instant the water under the jet erupted and the tip of the 80 hammered over.

Before I could wrench it from the holder it sprang straight, then jammed over again. 'TAKE IT YOU SONOFA-BITCH!' roared Alan. Twice, three times it took the lure but failed to hook up. I levered the stainless butt out of the holder and dropped it into the gimbal, holding the rod. I felt the tip bang down as the billfish hammered in again. 'ZZZzzz!' line buzzed off the reel and I banged the rod back. Nothing. Again it took, throwing a gout of water up behind the pink skirt. 'ZZZzzz!' Nothing. 'I don't believe this is happening' shouted Andy. I held the rod steady, waiting for him to come again. He didn't. I cranked back the big jet and Andy stripped the wire leader through his gloves, flipping the lure over the stern.

'See why Graeme?' asked Andy, 'the goddam skirt has slipped round the bend of the hook. The fish was just grabbing the plastic.' Even as he spoke the other set of 80 crashed over, line screaming from the International. I fell out of the fighting chair grabbed the rod and heaved back in short, nail-driving thumps. I had difficulty in standing up as *Challenger's* twin engines roared, trying to take the stretch out of the line, driving the iron into the marlin's bony jaw.

'Get in the chair Graeme . . . he's gonna drag you over the side' shouted Andy, readying the bucket harness, and dropping down the back of the fighting chair. I slotted the butt into the gimbal, fumbling as the boat canted over in a steep trough. Line screeched from the reel. 'He took the 'clone . . . keep him tight now!' I was tight alright, line still running off the spool while I struggled to screw up the drag. 'Let him run' said Andy, ' there's no rush . . . he ain't gonna cut you on anything.' It wasn't a spectacular fight. As far as I remember he came out five times, three straight leaps, and a couple of greyhounds from one wave to the next. I wanted him badly, so eased up the lever when I thought Andy wasn't watching. In twenty minutes he was at the back of the boat, a magnificent blue and silver form, rolling against the wash of the gameboat. 'Wired up Alan!' shouted Andy.

Alan shinned down the ladder, picked up the head of the flying gaff and hanging over the side, sank it into the fish. It went on thrashing and banging for several minutes while they tried to get a tail rope on it. All the time this was going on I sat in the chair feeling jubilant yet absolutely wretched. The nausea swept over me in waves, and the sight of white water coming at me on a level with the gunnel did nothing to ease the discomfort. We all shook hands but I found it difficult to force a smile from my blue lips.

'Hang in there Graeme' said Alan, slapping me on the shoulder, 'you did a good job in this sea.'

Taking that as a compliment of the highest order I stood up and started running out the 'clone again. After half an hour of constant rolling the exhilaration of looking at the billfish on the decks had subsided. Andy was rigging up some double hook rigs on piano wire for wahoo trolling, and I was again jammed in the fighting chair, trying to keep the sausages down. I don't remember anything about that second marlin hitting. All I can recall are Andy's words, flying on the wind as the big reel screamed its warning: 'JESUS . . . I ONLY JUST LOOKED AT THAT JET! WHERE'N HELL HE COME FROM!'

By the time I was awake enough to realise that something was stripping line from the reel like an out of control express train, the twin engines were driving the boat forward into a head sea. I tried to lift the rod from the chair holder, but the pressure was phenomenal. A quarter of the spool disappeared as an absolute monster of a marlin literally punched its way back through the sea away from us, an incredible power that to this date I have never, ever experienced since. It's hard to put a really good bend into a set of 80-lb class gear, yet mine was into a hoop. Andy helped me lift the butt out of the holder, thus discounting any chance if this was a potential record fish. In slow motion I struck, if you could call it striking, for such was the power of the driving fish that the rod tip barely lifted from the parallel. The sound made by the line being ripped from the spool rose in a crescendo to a crackle, as the monofilament blistered its protest at being dragged out so fast. Half a spool emptied, and I hadn't even got to take both hands from the foregrip.

'He ain't gonna stop Graeme . . . man, that's a helluva fish you're tied to!'

In the next few seconds more line was stripped and half a mile away a huge form thrashed the surface to a foam. I felt the tip kick and he was gone.

'Is he gone? No. Wind fast he may be running up on us!' I continued winding slowly.

'No, he's gone, I felt the line part.'

It took me fully five minutes to wind all that line back on

the reel. Half the 300-lb mono leader was there, it had parted half way along. Alan turned and put the engines on, Andy just fingered the cut end of the line. 'That was some kinda billfish Graeme, I don't understand what happened!'

I looked down at my hands. They were white and shaking . . . but not from the cold. Andy took the controls and Alan came down. 'Well you had a taste of billfish today Graeme. This one will go up near two hundred or so, but that last one . . . Jesus, that was some kinda billfish!'

'Did you see much of him from up on the bridge?'

'Not a lot, but what I saw was big. He was somewhere between six and eight hundred! But man, he ate that lure of yours! HE ATE IT GOOD!' I knew that for sure.

★ ★ ★

Hunting big fish is a repetitive procedure. The same old story of putting theory into practise. This is where the element of luck comes into play, for despite what many anglers may tell you, luck does play a very important part in the capture of any fish. We just do our best to eliminate the bad luck then call the remainder skill! So came about the capture of my biggest Pacific blue from the Baja peninsula in Mexico. I had been asked to act as angling consultant for the making of a TV commercial, and had in mind the striped marlin as the species. This high jumping billfish offered me the best chance of giving the film crew plenty of action in the high finance world of commercials. We were staying at the Hacienda hotel situated on the beach, allowing me a perfect view of Cabo Falso and the Pacific Ocean beyond. That, coupled to the fact that the film producer was getting satellite weather updates, meant I could go to sea at a moment's notice. My captain was Pete Groesbeck with crewmate Kenny Hughes. A finer honed billfish team would be harder to find, certainly this side of Hawaii.

The first day's fishing was spent in coming to terms with the conditions that existed at the time. Previous years had seen the striped marlin falling to the traditional Mexican technique of trolling a konahead from each flatline rod, and mounted flying fish from the two outriggers. The marlin were generally seen tailing through the wave troughs, where the boat would then increase speed in an attempt to drag the baits and lures across the path of the fish. If it failed to take either of these, the crewmate would immediately run a small lip-hooked livebait back into the wake, and it was generally this that enticed the 'striper' to strike. This season however was different as the billfish were feeding over an offshore bank a few miles from the cape. They were hunting shoals of mackerel and all the gameboats were frantically employed on drifts across the top of this bank, using the cabalitto livebaits, not unlike our native scad. The first day out was for test fishing. I was aboard Tortuga 7 and fought a fish on my 30-lb class outfit, Conoflex Blank and International reel to full advantage. The fish fought deep, unlike a marlin, yet hit the livebait softly, almost as though it had opened its mouth, engulfed the bait and simply swum on unperturbed. It proved to be a thresher shark. My largest on light tackle, at 130lb!

The next few days were spent in the area of the Cape Bank, working the depths with drifted livebaits and taking striped marlin each day. These fish were ideal filming material making plenty of tail walking jumps and grey-hounding through the waves. Hundreds of feet of film were shot and I took fish between 100lb and 130lb. Most were released after holding them in the wake to regain their strength. During the runs between the inshore Cape Bank and the Jamie Bank much further offshore, we ran straight running lures, and through this deep water I took several larger marlin, this time the Pacific blues. One fish weighed 160lb, another after a short, hard fight on heavy gear weighed 250lb, at the time my heaviest Pacific blue, although the Azores had given me six Atlantic blues to 400lb. Then came the day that would never be forgotten.

Climatically, no different from any of the others. I did not feel any particular excitement, in fact I was tired from fighting marlin from dawn to dusk every day. I was on a trial run with Carlos Cosa's boat the *Bacardi*. Carlos had previously hooked up on a broadbill swordfish on a day when I was supposed to have fished with him. Unfortunately after two men fought the fish for some time and succeeded in bringing it to the stern of the boat, it was mutilated and eaten by a pack of bronze whaler sharks. Shades of Hemingway's *Old Man and The Sea!* You get all the luck in the world to even hook up on a broadbill swordfish, then you get the bad luck that destroys your chance of glory at the last moment.

It was dawn, and in a chill breeze I held the 50-lb class outfit, jacket pulled around my hunched shoulders to ward off the chill. A soft take, and I found myself looking at a revolving spool as line ran smoothly between my fingers. Locking up the big reel I struck and watched in amazement as the water off our stern opened up with a huge marlin broaching on its side, head shaking, in an attempt to throw the iron. For a few seconds I remained mesmerised as I could not envisage myself attached to such a leviathan with my own line still slanting downwards through the depths. I had not taken into account the amazing speed of a really big marlin that could take a bait at eighty feet of water and clear it a couple of seconds later. As this fish, a huge Pacific blue, continued its relentless attack on the surface of the ocean, the line from rod top to fish gradually straightened, and I realised the full extent of the situation. Here I was, using my striped marlin tackle when along comes Mr. Blue and engulfs the bait. I looked round to see Carlos up on the bridge shaking his head in disbelief. We were in the position of losing a fine fish and there was nothing we could do about it. Or was there?

By frantic boat manoeuvering and almost suicidal attempts with the flying gaff in the crewmate's hands, we suddenly realised there was a chance. A fish that seemed likely to snap my line like cotton was now within striking distance. You've heard about the seconds dragging like hours? Well, as that crashing, leaping body of muscle came closer and closer the seconds seemed like days; it was agonising, both physically and mentally. Suddenly one of the Mexican crew sank a flying gaff and leapt clear of the twanging rope. Then the second flying gaff went in and I saw that fifteen minutes of frantic fighting had seen lady luck on my arm. A quarter of an hour ago I was shivering in a denim jacket, a hot mug of tea in one hand, the rod in the other. Now I was looking over the stern, soaked in sea spray and sweat from excitement, with my eyes raking the flanks of a huge Pacific blue marlin, certainly over the 400-lb mark, maybe nearer 500. If I had chartered the *Bacardi* myself I would have left for Cabo San Lucas immediately in order to get the fish weighed officially. As it was, my job was to stay and get hooked up to a striped marlin, radio the mother ship with the film crew aboard who were then to steam over and put a crew underwater filming while the boat crew ran celulloid on the action above. Through the remainder of that day we fished striped marlin and I took three fish, all over the 100-lb mark.

By the time we had finished the filming and returned to the port it was dark. *Bacardi* docked, and already there were a group of people standing dockside who had heard of the big fish. Tired, bruised and contented I watched as the crew attached a rope to the tail of the huge fish and hauled it to the scales. A silence descended over the huddled group on that cool night as we waited for the scale needle to settle. At 461lb it was my biggest Pacific blue marlin, but more important than the actual weight was the comradeship and teamwork involved in that frantic fifteen minutes. For let no man in a big gameboat allow himself the luxury of thinking that he has done it all himself. The boat, the captain and the crew play an important part. And let's not forget the fish and Lady Luck as well. If the fish is swimming your way, in the direction of your bait, then your luck is that much greater.

★ ★ ★

Fish strikes come when you least expect them, none more so than the really big ones. You could be forgiven, when reading some of the accounts in this book, for thinking that big fish always swim up and take my bait in front of all others. Not so. Although a certain amount of experience and knowledge will always swing the odds in my favour, I have no way of dictating exactly how big the fish that strikes my bait or lure is going to be. I can eliminate the very small fish simply by using a size of lure that makes it difficult, if not impossible for them to eat. But fish live in an 'eat-or-be-eaten' world and thus possess voracious appetites. While you may read here some of the accounts that stick in my own mind, there are hundreds of other big and medium size fish I've caught that limitations of space preclude me from writing about.

My biggest Pacific blue marlin came as a surprise, not because I wasn't expecting it, but because the average sized billfish being taken by the charter boats at that time wasn't particularly large. The venue was the Centre-de-Peche Club on the Indian Ocean island of Mauritius, the boat

Flipper 5, the skipper Jacques. My first day had been spent acclimatising and recuperating from jet lag, which, coupled with the heat of ninety degrees and the humidity, made getting aboard a gameboat the next day sheer heaven. The temperatures are so much more bearable out on the ocean, away from the reflective heat of the land mass. On the ocean the breezes and gentle lapping of the water past the hull relaxes you completely.

I was seen off from the jetty at 1 pm by the Centre-de-Peche Club manager, Ram Aneerow and Jacques who ran the boat bookings (as opposed to Jacques the skipper). It's strange how many Jacques there are on this tiny island, indicating the French influence in its cosmopolitan population. I had to wait for another client to return from his last day's fishing: a Frenchman who had fished four full days with the boat to himself for not even one strike. Now, he had one last morning's fishing which had allowed me a few hours in the afternoon to try my luck. I was quite pleased with this arrangement as in my experience with marlin throughout the world, I had concluded that early morning or late evening were the best periods for action.

I ran four lures, three of which had been supplied to me by Ed Murray of Murray Brothers tackle, the other was from Sevenstrand. I had been getting more and more keen on the use of straight running lures as opposed to the older fashioned konahead design which 'travelled' up to two or three feet across the boat's wake. The konaheads would raise fish well with their erratic action, but minimise any solid hook-hold as the billfish had trouble nailing them on that first rush. The straight runners on the other hand, were simply there in a straight line waiting to be eaten, and invariably gave a good hook-up. I ran two straight runners in close, a blue straight runner on the left outrigger and a big orange and pink Sevenstrand konahead on the right outrigger. At 4.30 pm I was up on the bridge mesmerised by the plastic lures churning through the wake. We were heading back to the clubhouse, but via the Le Morne mountain drop-off, a favourite marlin area due to the upwelling currents that pushed the baitfish near the surface.

At about 4.45 pm I saw an explosion of spray behind the Sevenstrand konahead and screamed out 'M-A-R-L-I-N!' Skipper Jacques had already seen it of course, and pushed up the *Flipper 5's* throttle, adding speed to the lures. 'He's on the blue murray' he shouted, 'see him! see him!' Try as I might there was no way I could distinguish any sort of a fish shape behind that lure which had a spume of bubbles like a jet stream snaking behind it. 'Here he comes!' shouted Jacques, 'he's going to hit it!' All I saw was a flat spot behind the lure. No violent splash, no rearing fish with its rapier-like bill slashing the surface. The lure stopped streaming bubbles for a second, and then I realised that there was in fact no lure, and the big International reel was shrieking in unison to the roaring boat engines. Clouds of black exhaust boiled away into the humid air as *Flipper 5* surged forward, driving the double hook rig deep into the marlin's lower jaw. Some 150 yards away a gout of white water rent the pure blue and I knew then I was into a nice billfish.

The journey from the bridge to the fighting chair was not memorable. If I had any joints that weren't banged en route I can't remember what they were. Always it seems a fumble trying to get that kidney harness clip snapped onto the reel lugs. Yet in reality it took no more than fifteen seconds. Then I could lean back, feel that satisfying creak as I straightened my legs and the harness began to take the strain. I could rest my arms from the constant weight of rod and reel and allow my shoulders and back to ease some of the pressure and distribute it more evenly. I decided at an early stage to take a workout on this fish, which I assumed to be in the 200-lb range. It was my first day and I needed to get used to that old familiar feeling of the physical battle between man and fish. In a couple of minutes the marlin had ceased to tear up the surface and began to settle down to a new rhythm: short hard runs that were unstoppable without risk of parting the line. Yet as soon as he stopped I upped the drag lever and leaned on him some more. Ten minutes hard labour and I had him coming my way. Fifteen, and I could sense this fish was mine.

'Could be a black' said Jacques 'I'm sure it is one. I saw him behind the lure when he took. A nice fish.' When a marlin skipper described a fish as being 'nice' it means it's getting into the realms of being big. Invariably professional captains slightly underestimate the size of the fish just in case it should turn out to be small. I renewed the pressure, standing up on the footplate, and leant my whole body weight against the harness, trying to bend the 130-lb class tackle, while waiting for the tip to straighten as I gained a turn of the reel handle. A few minutes more and the double line showed. Away off the back as Jacques manoeuvered the boat to keep the stern to the fish, I could make out a blue and silver form beneath the surface.

'A nice fish Jacques' I shouted, 'he'll go 250lb'. He shook his head, coiling up the flying gaff rope and inserting the massive steel hook onto the pole.

'No Graeme, this is a very big fish. I think over 400lb.'

What? How could it be? Had I not hauled this brute straight to the boat? The double line began to show and I could actually see the billfish outline beneath the surface. I lost the double line — three times — and each time after I had allegedly 'locked up' to prevent this happening. My breath was coming quicker now, my head and heart hammering. Sweat was running into the corner of my eyes. If this fish was 400lb, a fact which I still couldn't believe, then I could be in trouble. Having shot nearly all my strength in under twenty minutes on what I thought was a 200-lb fish, I had very little left in reserve. The difference in fighting time between 200lb and 400lb is substantial. From past experience I knew I could easily tack another three quarters of an hour onto the fight. It was time that my tortured body didn't have. At any moment this fish could wake up and depart on a run that could distance us 600 yards or more. I agonised at the thought of trying to retrieve it after spending most of my energy in that first twenty minutes. To me, with a 400-lb fish and the double line beneath the surface I had little choice. I had to take him there or lose him.

'I'm going to try for the double again Jacques, are you ready?' He coiled up another rope, stationing the second flying gaff in the opposite corner of the stern.

'I think we take him first time yes?' he said. I nodded grimly, and popped the lever drag up a touch. Taking him first time meant if I ever got to put a few turns of double actually on the reel spool again, it had to stay there. No matter what. I put on the pressure, slowly at first until I felt that great bulk stirring beneath the surface, still finding it difficult to believe this fish was double my previous estimate. The double line showed, reached the tip ring, snickered through the rollers and found itself on my reel spool. I increased the drag past strike, placed both thumbs on the spool and stood up, putting absolute maximum pressure on the rod. It straightened from the curve very, very slowly. Then, and only then did I realise that here was my biggest Pacific blue marlin.

The gloved hand of Jacques reached out and closed on the leader. No jerks. No snatches. Just a cool efficiency that had given him many big fish. I still kept the pressure on, helping him as much as I could. The leader went slack from the rod top and I was out of the fight. It was all up to Jacques. He cursed in Creole and shouted to the mate who was operating the controls in the cabin. In a second he was by Jacques' side, the two of them straining to contain the big marlin and get the flying gaffs in. A third man who had come out for the ride, helped, and between the three of them they got the gaffs in and I knew the fish was mine. Before I left the fighting chair I saw the dancing light in Jacques eyes, heard the excited jabber of Creole, their native language, saw the handshakes between them and the flashing white of their gleaming teeth. It was the big one alright, and I pushed between them to lean over the stern. I gasped at its size. The shoulders were thick and heavy, the tail as broad as could be; the bill that instrument of death that spelt doom for many a tuna or dolphin, was enormous.

'How big?' I asked Jacques. He cocked his head to one side and pushed the cap to the back of his head, estimating in his mind's eye, the length, girth and belly of the fish. 'He's over 500lb I think. A very big fish. My friend I tell you. You did a good job on him.' Such a compliment from a charter captain to me was meaningful indeed. I was not a tourist angler. I didn't need to be impressed with praise that was false. We were four men in a boat as a team. Nobody else had seen this strange scenario. Only four people had felt that electric atmosphere when we had latched into the fish and actually won. Winning and the kill is a primeval force that still drives men, thank God. At least some of us can experience it. A throwback to the Stone Age where survival was the spur. The bringing home of the meat a cause for celebration. The respect of a fine kill is great amongst fellow men. This marlin, this huge glorious fish would not be wasted. On the market in Port Louis it would feed dozens who really needed it. The women who bought it to take home and cook for their family would not care how or where it came from. Merely that it is there to be bought is sufficient enough. Only the men would look at that huge form and wonder about the sort of struggle and excitement involved in its capture. Dozens of men would wish they had been there. Only four were. Only four will truly remember.

It weighed, by the way . . . 561lb!